A student's guide to Corporate Finance and Financial Management

by David Evans

British library cataloguing-in-publication data
A catalogue record for this book is available from the British Library.
Published by:
Kaplan Publishing UK
Unit 2 The Business Centre
Molly Millars Lane
Wokingham
Berkshire
RG41 2QZ
ISBN 978-0-85732-488-7

© David Evans

First edition published 2011

Printed and bound in Great Britain.

Contents

A* denotes an advanced level chapter

Why do you need this book?

Financial management (or corporate finance) is a technically difficult and demanding part of many business related university degrees and professional accountancy and business qualifications. Students, especially those with limited experience of mathematics, often struggle with the theory underlying many areas of financial management and in relating the theory to the real world.

This book reflects many years of experience of teaching students to successfully pass financial management exams and aims to provide students with a completely different and fresh approach to studying the subject. How?

- The style throughout is relaxed, informal and chatty – difficult finance theories are introduced and discussed in a very friendly and approachable way with plenty of examples and illustrations – hopefully creating an enjoyable learning experience.

- Tutor guidance – the book has been written in a style which simulates a tutor being with you as you read through each chapter – the aim is that rather than reading a dry academic textbook and puzzling over what a point means, or where a number comes from, the reader feels that they are sitting in a classroom or lecture theatre 'listening' to a tutor explaining a point. Clear, straightforward, but where necessary detailed explanations accompany all topics and calculations.

- The mathematics is kept to a minimum – many academic textbooks on financial management bombard the reader with mathematical proofs of theories and formulae. One important myth to dispel - you do not need to be a maths genius to do really well in a financial management exam. You are likely to gain far more marks from being able to understand and explain the logic of a formula, and explain how and why it might be useful in real life, than from being able to work through a proof – this is the focus of the book.

- Diagrams and features – each chapter is packed with diagrams and features such as 'need to know' (more on this below) to appeal to different learning styles and provide some variety.

The book assumes no prior knowledge of finance, or financial management, and is suitable for a student studying for a first level financial management or corporate finance exam. It also, however, covers many of the most important advanced financial management topics and developments. The book should also, therefore, be an invaluable aid to someone who is studying for a more advanced financial management or corporate finance exam.

How to use this book

There are three main ways in which a student could use this book.

1. A student without any prior knowledge or understanding of financial management or corporate finance could read the book from cover to cover to develop a through understanding of the subject matter.

2. The book is broken down into 5 sections, each of which deals with a different area of financial management. The areas covered by these sections, and how they inter-relate is explained in more detail in chapter 1. Each of these sections can be read without reference to other sections and therefore if you need to focus more on one section than the others you can jump straight to that section. If your interest is, for example, in understanding business and equity valuation you could jump straight to section 5 of the book and start there.

3   The contents summary identifies the chapters that cover advanced financial management topics. If you are preparing for a first level financial management or corporate finance exam you could just work your way through the book leaving out the chapters marked as advanced. Similarly, if studying for a more advanced level financial management or corporate finance exam you could focus more on the advanced chapters. Clearly what is advanced is to an extent a matter of opinion and therefore you need to consult the syllabus for the specific exam that you are sitting before deciding on what to focus on or what to leave out.

What are the key features in each chapter?

You will find the following features in each of the chapters of the book.

Need to know

This highlights the most important points that, from experience, students 'need to know' before sitting an exam which covers that subject area. Many of these 'need to know' points will need to be committed to memory before you sit an examination – sorry!

Finance terminology explained

Whenever a new finance term is introduced this is explained in an informal, easy to understand way. If you have ever wondered, for example, what the term 'securitisation' means – well – you are going to have to turn to chapter 8 to find out.

Exam tip

This little feature highlights useful tips for students when answering an exam question. It sometimes highlights points that examiners expect to see in a 'good answer', sometimes highlights the best approach to take when producing an answer, and sometimes highlights common mistakes and pitfalls that need to be avoided – allowing you to learn from the mistakes of others.

Example

These are worked examples to illustrate how a topic is often examined. The solutions to the worked examples are broken down into simple steps and where appropriate, each step is accompanied by an explanation of how and why a calculation is performed.

In addition...

Finally, each chapter also has an introduction, an outline of the key sections of the chapter, and a key points summary at the end of the chapter, which can be used as a revision aid.

Formulae – a quick note

Many academic textbooks use subscripts extensively in mathematical formulae. In this book, in order to make the formulae clear, and easy to follow, the approach adopted throughout is to avoid using subscripts unless absolutely necessary.

Some words of thanks....

Thank you to everyone who has assisted me during the writing of this book including work colleagues and the wonderfully creative publishing team at Kaplan.

I'm also grateful to the many students that I've taught over the years whose questions, suggestions, comments and mistakes (!) have also, in many different ways, contributed, without their knowing, to the content of the book.

A special thank you to Janet, Rhys and Bronwen, to whom this book is dedicated, for their support and encouragement during the time that this book was being written.

Thanks also to family, friends and colleagues whose influence, over many years, have indirectly made this book possible. In particular I need to thank my parents, Jean and Alun, and also Dan Gidwaney, who first gave me the opportunity to teach financial management.

A final special thank you to Sharon Forbes who reviewed each chapter of the book as it was being written. Her wisdom, diligence and suggested improvements have made this book a far better one than it would otherwise have been.

If you find any errors in the content of the book – apologies – they are all my own.

"October. This is one peculiarly dangerous month to invest in stocks. The others are July, January, September, April, November, May, March, June, December, August and February."

Mark Twain

INVESTMENT APPRAISAL

INTRODUCTION TO FINANCIAL MANAGEMENT

1

Introduction
what is this chapter about?

This chapter introduces the ideas and themes that form the basis of this book. In this chapter we will consider the main types of decision that a finance manager will need to make. We will also explore the relationship between risk and return. This relationship lies at the heart of many of the theories that are covered in the book and if, by the end of the chapter, you understand this relationship – congratulations – you are well on your way to understanding what the whole book is about.

Key areas of the chapter are ....

1   **Investment, financing and dividend decisions** – which investment or investments should the business undertake? How should those investments be financed? What level of dividends should be distributed to investors? Financial management essentially involves making these three types of decisions (just three decisions I hear you ask – is that all? – ah but there is a lot to consider before each of the three types of decision can be made.) We also need to understand how these decisions relate to each other.

2   **Financial objectives** – what are the main objectives that a finance manager will consider when making decisions about investments, financing and dividends?

3   **Risk and return** – What is the relationship between the risk associated with an investment and the return from that investment? Is it possible to draw any general conclusions about the the way in which investors will behave in relation to risk and return?

INVESTMENT, FINANCING AND DIVIDEND DECISIONS

Financial management is essentially about managing the finances of an organisation engaged in business. As outlined in the introduction the three key decisions that a finance manager needs to make are decisions about investments, decisions about financing and decisions about dividends. The three decisions are interrelated.

A small scenario

Let's consider how these three decisions work. Assume you are the finance director at one of the world's major oil production companies. The key types of decision that you would be involved in making would typically be:

Investment decisions

Should the company invest in the exploration and development of potential new oil fields, perhaps in deep water or sensitive environmental areas? Should the company invest in research or new cleaner technology? Should the company invest significantly more in health and safety - perhaps appropriate for some oil companies you might think!

Making these decisions is, of course, a complex and in many ways a very subjective process involving consideration of strategic, economic, political, environmental, social and financial factors.

The **first section of this book (chapters 1 to 7)** is devoted to considering the **financial aspects of an investment decision**. There are techniques that can be used to help a finance director decide whether an investment is financially viable, that is, whether it is worth undertaking in financial terms. Of course, even if an investment is financially viable, the board of a company may still decide that the company will not proceed with the investment, perhaps because politically or environmentally it is too difficult to proceed, or perhaps because there are other investment opportunities that are better from a financial point of view.

Financing decisions

Any decision about a significant new investment cannot be considered without also considering **how that investment will be financed.** Suppose the oil production company has estimated that an investment in developing a potential new oil field will cost $300 million over the next five years, and will not generate any sales revenue until the development is complete. The next question to be asked therefore is how will that investment be financed?

The company could, perhaps, raise the finance from ordinary shareholders through issuing new shares. Alternatively the company could raise the finance through issuing debt capital, perhaps through borrowing from a number of different banks or through selling blocks of debt capital on a stock market. Different ways of financing new investments have different implications for a business.

The **second section of the book (chapters 8 to 15)** considers how a business raises long term finance and the implications for a company and its investors of raising finance in different ways.

Dividend decisions

When a company generates profit, provided that the profit also results in cash being generated (and the accountants amongst you will know that the two are not the same!!) an important decision to make is how much of the profit should be distributed to shareholders as a dividend payment, and how much should be retained and reinvested within the company.

This decision is really a special kind of financing decision, hence dividend policy is included in the second section of the book (chapter 15). If profits (and cash) are retained within the business then this can be used to finance (at least in part) new investments that a company undertakes. If, however, profits are not distributed to shareholders as a dividend, shareholders may not be happy with the decision and the company's share price may fall. A balance therefore needs to be found between paying cash dividends to shareholders and retaining profits, and cash, to reinvest.

The interaction between the three decisions

There is a strong link between all three decisions that you need to be aware of. We have already seen that in order to undertake a new investment a business must raise finance from investors. The link between the decisions does, however, go much further than this and as you read through the book you will understand more fully how these decisions relate to each other.

This leads to our first exam tip:

Exam tip – Investment, financing and dividend decisions

When discussing financial management in general in an exam question, or when discussing investment, financing or dividend decisions, marks are often available for exploring the link between the three decisions.

A common mistake in these types of question is to focus on one of the three decisions in isolation and completely ignore the other two.

What about the other sections of the book?

So, the first two sections of the book cover the three key decisions that a finance manager needs to make. Does this mean, I hear you ask, that the last three sections of the book can be ignored?

Unfortunately not. The last three sections of the book all cover different aspects of the three key decisions in the following way.

Section 3 – working capital management. This section considers both financing and investment decisions but **in the short term rather than the long term**. We consider how much a business should invest in inventory and receivables, and whether payables and a bank overdraft can be used as a form of financing. Could a business, for example, take longer to pay its payables than it is currently taking?

Section 4 – risk management and derivatives. The management of risk is a major part of the work of a finance manager, or at least it should be. (Perhaps, it could be argued, directors and senior managers of some of the major banks did not devote enough time and attention to managing risk during the period 2000 to 2010.)

Risk significantly affects both financing and investment decisions. A company might, for example, be considering investing in a new product or in a foreign country for the first time. If this is the case the risk may well be significantly greater than the risk associated with any of the existing investments of the company. This needs to be taken into account when assessing the financial viability of the investment. If the investment is in one currency and the financing is in another, a company faces potential currency risk. Some of the techniques that we explore in section 4 allow us to manage and therefore reduce this type of risk.

Section 5 – valuation. Why is this covered in the book? Rather than expanding by investing in a new project, a company could seek to expand by acquiring an existing company. This 'target' company would need to be valued before an offer could be made to purchase it. Alternatively, a company that wants to raise a significant amount of new finance by issuing new shares will need to obtain a listing on a recognised stock exchange. As part of this process a valuation of the company is necessary.

Valuation is therefore a necessary part of the process if making certain types of investment and financing decisions.

Finance terminology explained

Finance and capital

Before we go further it would be sensible to clarify what we mean by finance.

Finance is the cash that is raised from investors and then invested in the company. This could be cash raised from shareholders, either existing shareholders or new shareholders, or cash raised from investors in other ways, for example, through borrowing from a bank.

Finance = Capital

It is important to note at this stage that the terms finance and capital are often used interchangeably. They mean the same thing. When finance is raised from shareholders or from a bank, the amount of finance raised and invested in a company is often called capital.

Other terms related to the process of raising finance from investors, such as equity capital, preference share capital and bonds are all explained in chapter 8 (and if you really can't wait to cover these terms you could always dip into chapter 8 now!).

FINANCIAL OBJECTIVES

When a finance manager makes a decision is there a particular objective or a number of objectives that the finance manager would consider? The answer to this is that for private sector companies there is one key objective with which you will become very familiar.

Need to know!

Maximisation of shareholder wealth

The overriding objective of financial management is to maximise shareholder wealth. All of the main financial management theories that are covered in this book are based on this assumption.

A company is owned by its ordinary shareholders. It follows that anyone who works for the company, whether a director at board level or an employee below board level, is in effect 'employed' by the shareholders of a company to act in the best interests of those shareholders. This idea is sometimes called **'agency theory'** meaning that the directors (and employees) of a company act as agents of the shareholders. Every decision that they make should therefore be based (in theory) on what would be best as far as shareholders of the company are concerned. I'm sure that when you go into work the first thing that you think about each day is – what could I do today to maximise shareholder wealth!? In theory, if you work in the private sector, this is what you should do. The reality is, of course, more complex than that.

Other stakeholders and other objectives

A stakeholder is anyone who has a stake in the future of a company. Investors are stakeholders, as are employees, customers, suppliers and even parties such as the government or local community. All are influenced to some extent by the performance of a company and decisions about investment and financing.

Directors will need to consider all stakeholders in a company, and consider a wide range of specific objectives relating to these other stakeholders. This does not, however, contradict the overriding objective of shareholder wealth maximisation. It could be argued that properly **considering the interests of all stakeholders is necessary in order to maximise shareholder wealth in the long term**.

If, for example, a company fails to consider the working conditions of employees, key employees may leave, which may affect the ability of the company to deliver the product or service and which may damage shareholder wealth. Failure to meet health and safety standards may result in fines, or closure of the business, which would, of course, adversely affect shareholder wealth.

How is a change in shareholder wealth measured?

For a company that is quoted on a stock market, and where the price of the share on any date is readily available, the change in shareholder wealth over a period of time will always have two elements. They are the dividend income that a shareholder will receive, and the capital gain or loss based on the change in the share price over the time period.

Finance terminology explained

Total shareholder return and dividend yield

It is important not to confuse these two terms when discussing the actual return that a shareholder may receive over a period of time.

$$\text{Dividend yield} = \frac{\text{Dividend}}{\text{Share price at the beginning of the period}} \times 100\%$$

$$\text{Total shareholder return} = \frac{\text{Dividend + change in the share price}}{\text{Share price at the beginning of the period}} \times 100\%$$

Whilst both measures are important to ordinary shareholders in real life, the total shareholder return is the true return to the shareholder over the time period. The dividend yield only measures part of the return – the cash dividend element.

Example 1

The following information is available about a company quoted on the stock market:

Share price on 1/1/20X1 = 300c

Share price on 1/1/20X2 = 330c

Dividend paid on 31/12/20X1 = 20c

Requirement

If an investor purchases one share on 1/1/20X1 and then sells that same share one year later on 1/1/20X2 what is the dividend yield and what is the total shareholder return over that period?

Solution 1

$$\text{Dividend yield} = \frac{20c}{300c} \times 100\%$$

Dividend yield = 6.67%

To determine the total shareholder return we need to firstly determine the change in share price over the period of time. If the share price increases over the time period this is added to the dividend. If the share price falls then this is deducted from the dividend.

The increase in the share price = (330c – 300c) = 30c

$$\text{Total shareholder return} = \frac{20c + 30c}{300c} \times 100\%$$

Total shareholder return = 16.67%

Despite the dividend only representing a return of 6.67%, the true return that the investor received during the 1 year investment period was 16.67%.

RISK AND RETURN

Before delving into the following chapters which will greatly expand upon investment, financing and dividend decisions, we need to look at the relationship between risk and return which, as a concept, underpins much of the financial management theory that you will find in many of the following chapters.

Finance terminology explained

What is risk?

Risk, in finance, refers to the variability of returns. It is the amount by which the returns received from an investment will vary from period to period.

In example 1 the return that was received in the one period analysed was 16.67% - a very good return. If, however, we had analysed the return in previous time periods, the returns may well have been very different – in some periods, perhaps when the share price fell, the return have been a lot lower than 16.67% and in other periods it may well have been higher than 16.67%.

The standard deviation of the returns of an investment is a mathematical way of measuring risk. Risk can also be measured in terms of beta factors which are explored fully in chapter 11.

Finance terminology explained

Risk averse — what does this mean?

The term risk averse (or risk aversion) is used extensively when discussing finance. It is often one of the assumptions underlying a finance theory. What does it mean?

The term essentially means that investors do not like risk. Because investors do not like risk we can assume that the greater the level of risk, the greater the return that an investor would require from the investment. Investors require compensation for taking on additional risk. If two potential investments were available which both had the same level of risk, we can assume that a risk averse investor would choose the investment with the higher expected return.

Suppose an investor has $10,000 available to invest. Let's assume that the investor could invest this amount in short term treasury bills (short term government debt) and receive a return on this investment of 3% per annum in the form of interest. This type of investment is considered to be risk free (or as risk free as it is possible to be). The 3% rate of interest could therefore be considered to be a risk free rate of return.

An alternative way of investing the $10,000 would be to buy ordinary shares in one of the top companies quoted on a stock market. This investment, of course, carries a significantly higher level of risk. There is always a possibility of significant problems adversely affecting the share price, and the future dividend income, and therefore the returns received each year could vary considerably (remember that risk is simply the variability of returns). As a result an investor would expect a higher return than 3% from this investment before purchasing the shares.

Exam tip – Risk averse

A common error made by students when using the term risk averse is to assert that risk averse means that an investor wants to avoid all risk. This is not true.

A risk averse investor will seek to minimise risk **for a given expected return** but that is not the same as seeking to avoid all risk. A risk averse investor might be prepared to accept significant levels of risk if the expected returns compensate the investor for that level of risk.

Finance terminology explained

Risk premium

The additional return that an investor requires to compensate for the risk involved is called the risk premium. The term premium simply means that it is an extra amount added to the risk free rate of return to compensate investors for the risk that they face.

What are the different types of return to an investor?

In many of the chapters that follow the returns to investors are discussed and analysed. To make sense of the analysis it is important to clarify what is meant by a return to an investor. There are three main variations of the term to be aware of.

1 **Actual return** – this refers to the actual return that an investor has received in the past.

2 **Expected return** – this refers to a return that an investor would expect to receive in the future from the investment. The term expected implies that there is no certainty. We might, for example, expect to receive a return of 15% over the next 12 months if we buy shares in a company quoted on the stock market. In 12 months' time when we look back, the actual return achieved from the investment might, of course, be very different. It could be significantly greater or significantly less than 15%.

3 **Required return** – this refers to the return that an investor would require from an investment in the future. This will be linked directly to the risk of the investment. The greater the level of risk attached to the investment the higher the return that an investor would require.

What is the link between the different types of return?

Suppose we were considering buying shares in a food retailer called Paris foods. The company is quoted on a stock market and the shares are trading at 100c per share. How do we make a decision about whether to buy shares at this price?

The first thing to consider is the **actual return** that investors have achieved in the past when investing in Paris foods. We do this by measuring the total shareholder return for previous periods as we did in example 1. Let's suppose that the average actual return that an investor would have achieved over the last 5 years was **12%** per annum.

From this information about the average actual return achieved in the past, and other information about the company, we can predict the return that we expect this investment to generate in the future. Suppose we read that Paris foods has just taken over a competitor. We might conclude from this that we expect the average future returns to be, say, 3% per annum higher than the actual past return – this would give an **expected future return** of (12% + 3%) = **15%**

The next task would be to consider the risk associated with the investment. As well as measuring the actual return in the past it is also possible to measure the variability of returns, or risk. We could also bring in other information that we are aware of to predict the future level of risk. We might, for example conclude that because Paris foods has recently taken over a competitor, we expect a greater variability of returns in the future than has been the case in the past. To compensate for this let's assume that we **require a return of 14%**.

Because the expected future return is greater than the return required to compensate for the level of risk we would say that the investment is worthwhile. The required return is effectively a benchmark or a target against which the expected return is compared.

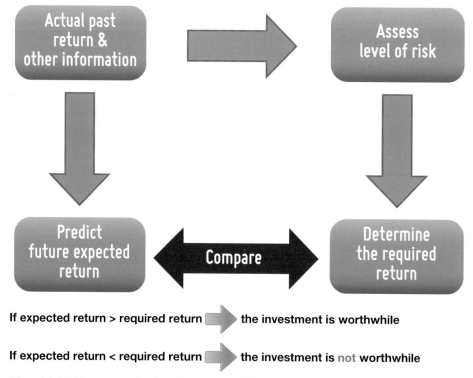

If expected return > required return ➡ **the investment is worthwhile**

If expected return < required return ➡ **the investment is not worthwhile**

Shouldn't the expected return equal the required return?

If you have already asked yourself this question when reading the above – congratulations. You have already jumped ahead to chapter 11 which covers the capital asset pricing model and chapter 14 which covers the efficiency of stock markets.

The expected return is partly based on the price paid for an investment and it could be argued that the correct 'price' of an investment would be where the expected return = required return. This is the essence of the **capital asset pricing model** – but more of that later in the book.

Chapter 1
key points summary

- There are three key decisions in financial management which are interrelated – we cannot consider one without the other two.

  - Investment decisions – how should we invest cash?

  - Finance decisions – how do we raise finance?

  - Dividend decisions – what level of dividend should be paid?

- The main objective in finance theory is to maximise shareholder wealth.

  - Other stakeholders (apart from shareholders) need to be considered in the short term in order to maximise shareholder wealth in the long term – e.g. employees, the wider community.

- Risk averse – means that investors require higher returns to compensate for higher levels of risk – it does not mean that investors want to avoid risk altogether.

- Total shareholder return = $\dfrac{\text{Dividend} \pm \text{Change in share price}}{\text{Share price at the beginning of the period}}$ x 100%

- Three types of return to be aware of are as follows.

  - Actual return – return achieved in the past by an investor.

  - Expected return – return investors expect to receive in the future (no guarantee).

  - Required return – return investors require to compensate for the risk involved.

- If expected return > required return then investment is worthwhile.

INVESTMENT APPRAISAL 2

Introduction
what is this chapter about?

In chapter 1 we saw that there were three key decisions for a finance manager to consider. They were the investment decision, the financing decision and the dividend decision. This chapter is the first of a series of chapters that focuses on the first of these decisions – the investment decision.

Key areas of the chapter are ....

1   **Basic investment appraisal techniques** – what are the more basic investment appraisal techniques that are available to finance managers? What are the benefits and drawbacks of each of these techniques?

2   **Net present value (NPV)** – the net present value technique is the most important of all of the investment appraisal techniques. What is it and how do we calculate it? Why is the net present value so important and what are the benefits of using this technique rather than any of the other investment appraisal techniques that are available?

3   **Internal rate of return (IRR)** – this is the main alternative to the net present value technique. How do we calculate the internal rate of return and what does it tell us? What are its benefits and limitations compared to the net present value?

BASIC INVESTMENT APPRAISAL TECHNIQUES

One important point to note before we consider investment appraisal techniques in detail is that the terms investment appraisal and project appraisal mean the same thing. A new investment that a company is considering can alternatively be described as a new project.

Need to know!

Investment appraisal = project appraisal

There are really two basic techniques that are used to appraise new investments that a business may undertake.

1 Accounting rate of return (ARR).

2 Payback period.

Finance terminology explained

Accounting rate of return

This technique involves calculating an average accounting rate of return for a proposed new investment, and comparing this to a target return.

The accounting rate of return is sometimes called the return on capital employed.

The accounting rate of return for a new investment can be calculated in one of two ways. It is either:

$$\frac{\text{Average annual accounting profit before interest and tax}}{\text{Initial capital invested}}$$

Or

$$\frac{\text{Average annual accounting profit before interest and tax}}{\text{Average capital invested}}$$

Points to note about the accounting rate of return

- It is based on the **average profit** generated by the investment. Interest and tax are a distribution of those profits, and therefore the relevant profit figure is the profit before interest and tax.

- As it's a profit measure it will include a deduction for the depreciation charge. Often in examination questions you will need to adjust for this depreciation charge in arriving at the average annual profit before interest and tax.

- The ratio measures the level of return being generated in relation to the capital invested. This could be based on the **initial capital**, or, it could be argued that a better measure would be to base the ratio on the **average capital** invested. This reflects the fact that as assets get older, they are less productive and generate less profit.

Example 1

Craig is a specialist car conversion company. Its main business activity is to convert cars to dual steering which it then sells on to driving schools nationwide. Craig is considering investing in new advanced production machinery which is expected to cost $2,800,000.

The machinery is expected to generate average profits each year, after allowing for depreciation, of $448,000. The machine will be used for 10 years after which it will be sold for an estimated $400,000.

Craig has a target accounting rate of return of 12% for all of its investments. Any investment that generates a lower return than this would be rejected.

Requirement

Should Craig invest in the new machinery?

Solution 1

The example does not specify how Craig calculates the accounting rate of return. We will therefore calculate this using both approaches.

Based on the **initial capital invested** the accounting rate of return would be:

$$\frac{\$448,000}{\$2,800,000} \times 100\% = 16\%$$

The **average capital invested** would be:

$$\frac{\$2,800,000 + \$400,000}{2} = \$1,600,000$$

This means that if the value of the machinery is $2,800,000 at the beginning of its life and is $400,000 at the end of its life, it will be worth an average of $1,600,000 during its life.

Based on the **average capital invested** the accounting rate of return would be:

$$\frac{\$448,000}{\$1,600,000} \times 100\% = 28\%$$

In both cases, the accounting rate of return is greater than the target figure, and therefore the recommendation would be to invest in the new machinery.

What are the benefits and drawbacks of using the accounting rate of return as an investment appraisal technique?

Benefits	Drawbacks
It is based on accounting profit. It is therefore consistent with accounting information.	Accounting profit is based on subjective assumptions, for example, the rate of depreciation used.
It is relatively simple to calculate and is easily understood.	Equal weighting is given to profit generated in different accounting periods. Profit generated, for example, in 7 years' time has the same impact on the result as profit generated in year 1.

Finance terminology explained

Payback period

The payback period is the length of time taken to recover the cash that is initially invested in an investment.

This method of investment appraisal is **based on cash** rather than accounting profit.

As a method of appraising investments it is particularly useful for analysing the liquidity of an investment, or how quickly a company can recover the cash that is invested.

The payback period is often used as a screening method when a large number of potential projects are being considered and there is a need to narrow this number down before further detailed analysis is carried out. A business may, for example, decide to analyse in detail only those projects that have a payback period of less than 5 years.

Example 2

Lowri is a major fashion retailer which currently operates 225 stores throughout the world. It is planning to open 30 new stores in the next 12 months as part of its expansion programme. Lowri has performed initial research on 60 potential new sites and now wishes to narrow this number down. Lowri has decided that any store with a payback period of greater than 4 years will not be considered further.

The following information is available about one potential site:

Initial investment required	=	$120,000
Net cash inflow in year 1	=	$20,000
Net cash inflow in year 2	=	$35,000
Net cash inflow in year 3	=	$50,000
Net cash inflow in year 4	=	$70,000
Net cash inflow in year 5	=	$25,000

Requirement

Will this potential site be suitable for further consideration?

Solution 2

We can determine the payback period as follows:

Time	Cashflow ($)	Cumulative cashflow ($)
Now	(120,000)	(120,000)
First year	20,000	(100,000)
Second year	35,000	(65,000)
Third year	50,000	(15,000)
Fourth year	70,000	55,000

The payback period is therefore somewhere between year 3 and year 4. If we assume that cashflows accrue evenly during the year, the point at which the investment pays back can be estimated as:

$$3 \text{ years} + \frac{15,000}{70,000} = 3.2 \text{ years}$$

The payback period is therefore less than the maximum allowed, and therefore this investment would be considered further.

Payback period – shortcut

If the future cash inflows are an equal annual amount each year (which is known as an annuity – see later in the chapter), then rather than set out a table as above, the payback period can be calculated quickly using the following formula:

$$\frac{\text{Initial investment}}{\text{Net annual cashflow}}$$

Example 3

Dawn has a minimum acceptable payback period for new investments of 7 years. It is considering the following new investment:

Initial investment required   = $90,000

Net annual cash inflow from time 1 to time 10 = $20,000

Requirement

Would this investment be acceptable?

Solution 3

The payback period can be determined as follows:

$$\frac{\$90,000}{\$20,000} = 4.5 \text{ years and is therefore acceptable as an investment.}$$

What are the benefits and drawbacks of using the payback period as an investment appraisal technique?

Benefits	Drawbacks
It is based on cashflow rather than profit. Cashflow is much less subjective than accounting profit and is more directly relevant to shareholder wealth.	Cashflows beyond the payback period are ignored. These may be much more significant for one investment compared to another.
It is relatively simple to calculate and is easily understood.	Equal weighting is given to cashflow generated in different time periods.

NET PRESENT VALUE (NPV)

The net present value, and the internal rate of return (that we see in the next section) are both known as discounted cash flow techniques. They are both based on future forecast cash flows rather than profit and also reflect the time value of money.

The time value of money

The time value of money is a fundamental principle which underlies a number of the financial management theories and ideas that we cover in subsequent chapters.

The time value of money suggests that $100 of cash received today will be worth more than the same $100 of cash received at a future date.

Why is this the case?

There are a number of reasons.

1   **Reinvestment possibility**

    When cash is received, it could be reinvested and therefore earn interest. If an investor received $100 today and was able to invest this amount at 10% interest per annum, then $10 of interest could be earned over the next year. An investment of $100 could be turned into an equivalent investment of $110 in a years' time.

2   **Inflation**

    Inflation eats away at the purchasing power of money. If there is inflation in an economy $100 received in one years' time would buy fewer goods in a supermarket, for example, than the same $100 received today.

3   **Risk**

    $100 received today is a certain return. If an investor expects to receive $100 in a years' time there is always an element of risk, even if the investment appears to be very secure (consider the banking crisis of 2009 – some investors in very 'secure' triple A rated bonds lost a significant part of their investment). In general, the further into the future the expected cashflow the more risk there is.

In this chapter we focus on the reinvestment possibility. The impact of inflation and risk are considered in later chapters.

Compounding

If the time value of money is an important concept for both investors and companies, how can we compare cashflows which arise at different points in time?

The first approach is to compound. How does this work?

Example 4

Suppose an investor has $100 of cash available to invest today. If we assume that an investor can invest cash at 8% interest per annum and that any interest earned is reinvested, how much will the investment be worth in 3 years' time?

Solution 4

If $100 is invested at 8% per annum then the investment will be worth:

In 1 years' time - $100.00 x (1+0.08)   = $108.00
In 2 years' time - $108.00 x (1+0.08)   = $116.64
In 3 years' time - $116.64 x (1+0.08)   = $125.97

Compound interest means that we expect the interest cash flow to grow each year as the interest from the previous year is added to the capital invested.

We can achieve the same answer more quickly by using the formula:

$$PV (1+r)^n = TV$$

Where:

r   =   interest rate
n   =   the number of periods for which we are compounding
PV =   present value, or the value today
TV =   terminal value, or the value at the end of the life of the project

For example 4, the interest rate is 8% or 0.08 and the number of periods (years in this case) is 3.

The solution to example 4 could therefore have been determined as follows:

$100 (1 + 0.08)^3 = $125.97

Discounting

Discounting is the term we use if we want to find the present value, or value today of a cashflow that is expected to be received at a certain date in the future. This is the opposite of compounding. It is much more useful for appraising investments than compounding.

Need to know!

Discounting

To discount, or find the present value of a known future cashflow we can rearrange the compounding formula seen above.

$$TV \times \frac{1}{(1 + r)^n} = PV$$

Where:

r = interest rate
n = the number of periods for which we are discounting
PV = present value, or the value today
TV = terminal value, or the value at the end of the project's life

Example 5

Suppose an investor expects to receive $500 in 4 years' time. If the relevant interest rate is 5% what would be the present value of this cashflow?

Solution 5

We can use the formula to find the present value as follows:

$$\$500 \times \frac{1}{(1 + 0.05)^4} = \$411.35$$

The significance of compounding and discounting

Discounting and compounding is all about equating cashflows which arise at different points in time.

In example 5 above, we can say that at a 5% rate of interest an investor is indifferent between receiving $500 in 4 years' time, and receiving $411.35 immediately. An investor receiving $411.35 immediately could invest that at 5% per annum on a compound basis and turn it into $500 in 4 years' time.

We could also conclude, from the information in example 5, that if an investor was offered, for example, a choice of $420 today or $500 in 4 years' time at 5% interest, then the investor would prefer $420 today. An amount of $420 today could be turned into more than $500 in 4 years' time.

So far we have assumed when discounting that the rate of interest can be used to reflect the impact of the time value of money on future cash flows. In reality, however, the concept of the time value of money is more complicated than simply assuming that cash can be reinvested to earn interest. When discounting therefore, we talk about a discount rate rather than an interest rate. This discount rate will reflect all factors affecting the time value of money.

Discount factor and tables for a single cashflow

Discount factor

In the formula

$$TV \times \frac{1}{(1 + r)^n} = PV$$

we know that r is now known as the discount rate.

Need to know!

Discount tables

The fraction $\frac{1}{(1 + r)^n}$ is known as the discount factor and is often quoted to 3 decimal places.

In example 5, the discount factor would be $\frac{1}{(1 + 0.05)^4} = 0.823$

The present value can then be found by **multiplying** the future cash flow by the discount factor:

$$\$500 \times 0.823 = \$411.50$$

The answer is virtually the same as in example 5. The difference is due to the fact that we have rounded the discount factor to 3 decimal places.

Discount tables

Because discounting future cashflows is a very important principle of finance and investment, a set of **tables** is often used as a quick alternative to the formula to find the present value of the future cashflow. An example of a typical set of tables is shown in the appendix at the back of the book.

If we read the tables we can see that at a 5% discount rate, the relevant factor for period 4 is 0.823.

Discounted cashflow techniques — timing assumption

Cashflows in real life arise on a continuous basis. Every day, for example, most businesses will generate cash inflows, and will need to make cash outflows. For investment appraisal purposes we need to make assumptions about the timing of cashflows in order to be able to produce a result in a cost-effective way.

Need to know!

Discounting will be carried out in real life, and in exam questions, on a **periodic** basis. This means that cashflows are assumed to arise at fixed points in time. Often the time period will be assumed to be one year.

Cashflows that arise **during a period of time** are assumed to arise **at the end of that period** of time. Suppose, for example, a question says that sales during the first year of operations will be $60,000. For discounting purposes, the sales would be assumed to arise at the end of the first year, which would be referred to as **year 1 or time 1** in an investment appraisal exercise.

Finance terminology explained

Net present value (NPV)

The net present value of an investment is the present value of the future cash inflows from the investment, less the present value of the future cash outflows from the investment.

Because discounting future cashflows equates cashflows that arise at different points in time we can make a decision about an investment using the NPV as follows:

If the NPV is positive the investment is worthwhile and should be accepted

If the NPV is negative the investment is not worthwhile and should be rejected

Example 6

Let's re-visit example 2 – Lowri. We assessed the payback period of the investment in example 2 and found that it was below the target payback period set. We can now calculate the net present value of the investment. The cashflows were as follows:

Initial investment required = $120,000
Net cash inflow in year 1 = $20,000
Net cash inflow in year 2 = $35,000
Net cash inflow in year 3 = $50,000
Net cash inflow in year 4 = $70,000
Net cash inflow in year 5 = $25,000

The discount rate that Lowri uses to appraise new investments is 10%.
What is the NPV of the investment at a 10% discount rate?

Solution 6

The present value of a cashflow at time 0 is the same as the cashflow itself. There is no discounting of this cashflow and therefore the relevant discount factor is 1.000.

Time	Cashflow ($)	Discount factor @ 10%	Present value ($)
T0	(120,000)	1.000	(120,000)
T1	20,000	0.909	18,180
T2	35,000	0.826	28,910
T3	50,000	0.751	37,550
T4	70,000	0.683	47,810
T5	25,000	0.621	15,525
		NPV	**27,975**

The net present value is positive at $27,975 and therefore this investment is worthwhile. The investment should therefore be accepted.

Net present value and shareholder wealth

One of the important points about using the net present value as an investment appraisal technique is the link between the result and shareholder wealth.

Need to know!

If an appropriate discount rate is used, and a company was to proceed with an investment that has a positive NPV, the **wealth of the shareholders should rise by exactly the same as the NPV itself**. We will see how this works in later chapters.

In example 6, if the business went ahead with the investment, shareholder wealth should rise by a total of $27,975.

Annuities and perpetuities

With certain types of cashflow, shortcuts are available which allow us to find the present value quickly. The main types of cashflow where this is a possibility are annuities and perpetuities. We will consider other types of cashflow where shortcuts are possible in the next chapter.

Finance terminology explained

Annuity

An annuity is an equal annual cashflow, beginning in one periods' time, and continuing for a certain number of periods. Very often a period will equate to a year.

Consider the following example:

Example 7

What is the present value of an annual cash inflow of $10,000 from time 1 to time 3 at a discount rate of 9%?

Solution 7

We could discount each cashflow separately as follows using the discount factors at 9%:

Time	Cashflow ($)	Discount factor @ 9%	Present value ($)
T1	10,000	0.917	9,170
T2	10,000	0.842	8,420
T3	10,000	0.772	7,720
			25,310

Because the discount factor is multiplied by $10,000 in each of the three years, we can find the present value more quickly by adding up the three separate discount factors, and then multiplying $10,000 by the total.

The sum of the three discount factors is:

0.917 + 0.842 + 0.772 = 2.531

We then multiply the equal annual cashflow by this amount to find the present value:

$10,000 x 2.531 = $25,310

Annuity factor

The sum of the three separate discount rates is called an annuity factor.

As with the discount factors for a single cashflow, a table of annuity factors that have already been calculated is often used. An example is shown in the appendix at the back of the book.

Need to know!

The annuity factor could also be calculated directly by using the following formula:

$$\frac{1 - (1 + r)^{-n}}{r}$$

Where:
r = discount rate
n = the number of periods, beginning in time 1, for which the annuity arises

Example 8

What is the present value of an annuity of $800 receivable from time 1 to time 8 at a discount rate of 4%?

Solution 8

Using the formula we can find the annuity factor as follows:

$$\frac{1 - (1 + 0.04)^{-8}}{0.04} = 6.733$$

The present value is therefore:

$800 x 6.733 = $5,386

Finance terminology explained

Perpetuity

A perpetuity is an equal annual cashflow from time 1 until an infinite time in the future.

To calculate the present value of a perpetuity we multiply the cashflow by the perpetuity factor.

How do we determine the present value of a perpetuity?

Need to know!

The perpetuity factor is

$$\frac{1}{r}$$

Where r is the discount rate.

Example 9

What is the present value of an equal annual cashflow of $400 from time 1 to infinity at a discount rate of 12%?

Solution 9

The present value is determined as follows:

$$\$400 \times \frac{1}{0.12} = \$3,333$$

Discount rate and cost of capital

The term discount rate has been used in most of the examples that we have considered so far. The relevant discount rate for a business to use in most situations is the cost of capital. This is covered in detail in chapter 8.

What are the benefits and drawbacks of using the net present value as an investment appraisal technique?

Benefits	Drawbacks
It is based on cashflow rather than profit.	It is not easy to understand or to explain to managers.
It takes into account the time value of money.	It is based on an estimated discount rate which estimates the cost of capital. The estimate of the cost of capital may be incorrect.
It is an absolute measure of the value of an investment to a business.	
It tells us the amount by which shareholder wealth would change if we went ahead with the investment.	

INTERNAL RATE OF RETURN (IRR)

The internal rate of return is the alternative way of using discounted cashflow techniques to evaluate a new investment. It is a measure of the true return that an investment offers when we take into account the time value of money.

Finance terminology explained

How is the internal rate of return defined?

The internal rate of return is the rate of return that gives an NPV of zero. In other words it is the rate of return at which the present value of the cash inflows is equal to the present value of the cash outflows.

Many managers in business feel more comfortable discussing a percentage return than a net present value and therefore prefer the internal rate of return method to the net present value method.

Don't confuse the internal rate of return (IRR) with the accounting rate of return (ARR). Although both are percentage returns, the IRR is based on cashflow and reflects the time value of money whereas the ARR is based on profit and does not reflect the time value of money.

Calculation of the IRR

To calculate the IRR we need to use the following approach.

1   Calculate the NPV of an investment at two different discount rates. Ideally the NPV at one discount rate will be a positive result and the NPV at the other discount rate will give a negative result.

2 Use linear interpolation to estimate the rate at which the NPV is zero. This means that we assume that there is a liner relationship between a change in the discount rate and a change in the NPV. A formula is often used to do this.

The formula for linear interpolation

Need to know!

The formula for estimating the IRR is as follows:

$$IRR = L + \frac{N_L}{N_L - N_H} \times (H - L)$$

Where:

L	=	lower discount rate
H	=	higher discount rate
N_L	=	NPV at the lower discount rate
N_H	=	NPV at the higher discount rate

Interpretation of the result of an IRR calculation

The IRR needs to be compared to a target figure for the return from an investment. The target figure is normally the company's cost of capital.

If the IRR > cost of capital **accept** the project

If the IRR < cost of capital **reject** the project

Example 10

Simon is a retailer of high quality kitchens. It is considering a major new investment in computer aided design technology which would enable the business to increase its productivity significantly as well as offer a better service to its customers.

The following cashflows are estimated to arise from the introduction of the new technology:

Initial investment required	=	$150,000
Year 1 net cash inflow	=	$38,000
Year 2 net cash inflow	=	$44,000
Year 3 net cash inflow	=	$58,000
Year 4 net cash inflow	=	$54,000

Simon only wishes to consider cashflows arising over the next 4 years as part of its evaluation.

Simon's cost of capital is 8%. This is also the target rate for new investments.

Evaluate the new investment using the IRR approach and determine whether the new investment should be undertaken.

Solution 10

Working 1

The first working is to calculate the NPV at two different discount rates. It is sensible to use the cost of capital as one discount rate. If this results in a positive NPV we will select a second discount rate which is higher than the first.

Time	Cashflow ($)	DF @ 8%	PV @ 8%	DF @12%	PV @ 12%
T0	(150,000)	1.000	(150,000)	1.000	(150,000)
T1	38,000	0.926	35,188	0.893	33,934
T2	44,000	0.857	37,708	0.797	35,068
T3	58,000	0.794	46,052	0.712	41,296
T4	54,000	0.735	39,690	0.636	34,344
		NPV	8,638	NPV	(5,358)

Working 2

We then use the IRR formula as follows:

L = 8% or 0.08
H = 12% or 0.12
N_L = 8,638
N_H = (5,416)

$$IRR = 0.08 + \frac{8,638}{8,638 + 5,358} \times (0.12 - 0.08) = 0.1047 \text{ or } 10.47\%$$

The IRR is estimated to be 10.47%. This is above the cost of capital and therefore the investment should be accepted.

Exam tip – IRR calculation

In the formula for estimating the internal rate of return the NPV at the higher rate needs to be taken away from the NPV at the lower rate. Often, as in the example above, the NPV at the higher rate is negative. A minus multiplied by a minus is a plus and therefore in the formula above we added $5,416 to the NPV at the lower rate.

The true relationship between the discount rate and the NPV

The linear interpolation formula used above assumes that the relationship between a change in a discount rate and a change in the NPV is linear. This is not the case; the relationship is curvilinear which means that the result obtained using the formula is only an estimate of the true IRR.

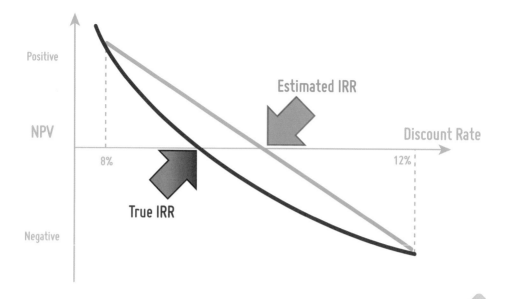

Exam tip – IRR calculation

Because the true relationship between a change in the discount rate and a change in the NPV is curvilinear, the choice of discount rates used to calculate the two NPV's will have an impact on the result. The estimated IRR will always be higher than the true IRR.

As long as the discount rates used are reasonable, an examiner will accept the estimate. When discussing the result, however, it is sensible to point out to an examiner that the estimated IRR is greater than the true IRR.

What are the benefits and drawbacks of using the internal rate of return as an investment appraisal technique?

Benefits	Drawbacks
It is based on cashflow rather than profit.	If there are non-conventional cashflows there may be more than one IRR.
It takes into account the time value of money.	When comparing mutually exclusive investments the result may not be consistent with the result when using the NPV technique.
It is a percentage return and therefore easily understood.	The IRR assumes that cashflows are reinvested at the IRR.

Drawbacks explained in more detail

1 Non-conventional cashflows

A conventional investment has an initial cash outflow followed by a series of cash inflows similar to the scenario in example 10. With such an investment, the NPV will always fall as the discount rate rises and therefore there is only one IRR as seen in the graph above.

Some investments have non-conventional cashflows. An example would be the construction of a nuclear power station. With this type of investment there will be a significant initial investment (cash outflow), then a series of net cash inflows during the operational phase, and then, at the end of the life of the investment there will be significant decommissioning costs (a further cash outflow).

With such an investment the relationship between a change in the discount rate and the NPV is more complex. There may be two IRRs or no IRRs depending on the specific cashflows!

2   Mutually exclusive investments

Mutually exclusive investments refer to a situation where undertaking one investment precludes another investment. An example would be where a business is considering a new piece of machinery in a manufacturing process and there are two potential suppliers of that machinery. The business can only buy from one supplier and therefore purchasing one piece of machinery precludes the other.

A problem with the IRR is that the machinery with the highest IRR may not have the highest NPV when discounted at the cost of capital. Choosing the machine that has the highest IRR may, therefore be the wrong decision.

3   Reinvestment at the IRR

If the IRR is referred to as the 'return' that a business obtains from an investment, this assumes that any cash inflows can be reinvested at the IRR for the life of the investment.

This is often unrealistic – the likely reinvestment rate for cash inflows would normally be significantly below this.

Need to know!

When there is a conflict between the results obtained using each of these two investment appraisal techniques, for example, when comparing mutually exclusive investments, the decision should be based on the result of the NPV analysis.

Because the NPV is an absolute measure of the value of the investment, and links directly to shareholder wealth it is considered to be a superior technique to the IRR.

Investment appraisal techniques – a summary

A summary of the key differences and similarities between the investment appraisal techniques is as follows:

	ARR	Payback period	NPV	IRR
Reflects the time value of money	✗	✗	✓	✓
Based on cashflow	✗	✓	✓	✓
Percentage return	✓	✗	✗	✓
Considers whole life of investment	✓	✗	✓	✓
Absolute measure of return	✗	✗	✓	✗
Easy to understand/explain	✓	✓	✗	✓

Chapter 2
key points summary

- There are two non-discounted cashflow techniques.

  - Accounting rate of return (ARR) – based on average profit.

  - Payback period – based on cashflow.

- Discounted cashflow techniques are superior because they take into account the time value of money.

- There are three main types of cashflow (covered so far!) to consider when discounting.

  1. A single cashflow – use formula or tables. Formula: $\dfrac{1}{(1 + r)^n}$

  2. An annuity (equal annual cashflow from time 1 to time n) – use formula or tables.

     Formula: $\dfrac{1 - (1 + r)^{-n}}{r}$

  3. A perpetuity (equal annual cashflow from time 1 to infinity) – can only find present value by using formula.

     Formula: $\dfrac{1}{r}$

- The NPV is the superior discounted cashflow technique. The NPV equals the change in shareholder wealth.

- The IRR is the rate at which the NPV is zero. It is found through using trial and error and then linear interpolation.

  Formula: $IRR = L + \dfrac{N_L}{N_L - N_H} \times (H - L)$

3

FURTHER DISCOUNTED CASHFLOW

Introduction
what is this chapter about?

In the previous chapter we looked at the main techniques that can be used by a business to appraise new investments, or projects, that are under consideration. We concluded that discounted cashflow (DCF) techniques are superior to other techniques because they take into account the time value of money.

This chapter further develops discounted cashflow techniques (great – I hear you say – more discounted cashflow!) and introduces real world complications such as dealing with the impact of inflation and taxation.

Key areas of the chapter are ....

1 **Presentation of an NPV** – how should an NPV calculation be presented in an examination question?

2 **DCF and inflation** – how is inflation taken into account in an NPV or IRR calculation? How will different assumptions about inflation impact on the result?

3 **DCF and taxation** – undertaking a new investment often has significant taxation implications. How are these taken into account in a discounted cashflow calculation?

4 **Relevant cashflows** – In performing a discounted cashflow calculation, which cashflows are relevant to the analysis and which cashflows should be ignored?

PRESENTATION OF AN NPV

Students are often under severe time pressure in an exam when carrying out an analysis of an investment using the NPV technique. When there are a significant range of cashflows with numerous complications, the presentation of the NPV can have a major impact on the ability to produce a good quality answer in the time available.

Approaches to presenting an NPV

There are two possible approaches to presenting an NPV calculation.

1 Years down the side of the page

This was the approach adopted in the last chapter. It is sensible when an investment appraisal exercise is relatively simple to the extent that we only have one or two cashflows arising in each time period.

The final column is the present value of cashflows, and by totalling the final column we obtain the NPV result neatly and quickly.

The pro-forma would be as follows:

Time	Cashflow	DF @ X%	Present value
T0	(X)	1.000	(X)
TI	X	X	X
		NPV	X

2 Years across the top of the page

This is the approach that is recommended whenever there are more complex cashflows or a greater number of cashflows to consider in each period. Presenting the analysis by setting the years out across the top of the page will be a neater and more sensible approach in a more complex question.

This approach is generally the best approach to take if dealing with the impact of inflation or taxation on an NPV (because, unfortunately, the cashflows are a bit more complex).

The pro-forma would be as follows:

Cashflow	T0	T1	T2	T3
Sales		X	X	X
Material costs		(X)	(X)	(X)
Labour costs		(X)	(X)	(X)
Taxation		(X)	(X)	(X)
Initial cost	(X)			
DF @ x%	1.000	X	X	X
Present value	(X)	X	X	X
NPV	X			

This will be the sum of the figures in the row above

Exam tip – NPV presentation

It is important to read the question very carefully, and think about the information presented before deciding on the specific layout.

Whilst the second approach of laying the years out across the top of the page is generally suitable for more complex NPVs, there are occasions where, even in a complex analysis, presenting the answer using the first approach is neater and quicker.

An example of this would be a complex analysis with significant annuities, for example if the sales revenue is $10,000 from time 1 to time 8. Using the first approach we can multiply a cashflow of $10,000 by the 8 year annuity factor to produce the present value of this cashflow as a single figure in the final column.

DCF AND INFLATION

Inflation is a real life problem which affects us all. In relation to appraising investments there are two impacts of inflation that you need to be able to deal with. These are firstly the impact on the estimated future cashflows and secondly the impact on the discount rate.

Specific and general inflation

1 Specific inflation – relevant to cashflows

This is the level of inflation that would be applicable to specific cashflows that are taken into account in an NPV calculation. A business may estimate, for example, that its material costs are likely to rise by an average of 5% per annum in the future as a result of inflation.

Other specific cashflows may be expected to inflate at a different rate. A business may, for example, forecast a lower rate of inflation in its sales revenue than in its material costs. It may be that, because of significant competition in a particular market, a business is unable to pass on the full material cost inflation into its selling prices.

2 General inflation – relevant to the discount rate

This refers to the general rate of inflation in the economy. There are a number of ways of measuring this in the real economy including the retail price index (RPI) and the consumer price index (CPI).

Capital invested in a business is provided by investors in the real economy. When we discount an investment the discount rate that we use reflects the cost of capital.

The general inflation rate is therefore the rate of inflation that would be relevant to the discount rate or cost of capital in an NPV calculation.

How do we take inflation into account when doing an NPV?

There are two acceptable approaches to dealing with inflation in an NPV analysis.

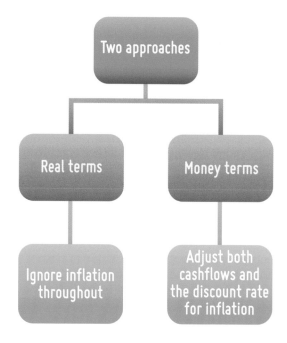

1   Real terms approach

Under this approach we completely ignore inflation in the calculation. This means that we do not inflate estimated future cashflows using the specific rate of inflation. Instead we present future cashflows in current prices, or today's prices.

To be consistent we also want to ignore the impact of inflation on the discount rate. The discount rate represents the cost of capital, and we therefore need to discount using a real cost of capital.

2   Money terms approach

Under this approach we inflate the cashflows using the specific rates of inflation applicable to each cashflow.

When discounting, we use a money cost of capital (sometimes called a nominal cost of capital). This is the cost of capital that includes the impact of general inflation on the returns that investors demand.

Money and real discount rate

We have already seen from the above that the difference between a money discount rate and a real discount rate is the level of general inflation.

How do we get from a real discount rate to a money discount rate or vice versa?

Need to know!

The relationship between the money discount rate and the real discount rate is a compound relationship and is given by the Fisher effect which is shown below

$(1+m) = (1+r) \times (1+i)$

Where

m = the money discount rate

r = the real discount rate

i = the general inflation rate

We will see how this equation is used in example 1.

Exam tip – Money and real rate

Assume that a discount rate or cost of capital quoted in an exam question is a money rate unless told otherwise.

Most rates quoted in an economy are money rates. If, for example, a rate of interest offered on a bank loan is 6% – this is a money rate. The bank would receive 6% as a money return each year, but inflation would mean that the 'real return' would be considerably less than this.

The weighted average cost of capital (WACC) that we see in a later chapter is a money rate.

Discounting in money and in real terms

Having established the different approaches to dealing with inflation we will now see how each approach works using an example.

Example 1

Kevin manufactures digital radios. It is considering investing in a new factory. The factory will cost $900,000 which would be payable immediately. The new factory is expected to generate an additional annual net cash inflow of $500,000 per annum in current prices for the next three years. The specific rate of inflation applicable to the net cash inflow is 10% per annum.

The real cost of capital is 20%, and the general rate of inflation in the economy is, in this case, 10%, the same as the specific rate applicable to the cashflows.

Requirements

(a) What is the NPV in real terms?

(b) What is the NPV in money terms?

(a) NPV in real terms

Annual cashflows are given in current prices, and we are also given the real cost of capital. In real terms this is therefore a relatively straightforward discounting exercise.

Time	Cashflow	DF @ 20%	NPV ($)
0	(900,000)	1.000	(900,000)
1	500,000	$\dfrac{1}{(1 + 0.20)}$	416,667
2	500,000	$\dfrac{1}{(1 + 0.20)^2}$	347,222
3	500,000	$\dfrac{1}{(1 + 0.20)^3}$	289,352
			153,241

(b) NPV in money terms

In this case the first requirement is to determine the money cost of capital using the Fisher formula:

$$
\begin{aligned}
(1+m) &= (1 + r) \times (1 + i) \\
(1+m) &= (1 + 0.20) \times (1 + 0.10) \\
1+m &= 1.32 \\
m &= 1.32 - 1 \\
m &= 0.32 \text{ or } 32\%
\end{aligned}
$$

We then need to convert the real cashflows into money cashflows by increasing the cashflows using the specific rates of inflation as follows:

Year 1 - $500,000 \times (1 + 0.10)$ = $550,000
Year 2 - $500,000 \times (1 + 0.10)^2$ = $605,000
Year 3 - $500,000 \times (1 + 0.10)^3$ = $665,500

The NPV in money terms can then be calculated.

Time	Cashflow	DF @ 32%	NPV ($)
0	(900,000)	1.000	(900,000)
1	550,000	$\dfrac{1}{(1 + 0.32)}$	416,667
2	605,000	$\dfrac{1}{(1 + 0.32)^2}$	347,222
3	665,500	$\dfrac{1}{(1 + 0.32)^3}$	289,352
			153,241

The answer is exactly the same in real terms and money terms

Is this magic? – no - however, this has only arisen because the specific and general rates of inflation are exactly the same, and there is only one specific rate of inflation applicable to all of the cashflows. The inflation applicable to the cashflow has been cancelled out by the inflation applicable to the discount rate. Moving from a real to a money approach, the cashflows have increased because of the specific inflation rate applicable to them, but this is cancelled out in present value terms because of a higher discount rate.

Money or real terms approach?

Which approach is it best to take in exam questions? – now this is the really important bit!

Need to know!

A money terms approach is appropriate if:

1   there is more than one specific rate of inflation e.g. if we assume that material costs inflate at 4% per annum and sales inflate at 5% per annum, or if the general rate of inflation applicable to the cost of capital is different to the specific rate of inflation applicable to the cashflows

2   capital allowances are given, or are calculated in a question. The capital allowance would be offset against the money cashflow that would arise in the future. The benefit of a capital allowance (which we will see in the next section) is therefore a money cashflow.

A real terms approach is appropriate if:

1   there is a single rate of inflation applicable to all cashflows and the discount rate. This was the case in example 1, and we saw that in this case the real terms approach was slightly quicker

2   we wish to take advantage of annuity factors. By keeping cashflows in current prices we often end up with annuities. In example 1, there was an annuity of $500,000 per annum when the cashflows were kept in current prices. We could have multiplied the annuity by the three year annuity factor to obtain the same answer more quickly. As soon as we inflate cashflows we have a separate cashflow each year and therefore lose the annuity.

DCF AND TAXATION

There are three important tax effects to take into account in a discounted cashflow calculation. They are:

1   **Taxation of operating cashflow**. The net operating cashflow generated by a project or investment will be taxed at the company's corporate tax rate and therefore is a relevant cashflow which needs to be included in the calculation.

2   **Tax benefits from available capital allowances**. Certain assets invested in will qualify for capital allowance tax relief. As a result a cash inflow will exist which needs to be included in the calculation.

3   **Tax relief on interest payments on debt**. If an investment is financed by issuing debt capital, the interest payment on the debt will be tax allowable. This is dealt with by adjusting the cost of capital or discount rate – we will see how this is done in chapter 9. For the examples in this chapter, the term 'post-tax discount rate' is used. This assumes that the cost of capital has been correctly adjusted for any tax relief available on interest payments on debt.

Taxation of operating cashflow

This would be found by multiplying the net operating cashflow by the relevant corporate tax rate. We would normally add an additional line into an NPV calculation to reflect this additional cash outflow.

Timing of taxation of operating cashflow

In any NPV analysis we need to make simplifying assumptions in order to be able to discount at fixed (normally) annual time intervals.

The normal assumption to make about the timing of tax payments on operating cashflow is to assume that tax is **either payable in the same year** as the profit or cashflow upon which it is charged, or that **tax is payable a year later**.

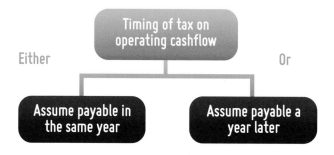

A question will normally suggest that one of these assumptions should be made. If the question doesn't say anything then either assumption would be acceptable.

Capital allowances

An exam question should always specify whether or not allowances are claimable on assets purchased by a company as part of an investment. The rate of capital allowances should also be specified in a question.

Timing of the first capital allowance

Normal taxation rules allow an ongoing business to claim the first capital allowance (also known as writing down allowances) at the end of the accounting period in which the asset in question is purchased. This is irrespective of when, during the accounting period, this purchase occurs.

All cashflows in an NPV calculation are assumed to arise at fixed annual points in time. As a result there is a need to make an assumption about when an asset is purchased in relation to an accounting period end. Two alternative assumptions are possible in exam questions.

1 First writing down allowance (WDA) at time 0

We could assume that the asset is purchased just before the end of the accounting period. The date that the asset is purchased is normally assumed to be time 0. If the asset is purchased just before the end of the accounting period we can assume that the first WDA is claimable immediately after the purchase – effectively at time 0.

2 First writing down allowance (WDA) at time 1

If we assume that an asset is purchased just after the end of an accounting period, we would have to wait until the end of the next accounting period before claiming the first WDA – effectively at time 1.

Year– end
31st Dec 20X0
Time 0

Year– end
31st Dec 20X1
Time 1

Buy an asset here
on 31 Dec 20X0
– 1st WDA at T0

Buy an asset here
on 1 January 20X1
– 1st WDA at T1

Note!

For the purposes of NPV calculations 31 December 20X0 and 1 January 20X1 are effectively taken as the same point in time – that is T0. For the purchase of this asset, the cash outflow will appear in the NPV calculation at T0, irrespective of whether purchased on 31 Dec or 1 Jan. However, the date of purchase will be relevant for the timing of the cash inflow associated with the writing down allowance.

Example 2

Joe is considering purchasing a machine at a cost of $100,000. It has a life of 4 years and can be sold for $30,000 at the end of the 4th year. The machine is eligible for writing down allowances on a reducing balance basis at 20% per annum.

The machine will generate the following annual net cash inflows, which we assume occur at the end of the year to which they relate:

year 1 - $35,000
year 2 - $42,000
year 3 - $51,000
year 4 - $36,000

The post-tax cost of capital is 11%. The relevant corporation tax rate is 28%. Tax is payable 1 year after the relevant cashflow arises. Assume that the asset is purchased at the beginning of an accounting period.

Requirement

Calculate the NPV of the machine project and evaluate whether or not the investment is worthwhile.

Working 1

We start by working out the cashflow benefit of the capital allowances that can be claimed. This is the amount of tax that would be saved as a result of offsetting the capital allowances against taxable profits.

We always assume that the company will be generating sufficient taxable profits to be able to absorb any capital allowances in full as soon as they arise. We also assume that an asset is in a pool of its own i.e. that there will be a balancing allowance or a balancing charge at the end of the project's life.

Time	Narrative	Written down value ($)	Cashflow benefit ($)	Timing of benefit
T0	Asset cost	(100,000)		
T1	1st WDA @ 20%	20,000	X 0.28 = 5,600	T2
	Net c/f	(80,000)		
T2	2nd WDA @ 20%	16,000	X 0.28 = 4,480	T3
	Net c/f	(64,000)		
T3	3rd WDA @ 20%	12,800	X 0.28 = 3,584	T4
	Net c/f	(51,200)		
T4	Sale proceeds	30,000		
	Net c/f	(21,200)		
T4	Balancing allowance	21,200	X 0.28 = 5,936	T5

As the asset is purchased at the beginning of an accounting period, the first WDA is assumed to arise at time 1. Tax is payable a year later and therefore the first tax saving, or cashflow benefit is assumed to arise at time 2.

Working 2

We can now work out the NPV of the investment.

Narrative	T0	T1	T2	T3	T4	T5
Cash inflows		35,000	42,000	51,000	36,000	
Tax @ 28%			(9,800)	(11,760)	(14,280)	(10,080)
Investment	(100,000)				30,000	
CA benefit (W1)			5,600	4,480	3,584	5,936
Net cashflow	(100,000)	35,000	37,800	43,720	55,304	(4,144)
DF @ 11%	1.000	0.901	0.812	0.731	0.659	0.593
Present value	(100,000)	31,535	30,694	31,959	36,445	(2,457)

The NPV therefore = $28,176 positive. As the NPV is positive the investment is worthwhile and should be undertaken.

RELEVANT CASHFLOWS

When carrying out a discounted cashflow analysis it is important to include only relevant cashflows in the analysis.

Finance terminology explained

What are relevant cashflow for a DCF analysis?

These are the incremental future cashflows. And so what does this mean?

This means that we should only include cashflows that have not yet been incurred, and are incremental to the decision. A cashflow would only be relevant to the DCF analysis if there is a change in the cashflows of the business because of a decision to go ahead with the investment.

Examples of what should be excluded.

1   **Depreciation** – this should not be included as it is not a cashflow. Depreciation is an accounting entry to reflect the fall in value of an asset.

2   **Sunk costs** – these are costs that have already been incurred and should therefore be excluded. If a business has already spent $30,000 investigating a potential new investment this cost should be ignored. This cost cannot be changed as a result of a decision to proceed with, or not to proceed with, an investment.

3   **Finance costs** – a finance cost, for example interest payments on debt financing used in the project is not relevant. Even if the finance is raised specifically for the project the interest payments would be irrelevant. The cost of capital, or discount rate, reflects the cost of financing, and therefore to also include the finance cost as a cash outflow would be double counting.

4   **Apportioned overheads** – a business may allocate or apportion existing overheads to the new investment. If the overhead is incurred anyway, irrespective of whether or not the new project goes ahead, then it should be excluded.

Examples of what should be included.

1   **Opportunity cost** – if, for example, a business loses potential sales revenue which could be generated from an alternative use of an asset, the loss of this revenue should be treated as a cost of the new project.

2   **Opportunity benefit** – a cost which would otherwise be incurred, but which is avoided if a decision is made to go ahead with the project, should be treated as a benefit (a cash inflow) of the new project. An example would be avoiding disposal costs of some material because the material can be used on the new project.

3   **Working capital investment** – cash tied up in working capital e.g. in inventory or receivables should be taken into account.

Working capital adjustment

When undertaking a major new investment, or project, there is often a need to invest in working capital in addition to non-current assets. In particular there will normally be a need to invest in inventory, and, if a credit period is offered to customers, a need to invest in receivables.

The cash invested in working capital needs to be taken into account in an NPV evaluation. Normally it is assumed that the cash invested is released at the end of the project's life, but because the time value of money is important, the timing of the investment in working capital, and the release of funds from the investment in working capital, becomes important.

How do we calculate the working capital adjustment?

The approach is as follows.

1   Calculate the **total working capital requirements** at each point in time. This is the total net amount that needs to be invested in working capital (the total amount of inventory and receivables less the level of payables).

2   Calculate the **net movement in working capital** from period to period. This net movement in working capital represents the amount that is tied up in, or released from working capital during that period.

Example 3

Sam is considering expanding its production process to generate greater sales revenue. The following incremental sales have been estimated:

Year 1 - $120,000
Year 2 - $140,000
Year 3 - $170,000
Year 4 - $210,000

The project has an estimated life of 4 years. Incremental working capital equal to 5% of the sales revenue will be needed to generate the extra sales revenue. This will need to be in place at the beginning of the period in which the sales revenue will be generated. All of the working capital will be released at the end of the project's life.

Requirement

Determine the net cash inflows or outflows relating to working capital that should be included in an NPV calculation.

The first task is to calculate the total working capital needs. This is 5% of the sales revenue figures given in the question but – timing is important. The working capital needs to be in place at the beginning of the period to which it relates. Sales revenue figures are quoted at the end of the year to which they relate, and therefore the total investment is effectively a year earlier than the relevant sales figure.

We then work out the net movement in total working capital during each period.

	T0	T1	T2	T3	T4	T5
Sales revenue		120,000	140,000	170,000	210,000	NIL
Total working capital	6,000	7,000	8,500	10,500	NIL	
Net movement	(6,000)	(1,000)	(1,500)	(2,000)	10,500	

5%

This is the difference between 6000 and 7,000

At time 4 the net movement is a release of working capital of $10,500. Given that the sales in period 5 are nil, then the total working capital needs at time 4 are also nil. The full amount 'tied up' in working capital up to the end of period 3 in therefore released during period 4.

The net movement in working capital represents the cash either invested or released in each period. These are the figures that would go into the NPV calculation.

Chapter 3
key points summary

- DCF and inflation – two approaches.

    - Money approach – inflate cashflows and use a discount rate that reflects inflation (money or nominal rate).

    - Real terms approach – keep cashflows in current prices and discount at a rate that is over and above inflation (real rate).

- DCF and inflation – when do we use each approach?

    - Money approach – if more than one inflation and/or capital allowances are given in a question.

    - Real approach – use if the same rate of inflation is applicable to all cashflows and the discount rate.

- DCF and taxation.

    - Capital allowance benefits – need to be clear about the timing of the first capital allowance – T0 or T1?

    - Operating cashflow taxed at corporate tax rate – need to be clear about timing of tax – same year or delayed a year?

- DCF and relevant cashflows.

    - Only include incremental cashflows – those that arise because of the decision.

    - Increase in working capital is a cash outflow in the DCF analysis.

ADVANCED DISCOUNTED CASHFLOW

Introduction
what is this chapter about?

In this chapter, the third of three that considers discounted cashflow techniques, we look at how to discount more complex cashflows (what – it gets more complex? – well – the cashflows that we consider are just really variations of the cashflows that we saw in chapters 2 and 3). We also consider an alternative type of internal rate of return calculation.

Key areas of the chapter are ....

1   **More complex annuities and perpetuities** – in chapter 2 we saw how is was possible to calculate the present value of an annuity or perpetuity quickly by using a formula or tables. How do we deal with more complex annuities or perpetuities?

2   **Non-annual discounting** – if we want to discount on a non-annual basis how could this be done?

3   **The modified internal rate of return** – the IRR has some significant drawbacks (we saw these in chapter 3). The modified internal rate of return is an alternative that overcomes some of these drawbacks. How does this work?

MORE COMPLEX ANNUITIES AND PERPETUITIES

In chapter 2 we looked at how the present value of an annuity could be determined using either the formula or the tables. We also saw how it was possible to determine the present value of a perpetuity using the formula.

What other possible annuities and perpetuities arise in discounted cashflow calculations?

Finance terminology explained

Advanced Annuity

A quick reminder (in case it is needed) - a 'normal' annuity is an equal annual cashflow that starts at period 1 and continues for a certain number of periods. The annuity tables, or the annuity formula, assume that the annuity is a 'normal' annuity.

An advanced annuity is an annuity where the first cashflow starts immediately, or at time 0 rather than at time or period 1.

How can we calculate the present value of an advanced annuity?

You may remember that the present value of a cashflow at time 0 is the same as the cashflow itself, that is, there is no need to discount (you are probably wishing that this applied to all cashflows) In an NPV calculation we normally show this by multiplying the cashflow by 1.

The quickest and neatest way to calculate the present value of an advanced annuity is therefore to add 1 to the 'normal' annuity factor that we find by using the tables or the formula.

Example 1

What is the present value of a cashflow £5,000 from T0 to T6 when discounted at 10% per annum?

Solution 1

An equal cashflow from T0 to T6 is the same as a cashflow from T1-T6 (i.e. a normal annuity) and an extra cashflow at T0. The annuity factor that we need to use to discount in this case is therefore the annuity factor from T1-T6 plus the discount factor at T0 (which is 1).

From the tables the annuity factor from T1-T6 @ 10% is 4.355

The relevant annuity factor from T0-T6 is therefore 1 + 4.355 = 5.355

The present value of the cashflow is therefore $5,000 x 5.355 = $26,775

Exam tip - Advanced annuity

If calculating the present value of an advanced annuity in a question you need to read the question carefully to determine how many cashflows arise, and the timing of those cashflows.

If a question, for example, asks for the present value of a cashflow from T0 to T6, there are seven cashflows, one at T0 and then T1-T6.

If, alternatively, a question suggested, for example, a 6 year annuity with the first cashflow starting immediately, this would mean one cashflow at T0 and then a further five cashflows from T1 to T5.

Finance terminology explained

Advanced perpetuity

An advanced perpetuity is an equal annual cashflow to infinity that starts at T0.

Like an advanced annuity the present value is found by adding 1 to the normal perpetuity formula that we covered in chapter 2.

Example 2

What is the present value of a perpetuity of $3,000 from T0 to infinity at a discount rate of 8%?

Solution 2

The present value of a' normal' perpetuity (starting at time 1) is found by multiplying the cashflow by $\frac{1}{r}$.

The present value of this perpetuity, with an extra cashflow at T0, is therefore:

$$\$3,000 \times \left(1 + \frac{1}{0.08}\right) = \$40,500$$

Finance terminology explained

Delayed annuity

A delayed or deferred annuity is where there is an equal annual cashflow for a certain number of periods, but where the cashflows start later than period 1.

There are two approaches that could be taken if we want to calculate the present value of a delayed annuity. (Oh no – isn't having to know one approach bad enough!) Both approaches are, however, potentially useful in different scenarios in exam questions and therefore it is worth learning how to use both approaches. The two approaches are as follows.

1   Deduct the annuity for the 'missing' periods from the annuity factor.

2   Discount in two stages. In the first stage we deal with the cashflows as if they are a 'normal' annuity starting at T1. In the second stage we discount as if we have a single cashflow at a certain date in the future.

Example 3

What is the present value of an equal annual cashflow of $7,000 from time 4 to time 7 at a discount rate of 9%?

Solution 3

First approach

An annuity factor from time 4 to time 7 is the same as an annuity factor from time 1 to time 7 (a 'normal' annuity) but with the annuity factor for the cashflows from time 1 to time 3 missing.

We can determine the annuity factor from T4 to T7 @ 9% as follows:

$$AF\ (T4\text{-}T7)\ =\ AF\ (T1\text{-}T7)\ less\ AF\ (T1\text{-}T3)$$
$$AF\ (T4\text{-}T7)\ =\ 5.033\ less\ 2.531$$
$$AF\ (T4\text{-}T7)\ =\ 2.502$$

The present value of the cashflow is therefore $7,000 x 2.502 = $17,514

Second approach

When we discount a 'normal' annuity, the first cashflow starts in 1 years' time. Another way to look at this is that using a normal annuity formula will always give us the present value of the annuity **the year before** the first of the cashflows arises.

An annuity from T4 to T7 is a four year annuity starting at T4. If we multiply by the 'normal' 4 year annuity factor, this will give us the present value at T3 of those cashflows (the year before the first cashflow arises).

The present value at T3 is therefore:

$7,000 x 3.240 = $22,680

Discounting is all about equating cashflows that arise at different points in time. We can therefore say that receiving a single cash amount of $22,680 at time 3 is equivalent to receiving an annuity of $7,000 from time 4 to time 7.

The $22,680 is a 'single' cashflow at T3. The present value at T0 can then be found by multiplying the cashflow by the single discount factor at T3 @ 9% as follows:

$22,680 x 0.772 = $17,509

The two approaches should give the same answer. The difference here is due to rounding differences which have arisen because we have used the discount tables which only quote the factors to 3 decimal places.

T0	T1	T2	T3	T4	T5	T6	T7
-	-	-	-	7,000	7,000	7,000	7,000

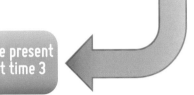

Multiply by the 4 year annuity factor @ 9%

Gives the present value at time 3

Finance terminology explained

Delayed perpetuity

A delayed perpetuity is an equal annual cashflow to infinity that starts later than period 1.

The present value of a delayed perpetuity is calculated in exactly the same way as a delayed annuity apart from the fact that we use the perpetuity formula instead of the annuity factor. As with the delayed annuity there are two approaches that could be used to find the solution (not again!)

Example 4

What is the present value of an equal annual cashflow of $400 from time 5 to infinity at a discount rate of 6%?

Solution 4

In this case we will only find the solution using the first method (thankfully – you say). A perpetuity factor from T5 to infinity is the same as a perpetuity factor from T1 to infinity with the annuity factor for the cashflows from T1 to T4 'missing'.

The present value of the delayed perpetuity is therefore:

$$\$400 \times (\frac{1}{r} - AF(T1 \text{ to } T4))$$

$$= \quad \$400 \times (\frac{1}{0.06} - 3.465)$$

$$= \quad \$5,281$$

Finance terminology explained

Growing perpetuity

A growing perpetuity is where a cashflow grows at a constant rate from period 1 to infinity

In this case we can find the present value by multiplying the cashflow by the formula for a growing perpetuity.

Need to know!

The formula for a growing perpetuity is:

$$\frac{1}{r - g}$$

Where:

r = the discount rate (expressed as a decimal)

g = the constant annual rate of growth in future cashflows (expressed as a decimal)

It is worth noting that you will see more of this formula later in the book in chapter 9 (and those of you who can't wait will no doubt jump to chapter 9 as soon as you have finished working through this one). This is because something called the dividend valuation model that we use to calculate a cost of equity is based on the concept of a growing perpetuity.

Example 5

What is the present value of a cash flow of $1,200 starting in 1 years' time and growing thereafter at a constant rate of 3% per annum to infinity? The discount rate is 7%.

Solution 5

The present value is found as follows:

$$\$1,200 \times \frac{1}{(0.07 - 0.03)} = \$30,000$$

Finance terminology explained

Delayed growing perpetuity

How many more complex annuities and perpetuities? Well the good news is that this is the last one.

A delayed growing perpetuity is where the cashflow grows at a constant rate each period to infinity, but the first cashflow starts at a later date than period 1.

The present value of a delayed growing perpetuity is calculated in the same way as the second approach that we used earlier to calculate the present value of a delayed annuity. The first approach that we used earlier will not work in this case, as by definition, the cashflows are not equal each year, and we cannot therefore remove 'missing' cashflows in the way that we did with a delayed annuity. (You see – I told you that knowing the two approaches would be useful).

Example 6

What is the present value of a cashflow at time 3 of $750, which subsequently grows at 5% per annum to infinity? Assume that the cashflows are discounted at 10% per annum.

Solution 6

If we treat this as a 'normal' growing perpetuity, we can find the present value the year before the first cashflow arises by using the formula for a growing perpetuity.

The present value at time 2 of the cashflows from time 3 to infinity is:

$$\$750 \times \frac{1}{(0.10 - 0.05)} = \$15,000$$

$$= \$15,000$$

We then discount this back to time 0 by treating it as if it were a 'single' cashflow arising at time 2.

The present value at time 0 is therefore:

$$\$15,000 \times DF\ T2\ @\ 10\%$$

$$= \$15,000 \times 0.826$$

$$= \$12,390$$

NON-ANNUAL DISCOUNTING

In the examples covered so far, cashflows have all been assumed to arise annually. The 'period' that we have used for discounting has always been one year, and all cashflows have been assumed to arise at the beginning or end of the year.

It is possible, however, to use discounted cashflow techniques when cashflows are assumed to be on a non-annual basis, for example, every three months or every six months. The 'period' for discounting would therefore be a three or a six month period.

In this type of situation a potential problem is that the discount rate quoted is likely to be the annual equivalent discount rate (only suitable if the 'period' is one year). In this case the annual equivalent discount rate would need to be converted to a periodic rate before performing a discounted cashflow evaluation.

Need to know!

Annual to periodic discount rate

If we want to find a periodic discount rate having been given an annual equivalent discount rate, we can do so using the following formula:

$(1 + R) = (1 + r)^n$

Where:

R = annual equivalent discount rate

r = periodic discount rate

n = no of periods per annum

Example 7

Evey is an investment company. It is considering investing in property which will cost $300,000. The property will generate net quarterly rental income, after all management and maintenance costs have been taken into account, of $4,000, payable in arrears over the next 4 years. The property is then expected to be sold for $350,000 based on current forecasts of property price movements.

Evey applies an annual discount rate of 10% to its investments.

Determine, using the NPV technique, whether the new investment is worthwhile.

Solution 7

Working 1

As the net cash inflow arises quarterly, we need to calculate the quarterly discount rate, and then discount the cashflows on a quarterly basis.

The period for discounting is therefore a quarterly period.

There are four quarterly periods in a year therefore:

R = 10% or 0.10

n = 4 and if we use the formula:

$(1 + R) = (1 + r)^n$

$(1 + 0.10) = (1 + r)^4$

$(1 + r) = \sqrt[4]{(1 + 0.10)}$

1 + r = 1.0241

r = 1.0241 – 1

r = 0.0241 or 2.41%

Working 2

Given that 2.41% is not in the tables, we will need to use the formula to discount. The quarterly rental income is payable over 4 years.

Each time period for discounting will be a quarter of a year, and therefore there will be 16 quarterly rental payments over the 4 year period.

To be able to find the present value quickly we need to find the annuity factor for 16 periods at 2.41%.

Using the formula for an annuity factor seen in chapter 2:

$$\frac{1-(1 + r)^{-n}}{r}$$

Where:

r = 2.41% or 0.0241

n = 16 periods

Then the annuity factor =

$$\frac{1-(1 + 0.0241)^{-16}}{0.0241} = 13.147$$

Working 3

We can then determine the NPV of the project as follows:

Time (periods)	Narrative	Cashflow ($)	DF @ 2.41%	NPV ($)
T0	Initial cost	(300,000)	1.000	(300,000)
T1 – T16	Net inflow	4,000	13.147 (W2)	52,588
T16	Property sale	350,000	$\dfrac{1}{(1 + 0.0241)^{16}}$	239,106
	NPV			**(8,306)**

The NPV is negative and therefore the investment is not worthwhile.

Exam tip – Non-annual cashflows

If given periodic non-annual cashflows in a question, it is important to find the periodic discount rate, and then discount using that period.

In the above example, if we were to add up the 4 quarterly payments to make an annual payment of $16,000, and then discount using the annual equivalent rate of 10% we do not get the same answer! This is because we would be assuming that the quarterly rental income can only be reinvested at the end of the year rather than as soon as it is received.

MODIFIED INTERNAL RATE OF RETURN (MIRR)

In chapter 3 we looked at the limitations of the internal rate of return as a discounted cashflow technique. Let's remind ourselves of these:

1   When comparing mutually exclusive projects, the result obtained when using the IRR technique may be different to the result that would be obtained using the NPV technique.

2   If projects have unusual cashflows, for example, an outflow, then a series of inflows, then a further outflow, there may be more than one IRR.

3   The IRR assumes that cash inflows can be reinvested at the IRR. This is often unrealistic.

The **modified IRR (MIRR)** is a variation of the IRR which overcomes these assumptions. Like the IRR, we still have a percentage return that can be compared to a target rate of return (normally the cost of capital) for decision making purposes. With the MIRR, however, we:

1   Always get the same recommendation when comparing mutually exclusive projects as we would get if using the NPV technique. This means that if we need to choose between two projects – the project with the highest NPV when discounted at the cost of capital will also have the highest MIRR.

2   Only have one MIRR irrespective of the nature of the cashflows.

3   Can assume that cash inflows can be invested at a realistic rate of return rather than at the IRR. If, for example, a company could realistically borrow at 8% but only invest at 6% – the MIRR can reflect these rates whereas the IRR cannot.

Exam tip – Modified IRR

Exam questions involving the MIRR will often require students to discuss the benefits of using the MIRR instead of the IRR. If so – use the three points above as the basis of your answer and be prepared to expand on these points, by, for example, using the information in the question to illustrate the three points.

How do we calculate the MIRR?

There are two ways in which the MIRR can be calculated. They are as follows.

Method 1

This approach involves three stages.

1   Calculate the **present value** of the investment phase (the 'investment phase' refers to the net cash outflows needed to invest in a project). These may be cash outflows that are incurred immediately, or it may be that some cash outflows are incurred in future periods, for example, if the project involves constructing a building over more than one period. The 'investment phase' would also include any benefits of the capital allowances that are available because of the decision to invest in assets.

2 Calculate the **terminal value** of the return phase (the 'return phase' refers to the net cash inflows that will subsequently arise after undertaking the investment). The terminal value is the compound value of the net cash inflows at the end of the life of the project.

3 The **MIRR** is the discount rate that equates the terminal value of the cash inflows with the present value of the cash outflows.

Method 2

The alternative approach (this chapter is full of alternative approaches – sorry – but there are situations where understanding the alternative approaches is very useful) is as follows:

1 Calculate the **present value** of the **investment phase** discounting at the company's cost of capital.

2 Calculate the **present value** of the **return phase**, discounting at the company's cost of capital.

3 Calculate the MIRR by using the following formula:

Need to know!

$$MIRR = \left(\frac{PV^R}{PV^I}\right)^{\frac{1}{n}} \times (1 + ke) - 1$$

Where
PV^R = the present value of the return phase
PV^I = the present value of the investment phase
ke = the cost of capital
n = life of the project

What is the difference between the two approaches?

Advantage of using method 1 – the main benefit of this approach is that it allows us to use a different discount rate for calculating the present value of the investment phase (which involves cash outflows and will therefore mean borrowing money) and the return phase (which involves net cash inflows which would be invested). Method 2 only works if we have the same rate for borrowing and investing – normally the cost of capital would be used for this.

It could therefore be argued that method 1 allows us to find a **more realistic MIRR** by taking into account the fact that a reinvestment rate for surplus cash, especially in the short term, would be lower than a borrowing rate, or financing rate.

Advantage of using method 2 - the main benefit of this approach is that we can use the same workings to calculate both an NPV and a modified internal rate of return. Because method 2 is based on the present value of both the net cash outflows (investment phase) and the net cash inflows (return phase), once these are calculated it only requires one small extra step to determine both the NPV and the MIRR. This is not the case with method 1.

Example 8

Sally manufactures circuit boards for the mobile phone industry. The company is considering manufacturing a new range of market-leading circuit boards which will require a major new investment. The estimated cashflows associated with the new investment are as follows:

Year 0	Cost of the investment	($7,600,000)
Year 1	Further investment	($1,500,000)
Year 2	Net cash inflows	$4,500,000
Year 3	Net cash inflows	$5,500,000
Year 4	Net cash inflows	$6,300,000

After 4 years it is believed that the new circuit boards will become obsolete and that cashflows beyond year 4 will therefore be negligible.

Sally has a cost of capital of 12% which is also its hurdle rate for all new projects. Sally assumes that surplus cash can be reinvested at the cost of capital.

Requirements:

(a) What is the modified internal rate of return of the new project using method 1?

(b) What is the NPV of the project and what is the modified internal rate of return of the project using method 2?

Solution 8

Part (a)

To determine the modified internal rate of return using method 1 we proceed as follows.

1   Calculate the **present value of the investment phase**.

The investment phase in this case involves cash outflows at time 0 and time 1. These are discounted at the company's cost of capital.

Time	Narrative	Cashflow ($)	DF @ 12%	PV ($)
T0	Initial cost	(7,600,000)	1.000	(7,600,000)
T1	Further cost	(1,500,000)	0.893	(1,339,500)
	Present value			**(8,939,500)**

2   Calculate the **terminal value of the return phase**.

This involves compounding up the net cash inflows to find their value at the end of the project's life i.e. at time 4 – assuming that the cashflows are reinvested at the company's cost of capital.

Time	Narrative	Cashflow ($)	Compound	TV @ T4 ($)
T2	Net cash inflow	4,500,000	$(1 + 0.12)^2$	5,644,800
T3	Net cash inflow	5,500,000	$(1 + 0.12)$	6,160,000
T4	Net cash inflow	6,300,000	1.000	6,300,000
	Terminal value			**18,104,800**

To find the terminal value we compound up, or assume that the cash inflow can be reinvested to give us the equivalent cash inflow at time 4. The cash inflow at time 2 can therefore be reinvested for 2 years, the cash inflow at time 3 can be reinvested for a year, and the cash inflow at time 4 will not be reinvested.

3   Equate the present value of the investment phase with the terminal value of the return phase to find the MIRR.

We effectively look at this as if there are just 2 cashflows, an outflow at time 0 of ($8,939,500) and an inflow at time 4 of $18,104,800. The MIRR is the rate that, when applied to the inflow, will give us a present value equal to the cash outflow.

$$\frac{18,104,800}{(1 + r)^4} = 8,939,500$$

$$(1 + r) = \sqrt[4]{\frac{18,104,800}{8,939,500}}$$

$$1 + r = 1.1929$$

$$r = 0.1929 \text{ or } 19.29\%$$

The MIRR is therefore 19.29%. As this is above the cost of capital, the new investment is worthwhile.

Part (b)

We have already calculated the present value of the investment phase in part (a). To find the NPV we firstly need to calculate the present value of the return phase.

1   The present value of the return phase is calculated as follows:

Time	Narrative	Cashflow ($)	DF @ 12%	PV ($)
T2	Net cash inflow	4,500,000	0.797	3,586,500
T3	Net cash inflow	5,500,000	0.712	3,916,000
T4	Net cash inflow	6,300,000	0.636	4,006,800
	Present value			**11,509,300**

2   The NPV is the present value of the return phase less the present value of the investment phase.

The NPV is therefore equal to $11,509,300 - $8,939,500 = $2,569,800
The NPV is positive and therefore the investment is worthwhile.

3   The MIRR

We can now work out the MIRR by using the formula.

$$MIRR = \left(\frac{PV^R}{PV^I}\right)^{\frac{1}{n}} \times (1 + ke) - 1$$

Where

PV^R = $11,509,300
PV^I = $8,939,500
ke   =   12% or 0.12

therefore

$$MIRR = \left(\frac{11,509,300}{8,939,500}\right)^{\frac{1}{4}} \times (1 + 0.12) - 1$$

MIRR = 0.1930 or 19.30%

The MIRR is the same using each of the two methods allowing for rounding. This would always be the case if it assumed that net cash inflows (return phase) can be invested at the same rate as that which is used to finance the net cash outflows (investment phase).

Chapter 4
key points summary

- Complex annuities and perpetuities.

    - Advanced annuity or perpetuity (starts at T0) – add 1 to the relevant annuity/perpetuity factor.

    - Delayed annuity or perpetuity (starts later than T1) – deduct annuity for the 'missing periods' from the normal annuity/perpetuity factor or discount in two stages.

    - Growing perpetuity – constant growth from T1 to infinity – formula: $\dfrac{1}{r - g}$.

    - Delayed growing perpetuity – constant growth to infinity but starts later than T1 – two stages – using the growing perpetuity formula for the first stage.

- Non-annual discounting.

    - Convert annual rate to periodic rate by using formula: $(1 + R) = (1 + r)^n$.

- The modified internal rate of return (MIRR).

    - Use formula: $\text{MIRR} = \left(\dfrac{PV^R}{PV^I}\right)^{\frac{1}{n}} \times (1 + ke) - 1$

    or equate the present value of the 'investment phase' with the 'terminal value' of the return phase.

    - Formula assumes same borrowing and investing rate – not using the formula allows different borrowing and investing rates.

    - Same recommendation as NPV method when comparing mutually exclusive projects (not true with IRR).

    - Only one MIRR whatever the cashflows of the project (may be more than one 'normal' IRR).

INVESTMENT APPRAISAL AND RISK

Introduction
what is this chapter about?

We saw in the opening chapter how risk and return were related. When there is a greater level of risk an investor will demand a higher return to compensate for that risk. In this chapter we consider how the risk affecting an investment could be analysed, measured, and incorporated into a discounted cashflow evaluation.

Key areas of the chapter are ....

1 **Risk and uncertainty** – is there a difference between the terms risk and uncertainty? What are the different techniques that could be used to analyse risk and uncertainty?

2 **Sensitivity analysis** – what is sensitivity analysis and how is it performed on a new investment?

3 **Other methods of analysing risk and uncertainty** – what are the other methods and how can they be used to analyse risk and uncertainty?

RISK AND UNCERTAINTY

All discounted cashflow calculations are based on forecast future cashflows. To analyse the results properly it would be useful to know how much risk is attached to those cashflows. How do we do this? Well – to start the process we need to distinguish between risk and uncertainty. The terms are often used interchangeably but in the world of finance there is a difference between the two.

Finance terminology explained

What is risk?

This is where there is an uncertain future event, for example, the level of sales revenue generated from a new investment in a year's time, but where probabilities can be assigned to possible outcomes and the range of outcomes can be quantified.

Finance terminology explained

What is uncertainty?

This is where there is an uncertain future event, but where probabilities cannot be assigned to possible outcomes, and therefore the range of outcomes cannot be quantified.

A technique that allows us to quantify outcomes is therefore a technique for analysing risk, whereas a technique that does not allow us to quantify outcomes is a technique for analysing uncertainty.

Methods of analysing risk and uncertainty

The main methods that could be used to analyse risk and uncertainty can be summarised as follows:

Risk	Uncertainty
Expected values	Sensitivity analysis
Risk adjusted discount rate	Best and worst case scenarios
Certainty equivalents	Payback period
Discounted payback period	
Simulation	

We will consider each of these techniques in the next few sections.

SENSITIVITY ANALYSIS

This is the main method used to analyse uncertainty within an investment.

Finance terminology explained

What is sensitivity analysis?

Sensitivity analysis is a measurement of how sensitive a discounted cashflow evaluation is to a change in one variable.

It is really providing a manager with answers to a series of 'what if' questions, for example:

- If the forecast sales volume fell by 20% what would be the impact on the NPV?

- If the discount rate rose by 3% what would be the impact on the NPV?

A critical point in any NPV evaluation is where a change in a variable turns a positive NPV into a negative NPV. The focus of the sensitivity analysis question is often therefore on the extent to which a variable can change **before the NPV becomes zero**. If so the sensitivity question would be phrased as follows:

- By how much could the sales volume fall before the decision to invest changes?

- By how much could the discount rate rise before the decision to invest changes?

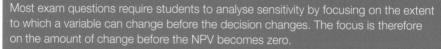

Exam tip – Sensitivity analysis

Most exam questions require students to analyse sensitivity by focusing on the extent to which a variable can change before the decision changes. The focus is therefore on the amount of change before the NPV becomes zero.

If in doubt – assume that this is the approach required.

Need to know!

How is sensitivity calculated?

If the approach is to determine the extent to which a variable can change before the decision changes then sensitivity is calculated as follows:

For an individual cashflow:

$$\text{Sensitivity} = \frac{\text{NPV}}{\text{Present value of the cashflow}} \times 100\%$$

For the discount rate:

The sensitivity is determined by calculating the IRR of the project and comparing it to the cost of capital. By definition the IRR is the rate of return that will give a net present value of zero.

Example 1

Polly is a company that manufactures equipment for the pet industry. It is considering a major new investment in an electronic cat flap that opens automatically when a cat, fitted with an electronic tag, approaches. The following cashflows have been estimated:

Year 0	Initial cost	$300,000
Years 1-6	Sales (12,000 units x $10 per unit)	$120,000
Years 1-6	Variable costs (12,000 units x $4 per unit)	$48,000
Year 6	Scrap value	$30,000

The relevant cost of capital is 8% per annum.

Requirements

(a) What is the project's NPV?
(b) What is the sensitivity of the project to a change in:
    (i)   the cost of the investment?
    (ii)   the selling price?
    (iii)   the sales volume?
    (iv) scrap value?
(c) How sensitive is the project to a change in the discount rate?

Part (a)

The NPV of the project can be calculated as follows:

Time	Narrative	Cashflow	DF @ 8%	NPV
0	Initial cost	(300,000)	1.000	(300,000)
1-6	Sales	120,000	4.623	554,760
1-6	Variable cost	(48,000)	4.623	(221,904)
6	Scrap value	30,000	0.630	18,900
	NPV			**51,756**

Part (b)

Sensitivity to cost of the investment

We use the formula:

$$\text{Sensitivity} = \frac{\text{NPV}}{\text{Present value of the cashflow}} \times 100\%$$

$$\text{Sensitivity} = \frac{\$51,756}{\$300,000} \times 100\% = 17.25\%$$

This means that a rise in the cost of the investment of 17.25% would result in the NPV falling to zero.

Sensitivity to the selling price

Using the same formula:

$$\text{Sensitivity} = \frac{\$51,756}{\$554,760} \times 100\% = 9.33\%$$

A fall in the selling price of 9.33% would result in the NPV falling to zero.

Sensitivity to the sales volume

This is a bit trickier! If the sales volume falls this will result in a fall in the sales revenue but will also result in a reduction in variable costs. To determine the sensitivity, the relevant cashflow is the present value of the contribution, or the present value of the sales less the variable costs.

$$\text{Sensitivity} = \frac{\$51,756}{(\$554,760 - \$221,904)} \times 100\% = 15.55\%$$

A fall in the sales volume of 15.55% would result in the NPV falling to zero.

Sensitivity to the scrap value

Using the same formula:

$$\text{Sensitivity} = \frac{\$51,756}{\$18,900} \times 100\% = 274\%$$

The scrap value would therefore need to fall by 274% before there is a zero NPV. This really means that even if the scrap value is zero, the project would still have a positive NPV.

Conclusion

The decision to invest is more sensitive to a change in the selling price than to a change in any other cashflow. A fall of just 9.33% in the selling price (i.e. from $10 to $9.07) would result in a different decision.

Part (c)

To determine the sensitivity to a change in the discount rate, the IRR of the project needs to be calculated. Because the NPV at 8% is positive then in order to calculate the IRR a second NPV needs to be calculated at a higher discount rate.

At a discount rate of, say, 15% the NPV will be determined as follows:

Time	Narrative	Cashflow	DF @ 15%	NPV
0	Initial cost	(300,000)	1.000	(300,000)
1-6	Sales	120,000	3.784	454,080
1-6	Variable cost	(48,000)	3.784	(181,632)
6	Scrap value	30,000	0.432	12,960
	NPV			**(14,592)**

The IRR can then be found by using the IRR formula:

$$IRR = L + \frac{N_L}{N_L - N_H} \times (H-L)$$

$$IRR = 0.08 + \frac{51,756}{(51,756 + 14,592)} \times (0.15 - 0.08)$$

IRR = 0.1346 or 13.46%

The discount rate can therefore rise from 8% to 13.46% before the decision changes. This is a rise of 5.46%.

OTHER METHODS OF ANALYSING RISK AND UNCERTAINTY

Let's now consider some of the other methods that could be used to analyse risk and uncertainty.

Risk adjusted discount rate (risk)

The capital asset pricing model (CAPM) provides a reliable method of adjusting a discount rate to reflect the risk of an investment. This is widely used in the real world and the approach will be covered in detail in chapters 11 and 12.

If a new project has a different level of risk compared to the risk of the existing activities of the company, perhaps because a company is diversifying, then the discount rate can be adjusted to reflect this.

Need to know!

Expected values (risk)

Expected value is based on probability theory. It is the sum of the probabilities of an outcome arising multiplied by the value of the outcome, or more formally:

Expected value = Σpx

Where

p = the probability of an outcome arising
x = the value of the outcome

Example 2

The following information about the cashflow arising from sales during the first year has been obtained:

Probability	Sales
0.2	$50,000
0.7	$20,000
0.1	$90,000

What is the expected value sales figure for the first year that should go into the NPV evaluation?

Solution 2

To find the expected value we multiply the probability by the outcome and add up the results as follows:

Probability	Sales	Expected value
0.2 x	$50,000	$10,000
0.7 x	$20,000	$14,000
0.1 x	$90,000	$9,000
Total		**$33,000**

The sales figure for the first year that would go into the NPV evaluation would therefore be $33,000.

In this example we have only considered one cashflow for one period. A similar exercise could be performed for a number of cashflows for each period of the life of the project, and the results incorporated into the NPV.

Some points to note about expected values

- The expected value of a cashflow is just a weighted average of the cashflows that could arise, based on probabilities. The expected value itself will never actually arise. In example 2, the actual sales figure has to be $50,000, $20,000 or $90,000.

- The expected value can give a distorted or misleading result. An example would be if there is a low probability of a high value cashflow arising. In example 2 there is a probability of 0.1 of a cashflow of $90,000. Although this is a low probability, the cashflow is considerably higher than the other cashflows and therefore this has pushed the average up significantly.

Payback period (uncertainty)

The payback period was covered in chapter 2. This considers how long it takes to recover the initial capital investment. We know that the further into the future the cashflow, the less certainty there is about the cashflow estimate.

If we set a minimum payback period for projects, of, for example, 4 years when considering a range of possible projects, then projects that may deliver high returns in the long term, but which are more risky because of the length of time before the high returns arise, would not be considered further.

Discounted payback period (risk)

This is calculated in exactly the same way as the payback period, except for the fact that all of the cashflows arising are discounted before the payback period is calculated.

The level of risk attached to an investment, can, using CAPM, be built into the discount rate. Discounted payback period therefore allows the risk attached to a particular investment to be built into the payback period. If we chose, for a range of projects, the project with the lowest discounted payback period, then it could be argued that we are choosing the project with the lowest level of risk.

Certainty equivalents (risk)

The normal approach to discounting is to estimate or forecast future cashflows, and then discount at a rate which reflects the risk of the investment.

The certainty equivalent approach looks at risk in a different way. Rather than adjust the discount rate to reflect risk, the cashflows are multiplied by a certainty equivalent factor.

The certainty equivalent factor is the proportion of the cashflow that is considered to be certain to arise. In other words, even in the worst case scenario this proportion of the cashflow would arise.

Suppose, for example, that forecast sales in the first year were $20,000, and in the second year were $30,000. If the certainty equivalent factors were 0.9 for the first year, and 0.8 for the second year, then the figures that would go into the NPV evaluation would be:

Year 1 $20,000 x 0.9 = $18,000
Year 2 $30,000 x 0.8 = $24,000

Because the risk has been removed from the cashflow, these cashflows are then discounted at the **risk free rate of return**, and not the company's normal cost of capital.

The certainty equivalent approach is not widely used, mainly because of the difficulty in determining the certainty equivalent. To determine the factor we should consider the certain cashflow that managers would be prepared to accept from an investment instead of the uncertain cashflow from the project. This is a much more difficult and subjective exercise than determining a risk adjusted discount rate.

Best and worst case scenario (uncertainty)

An NPV evaluation could be performed based on the manager's judgement about the best case scenario, or alternatively the worst case scenario, for the future cashflows.

The approach may produce some useful information, for example, if the NPV is still positive even in the worst case scenario it would give us some confidence when undertaking the investment.

Unlike the certainty equivalent, there is no attempt, in this case, to quantify the probability of various cashflows arising.

Simulation (risk)

Simulation or Monte Carlo simulation is a very sophisticated version of sensitivity analysis based on probability theory and random numbers.

Simulation allows the interdependence between variable to be taken into account (for example if the selling price is cut we might expect sales volume to increase). Under sensitivity analysis, that we saw earlier, only one variable at a time can be changed.

Simulation produces a range of NPV results allowing a manager to analyse the investment, and the risks associated with the investment, in some detail. Because the range of results follows a normal distribution it is a relatively straightforward task to determine, for example, the probability of the NPV being less than zero.

Chapter 5
key points summary

- The difference between risk and uncertainty is that:

    - risk is based on probability theory and can be quantified

    - uncertainty cannot be quantified.

- The main technique for analysing uncertainty is sensitivity analysis

    - sensitivity to a change in cashflow is found by using the formula:

    $$\text{Sensitivity} = \frac{\text{NPV}}{\text{Present value of the cashflow}} \times 100\%$$

    - sensitivity to a change in the discount rate – need to find the IRR.

- The main techniques for analysing risk are:

    - risk adjusted discount rate

    - expected values.

- Simulation is an advanced risk analysis techniques based on probability theory and normal distribution theory.

6

DCF – SPECIAL DECISIONS

This chapter considers how a finance manager can apply discounted cashflow (DCF) techniques to a number of specific areas of financial management. Using DCF techniques in these areas should enable a finance manager to make better financial decisions.

Key areas of the chapter are ....

1 **Lease or buy decisions** – leasing an asset over a long period of time is an alternative to borrowing money and purchasing an asset. How can we use DCF techniques to decide whether it is financially better to lease an asset, or, alternatively, borrow money and purchase the asset?

2 **Asset replacement decisions** – there are many situations in business when assets need periodic replacement by new, similar assets. In such situations how can DCF techniques help a finance manager decide when and how often such assets should be replaced?

3 **Capital rationing** – there are occasions where businesses have more potential investment opportunities available than the finance that is needed to undertake all of these opportunities. How, in such situations, can we decide which of these opportunities should be prioritised?

LEASE OR BUY DECISIONS

Leasing assets under long-term lease agreements is a widely available alternative to purchasing assets. Property, aircraft, motor vehicles, IT equipment and plant and machinery are often leased by companies on a long term basis. There are many attractions to leasing such assets rather than buying the assets. These include avoiding the complications and management time involved in acquisition and disposal of these assets, the ability to upgrade to newer models periodically as part of the lease arrangement (for example with photocopiers) and perhaps, most importantly, avoiding the enormous initial capital outlay that is often required when these assets are purchased.

DCF techniques can be used by a finance manager to decide whether it is financially better to lease an asset or alternatively borrow money in order to purchase the asset.

Need to know!

When comparing lease against buy decisions we always assume that the cash needed to buy the asset would be borrowed. This is because a long term lease is effectively debt financing – an interest charge will be built into the future lease payments. It is therefore logical to compare one form of debt financing (the lease) with an alternative form of debt financing.

Using DCF techniques to analyse lease or buy decisions

Whenever we use DCF techniques we always focus on incremental cashflows (do you remember that term from chapter 3?). This means that we only include in the analysis the cashflows that arise, or do not arise, as a direct result of the decision that we are making.

When using DCF techniques to analyse whether it is better to lease an asset, or borrow to buy the asset, many cashflows that would be important in an investment appraisal exercise, for example sales revenue, are irrelevant because they are not affected by the lease or borrow to buy decision. Whether an airline operator leases an aircraft or borrows money to buy the same aircraft should not have any impact on the sales revenue generated. It is the same aircraft and passengers travelling will have no idea whether it is leased or bought.

Because sales revenue is normally irrelevant, the present value result is often referred to as a present value cost rather than an NPV.

What are the incremental cashflows associated with each decision?

The main incremental cashflows associated with borrow to buy are as follows:

Purchase cost	The initial cost of purchasing the asset will be a relevant cash outflow. When an asset is leased this cost is avoided.
Resale/scrap value	At the end of the useful life of the asset it is expected that the asset could be sold for the estimated resale or scrap value.
Capital allowances	If an asset is purchased, any relevant capital allowances on the asset could be claimed. When an asset is leased, it is the lessor who has acquired the asset, and leased it to another party, who would normally claim the capital allowances.
Tax relief on interest payments	If the purchase of the asset is financed by borrowing, the interest payments can be offset against taxable profits and hence tax relief could be claimed.

The main incremental cashflows associated with leasing an asset are as follows:

Lease payments	The main cash outflow will be the lease payments that the company will be committed to make over the life of the lease agreement.
Tax relief on lease payments	All lease payments will qualify for some kind of tax relief. The tax treatment of the lease payments usually follow the accounting treatment (see point 2 in the next bit).

A couple of important points about tax!

1   If we borrow to buy an asset the interest payments are tax allowable. The way that this tax benefit is dealt with is not as a cashflow – instead the discount rate is used to calculate the present value of borrowing to buy, and the present value of leasing, is adjusted to reflect this.

2   If a lease payment is accounted for as an operating lease, the full lease payment is tax allowable. If, alternatively it is accounted for as a finance lease the interest element and the depreciation of the asset are tax allowable. Dealing with the different types of accounting treatment and hence tax consequences is beyond the scope of this book. In the example which follows we will therefore assume that the lease is accounted for as an operating lease.

How do we analyse these incremental cashflows?

Because we are comparing the cashflows associated with leasing to the cashflows associated with borrowing there are a number of alternative ways of presenting the information. These include comparing the present value cost of leasing with the present value cost of borrowing to buy.

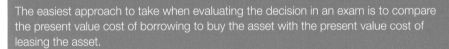

Exam tip – Evaluating lease or buy decisions

The easiest approach to take when evaluating the decision in an exam is to compare the present value cost of borrowing to buy the asset with the present value cost of leasing the asset.

The result of each calculation can then be compared. Whichever option gives the lowest present value cost would be the best option in financial terms.

Which discount rate?

We use the **post-tax cost of borrowing** to compare leasing with borrowing to buy an asset.

Because we focus purely on the financing cashflows, and not on the cashflows attached to a project we do not use the normal cost of capital of the company as a discount rate.

To take into account the tax relief on interest payments when we borrow money we adjust the cost of borrowing to reflect the tax saving. Applying the post-tax cost of borrowing to both sets of cashflows should then enable us to determine whether leasing or borrowing to buy an asset provides the lowest present value cost.

Example 1

Seren Airways is an international airline business operating mainly short haul flights across Western Europe. It needs to upgrade its fleet of aircraft and plans to purchase 8 new aircraft, at a cost of $40 million each. Seren likes to keep its fleet as new and up to date as possible and as a result the aircraft are expected to be sold in 5 years' time for $20 million each. Capital allowances are available at 20% per annum on a reducing balance basis. If purchased the aircraft would be financed by issuing bonds carrying an annual interest rate of 11%. Corporate tax is payable one year in arrears at a rate of 30%.

The CEO of Seren Airways, Ioan Evans, wants to evaluate the possibility of leasing the aircraft over a 5 year period as an alternative to the purchase. A leasing company has offered to lease the aircraft for an annual lease payment of $7 million, payable in arrears, for each aircraft. After the 5 year period has ended the aircraft would revert to the leasing company and Seren would not have any residual rights.

Requirement

Evaluate whether it would be better, in financial terms, for Seren to lease the aircraft, or alternatively borrow to buy the aircraft.

For this evaluation you may round the post-tax cost of borrowing to the nearest whole percentage and you can assume that the lease is accounted for as an operating lease.

You may round your workings to the nearest $1,000.

Solution 1

Working 1

Determine the post-tax cost of borrowing which will be used to calculate the present value cost of borrowing to buy and the present value cost of leasing. This is done by multiplying the interest rate by (1 – t) where t is the corporation tax rate. The logic of doing this is covered in more detail in chapter 9.

Post tax cost of borrowing = 11% (1-0.3)

= 7.7% or if rounded to the nearest whole percentage = 8%

Working 2

Calculate the benefit of the capital allowances that can be claimed.

We are not told when the asset would be purchased in relation to a tax year end and therefore we will assume that the first WDA can be claimed at Time 1.

Each aircraft cost $40 million. The total cost of all 8 aircraft is therefore 8 x $40 million = $320 million

The sale proceeds of the aircraft in 5 years' time will be 8 x $20m = $160 million

Workings are to the nearest $1000.

Time	Narrative	Written down value	Cash benefit (WDA x 30%)	When claimed?
T0		$320,000k		
T1	WDA@20%	(64,000k)	19,200k	T2
	Balance c/f	256,000k		
T2	WDA @ 20%	(51,200k)	15,360k	T3
	Balance c/f	204,800k		
T3	WDA @ 20%	(40,960k)	12,288k	T4
	Balance c/f	163,840k		
T4	WDA @ 20%	(32,768k)	9,830k	T5
	Balance c/f	131,072k		
T5	Proceeds	(160,000k)		
T5	Balancing charge	28,928k	(8,678k)	T6

Working 3

Determine the present value cost of borrowing to buy (workings to the nearest $1,000).

Narrative	T0	T1	T2	T3	T4	T5	T6
Cost	(320,000)						
Resale value						160,000	
WDA benefit			19,200	15,360	12,288	9,830	(8,678)
Net	(320,000)		19,200	15,360	12,288	169,830	(8,678)
DF @ 8%	1.000		0.857	0.794	0.735	0.681	0.630
Present value	(320,000)		16,454	12,196	9,032	115,654	(5,467)

Present value cost of borrowing to buy = ($172,131,000)

Working 4

Determine the present value cost of leasing (workings to the nearest $1,000).

The total annual lease payment will be 8 x $7m = $56 million

Narrative	T0	T1	T2	T3	T4	T5	T6
Lease payment		(56,000)	(56,000)	(56,000)	(56,000)	(56,000)	
Tax relief @ 30%			16,800	16,800	16,800	16,800	16,800
Net		(56,000)	(39,200)	(39,200)	(39,200)	(39,200)	16,800
DF @ 8%		0.926	0.857	0.794	0.735	0.681	0.630
Present value		(51,856)	(33,594)	(31,125)	(28,812)	(26,695)	10,584

Present value cost of leasing = ($161,498,000)

Conclusion

Leasing the asset is therefore cheaper in present value terms by ($172,131,000 - $161,498,000) = $10,633,000.

ASSET REPLACEMENT DECISION

Many assets used in a business need periodic replacement by similar assets. Common examples are IT equipment, motor vehicles used by the business and machinery used in manufacturing.

A key decision for the finance manager is when to replace these assets. Suppose a finance manager decides to delay replacement as long as possible – what are the advantages and disadvantages of doing this?

Advantages of delaying replacement

There is only one key advantage which is that the cost of purchasing the new asset is delayed. This provides a time value of money benefit – the longer we delay replacement the better. Over a long period of time, if the pattern of delaying replacement for as long as possible is repeated we also benefit from incurring the cost less frequently. If, for example we replace an asset every 4 years instead of every 3 years, then over a 12 year period we would save one total replacement cost.

Disadvantages of delaying replacement

1   **The asset becomes less efficient** – as an asset gets older it becomes less efficient. Maintenance, repair costs and insurance costs tend to rise, and the asset may well be operational for less time and therefore generate less sales revenue.

2   **Lower resale value** – as an asset gets older it will generate less value when eventually replaced and sold.

3   **Loss of technological improvements** – many assets can in practice be replaced by new assets that are technologically more advanced. They may well be more productive and efficient than the assets that they replace.

How do we evaluate the asset replacement decision?

The approach that we use is to convert the actual costs for each replacement cycle possibility into an equivalent annual cost and then compare the results.

What is a replacement cycle? Well – one cycle is the period of time between purchasing an asset and the purchasing another identical asset to replace it. If, for example an asset is purchased, owned and used for 3 years before being sold, and then another identical asset is purchased to replace it – the cycle is 3 years.

Need to know!

Equivalent annual cost

The equivalent annual cost is calculated as follows:

$$\frac{\text{Total present value over one replacement cycle}}{\text{Annuity factor for that cycle}}$$

The equivalent annual cost is an annuity i.e. an equal annual cashflow each year that is the same, in present value terms, as the actual costs incurred over one replacement cycle.

Assumptions

To be able to use the formula to determine the best time to replace an asset we need to make two assumptions:

1   When an asset is replaced we will assume that it is replaced by a financially identical asset i.e. one that would have exactly the same stream of cashflows in real terms as the asset that it replaces. This means that we cannot take into account, in calculations, the possibility of technological improvements.

2   We assume that the process of replacement by a financially identical asset will continue indefinitely. This means that if, for example, we say that the asset is replaced after 4 years, we also assume that the new asset will itself be replaced after a further 4 years and so on. This would be referred to as a 4 year replacement cycle.

Approach to questions

The approach to take is as follows:

Step 1 – total present value cost. For each possible cycle, calculate the total present value cost over one cycle. This would be the total present value costs from the point at which the new asset is purchased until the point at which the same asset is sold and replaced by an identical asset.

Step 2 – equivalent annual cost. For each possible cycle, calculate the equivalent annual cost using the formula.

Step 3 – the result. Compare the equivalent annual costs. The replacement cycle with the lowest equivalent annual cost will be the best replacement cycle.

As always, this is best demonstrated in an example.

Example 2

Plymouth is a manufacturing company. It makes a range of modern light fittings which are sold to high street retailers. Part of the manufacturing process involves using a specialist manufacturing machine. This machine needs replacing frequently. It is possible to replace the machine every year, every two years or every three years.

The finance director of Plymouth, Ben Forbes, has been presented with an analysis of the costs associated with each replacement possibility. They are as follows.

Cost of the asset when purchased will be $1,200k

Annual maintenance costs
year 1   = $200k
year 2   = $300k
year 3   = $450k

Resale value
after 1 year   = $900k
after 2 years = $700k
after 3 years = $550k

The maintenance costs are incurred at the end of each year of operation including the year in which the asset is sold.

Plymouth's cost of capital is 10%.

Determine the optimum replacement cycle for the machine.

Solution 2

Step 1 – total present value cost

We start by determining the total present value cost for each replacement cycle.

One year cycle ($'000)

Time	Narrative	Cashflow	DF@10%	PV cost
0	Cost	(1,200)	1.000	(1,200)
1	Maintenance	(200)	0.909	(182)
1	Resale value	900	0.909	818
	Total PV			(564)

Two year cycle ($'000)

Time	Narrative	Cashflow	DF@10%	PV cost
0	Cost	(1,200)	1.000	(1,200)
1	Maintenance	(200)	0.909	(182)
2	Maintenance	(300)	0.826	(248)
2	Resale value	700	0.826	578
	Total PV			(1,052)

Three year cycle ($'000)

Time	Narrative	Cashflow	DF@10%	PV cost
0	Cost	(1,200)	1.000	(1,200)
1	Maintenance	(200)	0.909	(182)
2	Maintenance	(300)	0.826	(248)
3	Maintenance	(450)	0.751	(338)
3	Resale value	550	0.751	413
	Total			(1,555)

Step 2 – equivalent annual cost

We then convert the costs to an equivalent annual cost using the formula:

$$\frac{\text{Total present value over one replacement cycle}}{\text{Annuity factor for that cycle}}$$

One year cycle

$$\frac{(\$564k)}{0.909} = (\$620k)$$

Two year cycle

$$\frac{(\$1,052k)}{1.736} = (\$606k)$$

Three year cycle

$$\frac{(\$1,555k)}{2.487} = (\$625k)$$

Step 3 – the result

The optimum replacement cycle is therefore to replace every 2 years. This minimises the equivalent annual cost of the asset and will also minimise the total cost, in present value terms, of using this asset up to some infinite date in the future.

CAPITAL RATIONING

This refers to a situation where a company has insufficient capital to invest in all of the potential investment opportunities that are available.

What types of rationing are possible?

There are two different ways in which capital may be rationed.

Finance terminology explained

Hard capital rationing

In this situation there is a limit on the amount of capital that a company is able to raise externally, that is from the providers of finance.

This may arise because of market conditions, or because of issues affecting the individual company, for example, investors may be unwilling to provide further capital to the company because of poor returns in the past.

Finance terminology explained

Soft capital rationing

This describes a situation where a company imposes its own internal limit on the amount of capital that it wants to invest.

The directors of a multinational business, split into divisions based on geographical lines may, for example, impose a limit on the amount of capital that each division is allowed to invest in any particular year. This allows the directors to manage growth and financing and ensure that all divisions are adequately resourced.

Single period and multiple period capital rationing

Capital rationing could be limited to one time period, or be present for more than one time period.

The approach to dealing with capital rationing in a single time period is to focus on the profitability index and to rank investment opportunities according to the **profitability index**.

Multiple period capital rationing is more problematic. To solve a multiple period capital rationing problem requires the use of linear programming techniques which are beyond the scope of this book.

Single period capital rationing — divisible projects

When a single period capital rationing problem exists, if projects are **assumed to be divisible** then we rank the projects according to the profitability index. Divisibility of projects means that that any proportion of a possible project could be undertaken, that is, the project could be scaled down in size.

Need to know!

Profitability index (PI)

The profitability index can be defined as:

$$\frac{\text{Net present value of an investment}}{\text{Capital investment}}$$

Or alternatively

$$\frac{\text{Present value of net cash inflows}}{\text{Capital invested}}$$

The profitability index measures the return generated, in present value terms from the capital invested.

Single period capital rationing – non-divisible projects

In a single period rationing problem, when it is assumed that projects are non-divisible, the solution to the problem is normally found through trial and error. A non-divisible project is one that cannot be scaled up or down in size.

The profitability index is still useful, however, even in a situation where projects are assumed to be non-divisible projects. Suppose we have a hard capital rationing situation where the available capital is only slightly less than the amount needed to finance all available investment opportunities. If each of the projects under consideration generates a high profitability index a finance director may decide that it is worth seeking to raise additional capital, perhaps from alternative sources where the interest payments are higher than normal, in order to overcome the rationing situation.

Exam tip – Non-divisible projects

Student often make the mistake of dismissing the Profitability index as being of no relevance when considering non-divisible projects.

Even though we use trial and error to determine the best combination of projects to invest in, the profitability index for each project is still useful information. A finance director could compare the profitability index with the cost of raising additional finance from alternative, more expensive, sources that have not yet been considered.

Example 3

Shadow operates a range of theme parks, safari parks and zoos in a number of different parts of the world. It has grown very steadily over the past few years. The CEO of Shadow, Bronwen Evans, is keen to avoid over expanding and has therefore imposed a total limit of $126 million on the amount of capital expenditure that will be approved by the board this year.

The following project requests have been submitted to the board by the regional managers as part of the annual approval process:

Project	Capital invested this year	Project NPV
A	$25 million	$10.0 million
B	$30 million	$12.9 million
C	$45 million	$17.1 million
D	$35 million	$16.8 million
E	$10 million	$3.5 million

Requirements

(a) Determine which projects should be approved by the board if we assume that projects are divisible?

(b) Would the decision change if projects are assumed to be non-divisible?

Solution 3

Part (a)

If projects are divisible they can be ranked according to the profitability index. The profitability index in this case will be calculated as

$$\frac{\text{Net present value of an investment}}{\text{Capital invested}}$$

Project	Profitability Index	Ranking
A	$10.0m / $25m = 0.40	3rd
B	$12.9m / $30m = 0.43	2nd
C	$17.1m / $45m = 0.38	4th
D	$16.8m / $35m = 0.48	1st
E	$3.5m / $10m = 0.35	5th

Therefore the capital should be invested in the following way:

Project	Capital ($million)	%age of project	NPV ($million)
D	35	100%	16.8
B	30	100%	12.9
A	25	100%	10.0
C	36	36/45 = 80%	13.68
Total	126		53.38

80% x
$17.1 million

Because the capital available is restricted to $126 million only 80% of project C will be undertaken and nothing will be invested in project E.

Part (b)

If the projects are assumed to be non-divisible the possible combinations of projects needs to be assessed as follows:

Project combination	Capital ($million)	NPV ($million)
A+B+C+E	25+30+45+10 = 110	10.0+12.9+17.1+3.5 = 43.5
A+B+D+E	25+30+35+10 = 100	10.0+12.9+16.8+3.5 = 43.2
A+C+D+E	25+45+35+10 = 115	10.0+17.1+16.8+3.5 = 47.4
B+C+D+E	30+45+35+10 = 120	12.9+17.1+16.8+3.5 = 50.3

The best combination of projects would be B+C+D+E. This provides an overall NPV of $50.3 million based on capital invested of $120 million (out of the $126 million available).

Whilst this combination provides the best overall NPV of the possibilities available it means that Shadow has to undertake project C and E (4th and 5th ranked based on the profitability index) before project A (3rd ranked based on the profitability index). To undertake the combination A+B+C+D, that is, the top 4 projects in terms of ranking, would require $135 million of capital and would provide an overall NPV of $56.8 million. If Shadow could therefore find an extra ($135m - $126m) = $9 million of capital, the overall NPV could be increased by ($56.8m –$ 50.3m) = $6.5 million. This would be worth considering.

Chapter 6
key points summary

- Lease or buy decisions – compare the present value of leasing with the present value of borrowing to buy.

  - Relevant cashflows if borrow to buy:

    - purchase cost

    - resale value

    - capital allowances.

  - Relevant cashflows if leasing:

    - lease payments

    - tax relief on lease payments.

- Asset replacement decisions – when to replace assets which need replacing periodically?

  - Approach.

    - Calculate the total present value cost over each cycle.

    - Calculate equivalent annual cost (EAC) over each cycle by using formula

      $$\frac{\text{Total present value over one replacement cycle}}{\text{Annuity factor for that cycle}}$$

    - Choose cycle with lowest EAC cost

- Capital rationing – limit on amount of capital available.

  - Hard rationing – external restriction.

  - Soft rationing – internal restriction.

  - Single period or multiple period rationing possible.

  - Single period rationing – how to decide between projects?

    - Projects divisible – rank according to PI – the formula for PI is

      $$\frac{\text{Net present value of an investment}}{\text{Capital investment}}$$

    - Projects not divisible – use trial and error.

FOREIGN INVESTMENTS

Introduction
what is this chapter about?

In this chapter we consider the decision by a business to make an investment in a project located in a foreign country (which we will define as a foreign direct investment). We assess some of the reasons for making such an investment as well as the additional risks and complications that would be faced by a company considering such a decision. We also consider how an investment can be appraised using discounted cashflow techniques, and how the appraisal differs from that which would be carried out on an investment within the same country.

Key areas of the chapter are ....

1   **Considerations when undertaking foreign direct investment –** what are the reasons for investing in a foreign country? What are the additional risks and complications when investing in a foreign country and to what extent can these be mitigated?

2   **Evaluating foreign direct investment** – how can a foreign direct investment be evaluated using discounted cashflow techniques? What are the additional elements that need to be incorporated into the discounted cashflow evaluation?

CONSIDERATIONS WHEN UNDERTAKING FOREIGN DIRECT INVESTMENT

Finance terminology explained

What is foreign direct investment?

Foreign direct investment is a significant long term investment in an enterprise in another economy. This can take the form of an investment in assets i.e. setting up a new project, or, alternatively it could be through the acquisition of an existing enterprise.

Foreign direct investment is often seen as an alternative way of expanding into foreign markets compared to exporting, or to licensing. It will generally involve a far greater commitment, and a far greater level of capital expenditure than either exporting or licensing involves and therefore requires a long term commitment.

Reasons for foreign direct investment

There are many possible reasons why a business may decide to undertake significant foreign investment. These include the following:

1   **To gain access to new markets**. Foreign direct investment may offer a company access to new markets which may not otherwise be accessible. The decision by Nissan to set up production facilities within the European Union allowed it to bypass import quotas into the European Union, and gave it access to the European market which would not have been possible through exporting alone.

2   **To gain access to raw materials**. Many companies that are involved in raw material extraction and distribution, such as oil, gas and mining companies will undertake significant foreign direct investment in order to ensure continued supply of raw materials. The announcement by BP in early 2011 of its decision to seek a joint venture with Russian energy firm Rosneft, would, if successful, allow it to access potentially huge deposits of oil and gas in Russia's Arctic shelf.

3   **To take advantage of favourable financial conditions**. A company may be attracted to invest in a foreign country by favourable financial conditions, for example, corporate tax rates or government grants or subsidies. The low rate of corporate tax, relaxed transfer pricing rules and the adoption of the euro in Ireland appear to be have been significant factors in the decision by many multinational companies to relocate significant parts of their operations there.

4   **To increase cost efficiency**. A business may relocate production to a foreign country because labour costs are significantly cheaper than in the home country, or because the workforce is perceived to be more efficient, or more highly trained and skilled, or because there is greater access to resources.

5   **To access intellectual property**. A significant motivation for acquiring foreign companies in technology based industries is to access and control intellectual property such as research and development, skills and experience, production processes and patents.

Risks of foreign direct investment

There are a number of specific risks arising from foreign direct investment such as the following:

1   **Political risk**. This can take many forms and there is strong overlap between political risk and other types of risk, for example, economic, and currency risk. In its extreme form political risk could involve a decision by a government to expropriate or nationalise assets owned by a foreign investor, or extreme civil strife or conflict which could significantly damage the value of the investment.

2   **Currency risk**. A foreign direct investment in an economy with a different currency could expose a business to a number of different types of currency risk. The risks involved, and how these could be mitigated, are covered in detail in chapter 19.

3   **Restrictions on profit repatriation** (that is returning or remitting profits from the foreign country to the home country). There may be significant restrictions on the ability of a business to repatriate profit generated by a foreign operation, or on repatriating the initial capital invested. A foreign government may impose exchange controls, or witholding taxes, to prevent repatriation of profit.

4   **Financing risk**. A business may find it more difficult to finance a foreign investment than to finance a home investment. From a currency risk management point of view it would be sensible to finance an investment in a foreign currency by raising capital in the same foreign currency. This may, however, be difficult to achieve especially when the investment is in an economy with relatively undeveloped capital markets.

Overcoming barriers to profit repatriation

There are a number of techniques that a business can seek to employ to overcome barriers to profit repatriation. The success of these techniques depends, to a large extent, on the type and level of restriction imposed by a foreign government on profit repatriation. Possible techniques include:

1   **Transfer pricing**. This is the price charged by the parent company for goods or services provided by the parent company to the foreign operation. The price therefore becomes a revenue stream in the parent company and a cost in the foreign operation. Setting a transfer price at a level that is well above the true arm's length market price is a controversial but potentially effective way of remitting profit and cash from the foreign operation.

2   **Management charges**. This is very similar to transfer pricing. A parent company may charge the overseas operation for management activities performed by a parent company for the foreign operation.

3   **Royalty payments**. If the parent company controls patents used by the foreign operation as part of its manufacturing process, the parent company can charge the foreign operation a royalty fee. As with a transfer price, the royalty may, or may not, be at arm's length.

4   **License payment**. The parent company may charge the foreign operation a licence fee for the use of the parent's intellectual property. A licence fee is often charged, for example, for the use of a brand name, owned by a parent company but used by a foreign operation in the manufacture and sale of a product within a foreign country.

5   **Interest payment on a loan**. A parent company may provide a loan to finance a foreign operation. It could then charge a rate of interest above the market rate, increasing revenue in the parent and costs in the foreign operation.

International diversification

One of the reasons sometimes cited for foreign direct investment is to diversify risk. From a practical point of view this may be a valid, sensible, benefit of foreign direct investment. Ford, historically, for example, has often duplicated production capabilities for its products such that it is able to produce the same product in more than one country. This has allowed it to expand production in one plant if it faced industrial unrest or other problems in the other plant. By operating in this way it could be argued that Ford is able to diversify away some of the political risk arising from foreign direct investment.

There is, however, a theoretical argument, based on the principles of the capital asset pricing model, CAPM (which will be developed in a later chapter), that it is always cheaper and more effective for an investor to diversify internationally than for a company to do so. An investor in the share capital of Ford, could, for example, buy shares in a range of car manufacturers in different geographical locations to achieve the same risk reduction effect.

We will consider the impact of diversification on risk in more detail in the chapter on portfolio theory and CAPM.

Exam tip – International diversification

In an exam question involving a discussion of the merits or otherwise of foreign investment, good marks can often be gained by mentioning the point above about international diversification.

The point links finance theory with practice, and if well explained it demonstrates a good understanding of the material.

EVALUATING FOREIGN DIRECT INVESTMENT

If a business is considering a foreign direct investment the decision can be evaluated by using the NPV technique. There are a number of additional complications when carrying out an NPV analysis in this situation. The main complications are as follows.

- How to approach the NPV evaluation if the investment is in a foreign currency and how to present the result of the evaluation.

- Forecasting future exchange rates if the investment or any of the future cashflows are in the foreign currency.

- Dealing with additional taxation issues arising from an investment in the foreign country.

- Incorporating different ways in which the business undertaking the investment may remit the cashflows generated back to the home country.

- Ensuring that the discount rate used for the evaluation properly reflects the risk involved. The risks of investing in a foreign country are likely to be significantly different to the risks faced by a business undertaking a similar investment in the home country.

Need to know!

Approach to an NPV evaluation

A fundamental principle of finance theory, as we saw in chapter 1, is that managers aim to maximise shareholder wealth. We also saw in chapter 2 that undertaking an investment with a positive NPV should, in theory, increase shareholder wealth by that amount.

In order to assess the impact of a foreign investment on shareholder wealth, it is therefore important that the **final NPV** result is **presented in the home currency** of the company undertaking the investment. The result of the investment or project can then be compared to the result of other projects including those that involve an investment in the home country, and a decision can be made about which investments will maximise shareholder wealth.

In theory there are two technically correct approaches to evaluate the NPV. They can be illustrated as follows:

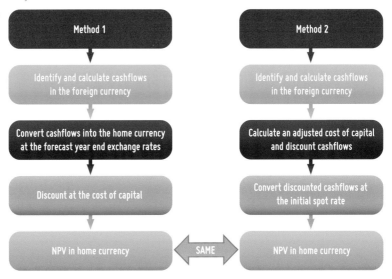

The two approaches will give the same answer (if the analysis is performed correctly!!)

Example 1

Sue is a Spanish company that owns and operates luxury hotels in the South of Spain. It is considering investing in a range of hotels in the United States. The investment will cost $120,000,000 and is expected to generate the following cashflows:

Year 1	Net cash inflow	$20,000,000
Year 2	Net cash inflow	$32,000,000
Year 3	Net cash inflow	$36,000,000
Year 4	Net cash inflow	$42,000,000

After 4 years the investment is expected to be sold for $100,000,000. Tax is payable on the operating cashflows in the United States at 20% per annum. The tax is payable in the same year as the cashflow to which it relates. No additional tax is payable in Spain.

A suitable cost of capital for the investment is 10%. The current spot rate is $2 per euro. The euro is expected to strengthen against the dollar by 5% per annum over the life of the investment.

Requirements

(a) What is the NPV in euro using method 1?
(b) What is the NPV in euro using method 2?

Solution 1

Part (a)

This approach involves converting the dollar cashflows at the end of each year into euro cashflows, using the forecast exchange rates. The exchange rates therefore need to be forecast. In this example, a strengthening of the euro by 5% per annum means that there will be 5% more dollars for every euro.

Forecast exchange rates are:

Year 1	-	$2 x (1+0.05)	=	$2.10 per euro
Year 2	-	$2.10 x (1+0.05)	=	$2.205 per euro
Year 3	-	$2.205 x (1+0.05)	=	$2.3153 per euro
Year 4	-	$2.3153 x (1+0.05)	=	$2.4311 per euro

We can then calculate the present value as follows (all figures are in '000):

	T0	T1	T2	T3	T4
Operating cashflows ($)		20,000	32,000	36,000	42,000
Tax @ 20% ($)		(4,000)	(6,400)	(7,200)	(8,400)
Cost ($)	(120,000)				
Resale ($)					100,000
Net cashflow ($)	(120,000)	16,000	25,600	28,800	133,600
	÷	÷	÷	÷	÷
Exchange rate	2	2.10	2.205	2.3153	2.4311
Netcashflow (€)	(60,000)	7,619	11,610	12,439	54,955
DF @ 10%	1.000	$\frac{1}{(1+0.10)}$	$\times \frac{1}{(1+0.10)^2}$	$\times \frac{1}{(1+0.10)^3}$	$\times \frac{1}{(1+0.10)^4}$
Present value (€)	(60,000)	6,926	9,595	9,346	37,535

The NPV in € is therefore = €3,402k

Part (b)

The alternative approach involves working out an adjusted cost of capital. In this context the cost of capital is adjusted to take into account the forecast exchange rate changes between currencies.

In this case the euro is forecast to strengthen by 5% per annum. If this is the case, any cashflows generated in dollars are effectively worth 5% less per annum when converted into euros.

If the cashflows are worth 5% less per annum because of forecast exchange rate changes this is like discounting the cashflows at an extra 5%.

The adjusted discount rate can then be found by using a similar approach to the Fisher formula for inflation seen earlier.

If r = adjusted discount rate
    c = cost of capital for the project
    e = exchange rate changes

Then

$(1+r)$ = $(1+c) \times (1+e)$

In this case

$(1+r)$ = $(1+0.10) \times (1+0.05)$
$(1+r)$ = 1.155
r = 0.155 or 15.5%

The NPV can then be found as follows (all figures are in '000).

	T0	T1	T2	T3	T4
Operating cashflows ($)		20,000	32,000	36,000	42,000
Tax @ 20% ($)		(4,000)	(6,400)	(7,200)	(8,400)
Cost ($)	(120,000)				
Resale ($)					100,000
Net cashflow ($)	(120,000)	16,000	25,600	28,800	133,600
Discount @ 15.5%	X 1.000	$X \dfrac{1}{(1 + 0.155)}$	$X \dfrac{1}{(1 + 0.155)^2}$	$X \dfrac{1}{(1 + 0.155)^3}$	$X \dfrac{1}{(1 + 0.155)^4}$
Present value ($)	(120,000)	13,853	19,190	18,691	75,072
Exchange rate	2	2	2	2	2
Present value (€)	(60,000)	6,927	9,595	9,346	37,536

The net present value is = €3,404k

The answer is therefore almost exactly the same using both methods - the difference is purely a result of rounding.

In this example, the forecast exchange rate is shown to four decimal places and discounting has been performed by using the formula rather than the tables. This is to avoid rounding errors having too big an impact on the result. In an exam it would be perfectly acceptable to round exchange rates (to the number of decimal places to which they are shown in the question) and to use the tables for discounting rather than the formula.

Which method should be used in answer to exam questions?

Need to know!

Method 1 is, in most cases, the best method to use when answering an exam question.

When cashflows become more complex, and there are additional cashflows in the home country currency, method 1 will allow you to is to produce an answer more quickly.

Additionally, if the exchange rate forecasts are more complex than those shown in example 1, when method 2 is used a separate discount rate may need to be calculated each year. If there is a long time horizon method 2 tends to create additional work.

Forecasting future exchange rates

We saw in example 1 that there is a need to forecast future exchange rates in order to be able to appraise a foreign investment using the NPV technique. In example 1 we were told that one currency would strengthen against another by 5%.

The most common way of estimating future exchange rates used in exam questions is purchasing power parity theory. This theory is covered in detail in chapter 19.

Additional taxation issues

If a business invests in a project in a foreign country, any earnings generated will be taxed in that foreign country at the relevant tax rate, and may then be taxed again in the home country.

In carrying out an NPV analysis on a foreign investment in the real world, a company would employ tax specialists to estimate the tax consequences of investment decisions and would then incorporate their suggestions into the investment appraisal exercise.

An exam question, however, needs to simplify tax assumptions in order to be able to incorporate tax calculations into an NPV analysis that can realistically be carried out under exam conditions. The main simplifying assumptions are:

1   The rules for taxation of profits are normally assumed to be the same in both the foreign country and the home country. This means that we will have **exactly the same taxable profits in both countries**.

2   **Full double taxation relief** is normally assumed to arise. This means that any tax paid in a foreign country can be fully offset against tax payable in the home country.

Need to know!

Impact of the above assumptions

The simplifying assumptions that are normally made leads to the following general rule about dealing with double taxation in an exam question:

If the home tax rate > foreign tax rate tax is payable in the home country at the difference between the two rates.

If the home tax rate < foreign tax rate no extra tax payable in the home country.

Example 2

Julie is a company based in the Eurozone. It is considering investing in the United States. Forecast pre-tax net cash inflows in dollars for the first 3 years are as follows:

Year 1 – $30,000
Year 2 – $45,000
Year 3 – $55,000

These net cash inflows can be assumed to be equal to taxable profit and are taxed in the United States at 20% per annum. The tax rate in the Eurozone is 30%. Full double taxation relief is available in the Eurozone for tax already paid in the United States on the profits generated. Tax in both countries is payable in the same year as the relevant taxable profit.

Assume a discount rate of 8%, and a constant exchange rate of $1.50 per euro.

What would be the present value in euros of the post-tax cashflows generated during the first 3 years of the project's life?

Solution 2

Working 1 – tax payable in dollars

The tax payable in dollars can be calculated as follows:

Year 1 $30,000 x 20% = $6,000
Year 2 $45,000 x 20% = $9,000
Year 3 $55,000 x 20% = $11,000

Working 2 – tax payable in euro

Tax will be payable in euro on the same profits (translated at the relevant exchange rate) at a rate of 30%.

If, however, there is full double taxation relief, and we are using the same taxable profit in both countries, this means that there is effectively just another 10% (30%-20%) of tax to pay on those profits.

The tax payable in euro will be:

Year 1 $30,000 ÷ 1.50 x 10% = €2,000
Year 2 $45,000 ÷ 1.50 x 10% = €3,000
Year 3 $55,000 ÷ 1.50 x 10% = €3,667

Working 3

The present value of the cashflows can then be calculated using method 1 as follows:

	T1	T2	T3
Pre-tax cashflow ($)	30,000	45,000	55,000
Tax @ 20% ($)	(6,000)	(9,000)	(11,000)
Net cashflow ($)	24,000	36,000	44,000
Exchange rate	÷ 1.50	÷ 1.50	÷ 1.50
Net cashflow (€)	16,000	24,000	29,333
Tax in euros (W2)	(2,000)	(3,000)	(3,667)
Net cashflow (€)	14,000	21,000	25,666
DF @ 8%	0.926	0.857	0.794
Present value	12,964	17,997	20,379

The present value of the cashflows in euro is therefore = €51,340

Incorporating different methods of remitting profit into an NPV evaluation

In the first section of this chapter we considered ways in which a business can remit profits to overcome barriers, or remittance restrictions imposed by a foreign government. How are these methods incorporated into an NPV evaluation?

The approach is to treat the payment as a **cash outflow** in the foreign part of the NPV evaluation, as if the payment is to a third party, and then a **cash inflow** in the home part of the evaluation, as if there is a receipt from a third party.

The cash outflow in the foreign part of the NPV evaluation will be allowable in full against foreign tax, and will therefore be **taxed in full** in the home part of the evaluation.

Example 3

We will use the same information as example 2.

In this case, however, we will assume that Julie decides to charge a royalty of $3,000 per annum to the foreign investment for each of the three years.

What would be the present value in euros of the post-tax cashflows generated during the first 3 years of the project's life?

Working 1 – tax payable in dollars

In this scenario, the annual royalty payment can be offset against the profit generated in dollars before the tax is calculated

The tax payable in the dollars can be calculated as follows:

Year 1   ($30,000-$3,000) x 20% = $5,400
Year 2   ($45,000-$3,000) x 20% = $8,400
Year 3   ($55,000-$3,000) x 20% = $10,400

Working 2 – tax payable in euro

The same taxable profits are then translated at the relevant exchange rate and then a further 10% tax is payable.

The tax payable in euro will be:

Year 1   ($30,000-$3,000) ÷ 1.50 x 10% = €1,800
Year 2   ($45,000-$3,000) ÷ 1.50 x 10% = €2,800
Year 3   ($55,000-$3,000) ÷ 1.50 x 10% = €3,467

Working 3 – the royalty

The royalty will be a cash outflow in the foreign currency part of the evaluation and will be allowable against foreign tax. As a result the royalty will be taxed in full at 30% in the home country.

The royalty in € will be:

$3,000 ÷ 1.50 = €2,000 per annum.

Working 4

The present value of the cashflows can then be calculated using method 1 as follows:

	T1	T2	T3
Pre-tax cashflow ($)	30,000	45,000	55,000
Royalty ($)	(3,000)	(3,000)	(3,000)
Tax @ 20% ($) (W1)	(5,400)	(8,400)	(10,400)
Net cashflow ($)	21,600	33,600	41,600
Exchange rate	÷ 1.50	÷ 1.50	÷ 1.50
Net cashflow (€)	14,400	22,400	27,733
Tax in euros (W2)	(1,800)	(2,800)	(3,467)
Royalty (€) (W3)	2,000	2,000	2,000
Tax on royalty @ 30%	(600)	(600)	(600)
Net cashflow (€)	14,000	21,000	25,666
DF @ 8%	0.926	0.857	0.794
Present value	12,964	17,997	20,379

The present value of the cashflows in euros is therefore = €51,340

The present value of the cashflows is exactly the same as in example 2.

This is because all profits generated by Julie from the foreign investment are effectively taxed within the group at 30%. If the profits are taxed at 20% in the dollar, there is a further 10% tax to pay in the euro. If the profits are not taxed in the dollar (which applies to the profits generated in the dollar which are then remitted via a royalty payment) they will be taxed in full at 30% in the euro.

Discount rate and risk

The risk of a new foreign investment is likely to be different to the risk of the company's existing activities. As a result, the company's current cost of capital is unlikely to be a suitable discount rate to use to appraise the new investment.

A suitable discount rate is more likely to be found using the techniques of CAPM and the risk adjusted WACC. These are covered in later chapters.

Chapter 7
key points summary

- Foreign direct investment offers significant opportunities to a business but also involves considerable additional risks.

- When appraising a foreign direct investment using the NPV technique – the final NPV result should always be presented in the currency of the home country.

- There are two ways of working out the NPV of a foreign investment:

    – convert cashflows at forecast exchange rates – approach normally used

    – adjusted discount rate.

- Additional complications when calculating the NPV of a foreign investment.

    – Forecasting exchange rates (often using purchasing power parity – see chapter 19).

    – Double taxation.

    – Different ways of remitting profit from a foreign investment.

    – Using a discount rate that properly reflects the risk of the foreign investment.

"This paper (Modigliani and Miller's gearing proposition) . . . has been assigned to students in business and finance all over the world. They think it's a terrible paper, a very hard one to understand – and they are right!"

Franco Modigliani
1985 Nobel Prize Winner for Economics

LONG TERM FINANCE

SOURCES OF LONG TERM FINANCE

8

Introduction
what is this chapter about?

In the first section of the book we considered how a business could appraise new potential investments using both DCF and non-DCF techniques. All new investments require long term finance. In this chapter we explore the different types of long term finance that are available to both large and small companies. Long term finance is also known as capital. The terms mean the same thing. When investors provide long term finance to a business we could say that they have invested capital in the business.

Short term finance is considered in section 3 of the book.

Key areas of the chapter are ....

1   **Equity finance** – this is finance raised from the company's ordinary shareholders. In what ways can finance be raised from ordinary shareholders? What is the impact of each method of raising equity finance on shareholder wealth?

2   **Preference share finance** – is this really debt or equity finance? When is this a useful form of finance to use?

3   **Debt finance** – debt finance can be raised in a number of different ways including bank borrowing and issuing bonds. What are the different characteristics of each type of debt finance?

4   **Other sources of finance** – what alternative sources of long term finance are available to companies in specific scenarios e.g. a rapidly growing private company?

EQUITY FINANCE

Equity capital is the ordinary share capital in a business. The providers of equity capital are therefore the investors who own the ordinary shares in a business. Ordinary shares give the holder the right to vote on major decisions and effectively give ownership in a business. The ordinary shareholder therefore 'owns' any profits generated in the business after interest and tax has been paid.

The company's directors may decide (on behalf of the shareholders) to distribute these profits as a dividend, or, alternatively, retain and reinvest the profits in the business. If the profits are retained and reinvested wisely, the ordinary shareholder should benefit from this through growth in future profits and dividends.

The ordinary shareholder, or provider of equity capital, therefore has a higher potential return but also bears more risk than the providers of any other type of finance.

Exam tip – What is the value of equity?

Students often confuse market values, book values and nominal values of equity.

When discussing equity financing the market value of equity is the most important figure to focus on. A lot of finance theory is based around the market value of equity. This is simply the number of shares multiplied by the current market price of each share (assuming that the ordinary shares are quoted and traded on a stock market).

The book value of equity is sometimes used as an alternative. The book value of equity is the value, based upon the latest statement of financial position, of share capital, share premium, retained earnings and other reserves (such as a revaluation surplus). It represents the amount, based on the latest statement of financial position, that the ordinary shareholder 'owns'.

The nominal value of equity is simply the number of ordinary shares in issue multiplied by the nominal value of each share. It does not include the value of share premium, retained earnings and other reserves.

Types of equity finance

There are three main types of equity finance:

1   Retained earnings - retaining some of the profits, or earnings, that have been generated rather than pay a dividend.

2   A rights issue of shares – where **existing shareholders** are offered the right to buy new shares to be issued by a company.

3   A new issue of shares to new investors – where shares are offered for sale to **new shareholders** rather than existing shareholders.

Retained earnings

This is where the directors of a company decide to retain and reinvest profits that are generated rather than distribute those profits to the shareholders in the form of a dividend.

A couple of important points to be aware of:

1   The term earnings means the same thing as profits. Using retained earnings as a form of finance therefore means the same thing as using retained profits.

2   In order to use retained earnings to finance new investments the earnings or profits generated must also result in a generation of cash.

This is the simplest form of equity finance and it avoids incurring the issue costs associated with a rights issue of shares or a new issue of shares.

Exam tip – Retained earnings

A common mistake made by students when discussing equity financing is to say that using retained earnings is a 'free' form of financing.

When a company retains earnings the financing is not 'free'. The company will avoid incurring issue cost but there is still a real, long term cost.

If a company retains earnings, the shareholders forego dividends that they would otherwise receive. The dividends could have been invested elsewhere by shareholders to earn a return. This return to the shareholder is 'lost' when earnings are retained and reinvested and is therefore an opportunity cost.

The decision as to whether or not to use retained earnings as a form of finance is really a dividend policy decision. This will be considered further in chapter 15.

Rights Issue

The existing shareholders are offered the right to buy new shares in proportion to their existing shareholding. Directors must give existing shareholders the right to buy new shares that are issued before they are offered for sale to new investors. This is known as 'pre-emption rights'. A shareholder who is offered the right to buy new shares in the company has three options available:

1 to take up the rights
2 to sell the rights to another investor
3 to allow the rights to lapse.

In practice the third option never happens. If the existing shareholders don't respond to a letter offering the rights, the default position is that the company will sell the rights on their behalf.

How does a rights issue work?

Suppose a manufacturing company, Perry, has 2 million shares in issue. Each share is currently trading at $4.00 on the stock market.

Perry needs to raise $1,120,000 of new finance to invest in new advanced manufacturing machinery. It plans to raise the finance by selling new shares to existing shareholders at a price of $2.80 per share.

How many new shares will Perry need to issue?

In order to raise $1,120,000 by issuing shares at $2.80 a share, Perry will need to issue a total of $1,120,000/$2.80 = 400,000 shares.

What is the issue price of new shares under a rights issue?

When a rights issue is made, the issue price of the new shares will be set at a level which is below the current market price of the existing shares. This gives the existing shareholders an incentive to purchase the new shares i.e. to take up the rights.

In this example, the new shares will be issued at a price of $2.80 per share, which is $1.20 below the current share price of $4.00. This equates to a discount of 30% on the existing share price.

What are the terms of the rights issue?

The terms of the rights issue refers to the number of new shares that each existing shareholder is entitled to buy. If Perry needs to issue 400,000 new shares, and the company currently has in issue 2 million shares, the terms of the rights issue need to be 400,000 new shares for the 2 million existing shares, or 1 new share for every 5 existing shares. A shareholder who owns 5 existing shares will therefore be offered the chance to buy 1 new share at $2.80.

Exam tip – Terms of a rights issue

In exams you will either be given

(a) The amount of new finance that the company wishes to raise, and from that you will need to work out, firstly, the number of new shares to be issued and, subsequently, the terms of the rights issue. This is the approach taken above.

Or alternatively you will be given

(b) The terms of the rights issue e.g. 1 new share for every 5 shares, and from that you will need to work out the number of new shares issued, and then, finally, the total amount of new finance raised.

Be prepared for either approach!

The Theoretical Ex-Rights Price (TERP)

This is the price at which the shares are expected to settle after the rights issue if we assume that the company's value will increase by the proceeds of the rights issue.

The TERP is a weighted average of the pre-rights share price (that is the price of a share immediately before the rights issue) and the price at which the new shares are issued under a right issue.

For Perry we can calculate the TERP as follows:

	Number of Shares		Price ($)	Total Value ($)
Existing	5	x	4.00	20.00
New	1	x	2.80	2.80
Total	6			22.80

TERP = $22.80/6 = $3.80 per share

Significance of the TERP

Following the rights issue both the existing and new shares will start trading on the stock market. Investors will be very interested in the actual share price after the rights issue, and, in whether or not they will be better off financially after the rights issue.

If the **total value** of a company rises by the same as the amount of new finance raised, then the **actual share price** following the rights issue **should equal the TERP**.

In the case of Perry's rights issue:

The rights issue will raise $1,120,000. Before the rights issue the company's equity was worth a total of 2m shares x $4.00 = $8,000,000. If the total value of the company's equity rises by the amount of new finance raised then it would rise to $9,120,000.

After the rights issue the company will have 2,000,000 + 400,000 shares in issue = 2,400,000 shares.

A total value of $9,120,000 would therefore result in a share price of $9,120,000/2,400,000 shares = $3.80 per share i.e. the TERP.

Of course – whether or not the share price after the rights issue settles at this level depends on shareholders perceptions of the rights issue, and on how the company will use the new finance raised. If shareholders believe that the new finance will produce long term benefits worth significantly more than the amount of new finance raised the actual share price post-rights may settle at an amount greater than the TERP.

Sale of the rights

If an investor decides not to take up the rights, or does not have the finance available to take up the rights, then the rights can be sold.

The amount that the rights could be sold for, in theory, is equal to:

TERP – rights issue price

In the case of Perry – this means that the rights could be sold for $3.80 – $2.80 = $1.00

An outside investor would, in this case, pay $1 for the right to buy one new share that is issued. They would pay $2.80 to the company to purchase the share, and if the shares settle at the TERP i.e. $3.80, then the new investor would be in a no gain/no loss position.

 ## Need to know!

If the actual share price settles at the TERP following a rights issue, an investor taking up a rights, or an investor selling the rights for the theoretical value of the right, will be in a no gain/no loss position.

Example 1

Suppose a shareholder, Baz, owns 10% of the shares of the quoted company Perry before the rights issue.

(a) How much were Baz's shares worth before the rights issue took place?

(b) If Baz took up the rights, how would his wealth have changed if the actual share price post-rights equals the TERP?

(c) If Baz sold the rights, how would his wealth have changed?

Solution 1

(a) Baz owns 10% x 4m shares = 400,000 shares, before the rights issue. Each share was trading at $4.00 on the date of the rights issue and therefore Baz's wealth before the rights issue was:

Value of Baz's shareholding pre-rights:		$
400,000 shares x $4.00	=	**1,600K**

(b) If Baz takes up his rights he will receive 1/5 x 400,000 shares = 80,000 shares.

		$
The value of Baz's shareholding post-rights:		
480,000 shares x $3.80	=	1,824k
Less the cost of purchasing the new shares:		
80,000 shares x $2.80	=	(224k)
Net wealth after taking up the rights	**=**	**1,600K**

(c) If Baz sells the rights

		$
The value of Baz's shareholding post-rights will now be:		
400,000 shares x $3.80	=	1,520k
Add the amount received from the sale of the rights:		
80,000 rights x $1.00	=	80k
Net wealth after the sale of the rights	**=**	**1,600K**

Baz has a wealth of $1,600k in each case. Selling the rights would therefore have the same impact on Baz's wealth as taking up the rights. These calculations do not, however, take into account the dilution of Baz's shareholding that would arise if the rights are sold. If the rights are sold Baz would no longer own 10% of the company's equity.

Underwriting

In practice all issues of new shares (whether a rights issue, or an issue of shares to new investors) are underwritten. In essence this is a form of insurance provided by the bank that arranges and manages the new share issue. If the shares are not taken up by investors, then the underwriters will agree to buy those shares at the issue price.

By underwriting the issue a company can guarantee that the shares will be sold, and hence that the finance that the company needs to raise will be raised. The main disadvantage of underwriting is the cost. This will depend on many factors e.g. the volatility of the stock market and the risk of the existing share price falling below the issue price, but will always be a significant amount.

Real life illustration – HBOS

In July 2008, a rights issue by HBOS, to raise $4bn, failed spectacularly. The funds were needed to bolster its tier 1 capital ratio. Only 8.29% of the existing shareholders took up the rights. As a result, the underwriters of the rights issue, Morgan Stanley and Dresdner, were left with the remainder of the shares, the bulk of which they then placed with other financial institutions.

The rights issue price was 275p per share. When the rights issue had been announced in April 2008 this price had been at a significant discount on the share price at the time of 500p a share. Between the announcement of the rights issue in April 2008, and July 2008, when the rights issue took place, the bank's shares plunged in value to 228p – significantly below the rights issue price.

A new issue of shares to new investors

There are many occasions when shareholders would be willing to forego their pre-emption rights in order to increase their wealth in the long term. A company, for example that wishes to grow rapidly may need to raise significantly more finance than the existing shareholders can provide. In order to raise a significant amount of new finance, and provide an incentive for new investors to invest, the existing shareholders will be willing to forego their pre-emption rights and allow the directors of the company to offer new shares to new investors.

There are three main ways in which this can be done:

(a)   an offer for sale
(b)   an offer for sale by tender
(c)   a placing.

An offer for sale

An offer for sale is often made when a company first obtains a listing on a stock exchange. When a company first obtains a listing on a stock exchange this is often called an Initial Public Offering (IPO).

The company and its advisors set an issue price and then invite the investing public to buy the new shares issued at that price.

If the issue price is attractive, this method should attract a wide range of shareholders, and, as a result, an active secondary market in the shares should be created i.e. there should be enough buyers and sellers to mean that there is a proper market in those shares following the issue.

The main disadvantage of an offer for sale is that costs of issuing are high (significantly higher than a rights issue) e.g. costs of advertising and underwriting the issue. There is also a risk that the pricing of the issue is too high, or too low. If too high – there will be insufficient investors and the new issue will not be fully subscribed. As well as not raising the finance this will generate bad publicity for the company.

Offer for sale by tender

Rather than set an issue price, in this case a minimum price for the shares is set and investors are invited to bid for the shares at or above this price.

After all of the bids have been received an issue price is then set in one of two ways:

(a) The highest price at which all of the shares can be sold. Any investor who has bid at or above this price will then receive the full amount of the shares that they bid for.

(b) A lower price and allow each investor who has bid at this price or above to receive a proportion of the shares that they bid for. This method of allocating shares results in wider share ownership and therefore greater marketability of shares.

Whichever method is adopted all shares must be issued at the same price.

When is an offer for sale by tender appropriate?

It is particularly useful as a method of issuing new shares when there is significant uncertainty or difficulty in determining the appropriate issue price. If, for example, a rapidly growing high technology company, with a unique product seeks to list on a stock market it would be extremely difficult to value the company and set an issue price.

An offer for sale by tender avoids the problem of underpricing or overpricing the issue. If there is significant demand for the shares and therefore the final issue price is higher than expected, it may also result in the company raising more capital than originally planned.

A placing

In a placing, new shares are sold or 'placed' by a merchant bank directly with an institutional investor, or a number of institutional investors e.g. a large pension fund, thus avoiding open market competition for the shares.

This has the advantage of ensuring that the issue will be successful before it takes place, and as a result the issue costs will be lower than in the case of an offer for sale, or an offer for sale by tender.

A placing would, however, limit the number of shareholders in a company, and as a result there may not be a proper secondary market in the buying and selling of shares in the company. When a company proposes to raise finance via a placing, a stock exchange may therefore insist that a proportion of the new shares issued, are issued via an offer for sale, or an offer for sale by tender, to widen share ownership.

PREFERENCE SHARE FINANCE

Preference share capital offers an investor a fixed dividend each year which is a percentage of the nominal value of the capital. An example would be 8% preference shares with a nominal value of 50 cents per share. An investor in the preference share capital would receive an annual dividend of 50c x 8% = 4c per share. Preference shares can be redeemable on a certain date in the future or, alternatively the capital can be irredeemable.

Key characteristics of preference share capital

These are as follows.

- An investor will receive **a fixed dividend** each year, and therefore the return is much less volatile and hence less risky than the return that an ordinary shareholder would receive.

- Unlike an ordinary shareholder, a preference shareholder cannot benefit if the company, and its profits, grow very significantly in the future.

- A company **does not have to pay the fixed dividend** in a year when performance is poor e.g. if there are insufficient profits or cashflow being generated. Most preference shares are cumulative which means that a company would not be allowed to pay a dividend to ordinary shareholders before any arrears of dividends on preference shares has been paid.

- The ability of a company to delay or defer a dividend in a bad year makes this a more risky form of investment than debt capital. A preference shareholder would therefore demand a higher rate of return than a provider of debt capital.

- Dividends paid to preference shareholders are a distribution from post-tax earnings, like dividends on ordinary shareholders. Interest paid to the providers of debt capital is a distribution from pre-tax earnings. Preference share capital is therefore not as tax efficient to a company as raising debt capital.

When is preference share finance attractive to a company?

If a company wants to raise capital from new investors, avoid a dilution of equity and hence control, but also avoid the risk of having to meet interest payment obligations, then preference share capital is an appropriate form of finance.

DEBT FINANCE

Debt finance is where an investor receives a guaranteed return each year on the capital invested, normally in the form of interest payments. A company must pay interest to the providers of debt finance before paying dividends to preference and ordinary shareholders. The interest payment is tax allowable from a company's point of view – we will explore this more in the chapter on the cost of capital (chapter 9).

There is a significant range of possibilities if a company wishes to raise long term debt finance. The main types of debt finance to be aware of are:

1   bank term loan
2   straight bond
3   zero coupon or deep discounted bond
4   unsecured bond (mezzanine finance)
5   convertible bond
6   straight bond with warrants attached
7   leasing.

A bank term loan

This is a loan by a bank or other financial institution that is repayable on a certain date in the future. The interest rate charged by the bank can be fixed or floating (variable). Loans are normally secured on the assets of the company. Repayment of the principal can be at the end of the period in one lump sum, or in instalments.

The interest rate charged by the finance provider depends on the risk they perceive of the borrower defaulting on the repayment.

This is the simplest form of debt financing and can be arranged by companies of all sizes. Repayment terms can also be arranged to suit the needs of the borrower.

A straight bond

A bond is marketable debt i.e. debt that is bought and sold on the stock market in the same way that shares are bought and sold on the stock market. Before being able to raise finance of this type a company therefore needs to be listed on a stock market.

The market price of a straight bond is normally quoted per $100 nominal value of the bond. Interest is calculated on the basis of the nominal value. If a 12% bond was trading at $92 for example, this would mean that an investor would be prepared to pay $92 for a block of debt with a nominal value of $100. The investor would then receive 12% x $100 = $12 of interest each year.

Finance terminology explained

Straight bond, marketable debt, loan note, debenture

These terms all essentially mean the same thing! They refer to a situation where a company issues a block of debt to investors which is normally secured on the assets of the company. The debt carries a fixed rate of interest set on the date that the debt is issued. A crucial difference between this type of debt and bank lending is that an investor buying a bond would be able to sell the bond at any time. This type of debt finance is therefore a lot more 'liquid' to an investor, than bank lending.

A bond compared to a term loan?

The key differences between debt financing via a bond, and debt financing via a term loan are:

- An investor in a bond has the ability to sell the investment on the stock market to another investor at any time. This ability to liquidate the investment at short notice makes bonds a very attractive form of investment and as a result there are many more potential investors available than in the case of a term loan.

- The cost and risks of raising finance via issuing a bond are significantly greater than when finance is raised via a term loan. As with issues of new equity, there are significant market related issue costs involved in the issue of bonds.

Finance terminology explained

Zero coupon or deep discounted bond

Zero coupon bond

A zero coupon bond is one that is issued at a significant discount to the redemption value. No interest is paid but the investor will obtain a significant known return in the form of a capital gain between the date of issue and the redemption date.

Deep discounted bond

A deep discounted bond is similar except that a small amount of interest is payable each year. A significant proportion of the return, however, will still be in the form of a capital gain.

Example 2

Manon issued a bond at $65. The bond is redeemable in 5 years' time for $100. The coupon rate is 0% i.e. the bond will not pay any interest to the investor.

What is the annual percentage return that the investor would receive if the bond was purchased on the issue date and held until redemption?

 ## Solution 2

If r is the return that the investor receives, then using the principles of compounding and discounting that we covered in an earlier chapter:

$$65 (1+r)^5 = 100$$

rearranging

$$1 + r = \sqrt[5]{\frac{100}{65}}$$

$$1 + r = 1.09$$
$$r = 1.09 - 1$$
$$r = 0.09 \text{ or } 9\%$$

The investor therefore receives a true overall return of 9% per annum.

What are the benefits and drawbacks to a company of deep discounted and zero coupon bonds compared to a normal bond?

Benefits	Drawbacks
A company avoids having to pay significant amounts of cash to an investor until the debt is redeemed. This is very useful if a company is financing a long term investment that will not generate cash returns for some time e.g. a long term construction project.	The overall percentage return that an investor will demand will be higher than the return on a normal bond. It is therefore a relatively expensive form of debt finance.
	The company will need to find a large amount of cash to redeem the debt on the redemption date.

Finance terminology explained

An unsecured bond (mezzanine finance)

What is mezzanine finance?

This is a bond issued without security on the assets of the company. An investor in mezzanine finance would therefore rank below an investor in secured debt in the event of a winding up.

Mezzanine finance is high risk debt and therefore the return that the company needs to offer to investors in this type of debt is often extremely high – sometimes very similar to the returns offered to the providers of equity capital.

In the United States, mezzanine finance is often referred to as **junk bonds**.

Finance terminology explained

Convertible bond

A convertible bond is a type of bond which provides the holder with the option to convert into a certain number of ordinary shares at a future date, or, alternatively, to have the bond redeemed for a cash lump sum. Interest is paid on the bond each year up to the date of conversion or redemption.

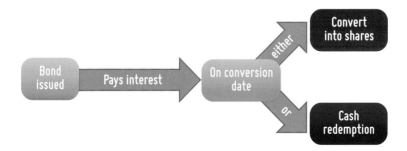

A company might have in issue, for example, 9% convertible bonds, convertible in 5 years' time into 50 ordinary shares. The bonds could, alternatively, be redeemed at nominal value.

This means that an investor would receive $100 x 9%= $9 of interest every year for the next 5 years and could then either take $100 of cash for each $100 nominal value of the bond, or alternatively convert the $100 into 50 ordinary shares. If the shares were worth $2.20 each in 5 years' time the shares will be worth 50 x $2.20 = $110 per $100 nominal value and therefore the investor is likely to convert the bond into ordinary shares.

Key points to note about convertible bonds

- Because the investor has the option to convert the bond into a certain number of ordinary shares, the investor will benefit from any share price growth in exactly the same way as an ordinary shareholder will benefit.

- As a result the interest payable on the bond will be lower than the interest payable on normal bonds redeemable at the same time.

- The company will therefore benefit in the short term from paying less interest each year than if a similar amount of new finance had been raised by issuing normal convertible bonds.

- When conversion takes place, the company will have a big cashflow & financing benefit compared to straight bonds i.e. the company will not need to find the finance to redeem the bonds.

- When conversion takes place, however, there will be dilution of control.

Straight bond with warrants attached

This is a straight bond, as described above, but in this case, when an investor purchases the straight bond they are also 'given' warrants to buy shares in the company which normally mature on the redemption date of the straight bond.

Finance terminology explained

What is a warrant?

A warrant is an option to buy shares in the company, issued by the company itself. If the warrant is exercised by the holder the company issues new share capital for cash.

A warrant should not be confused with a traded option. A traded option is an option created on shares that are already in existence. If the holder of a traded option exercises the option no new capital is created.

Implications of issuing straight bonds with warrants attached

When a company issues a straight bond with warrants attached, it is expected that the warrants will be worth exercising on the exercise date. The implication is that an investor will use the proceeds on redemption to buy shares in the company.

Therefore on the date that the debt is redeemed:

Bond is redeemed → **Investor receives cash** → **Investor immediately uses cash to exercise warrants and buy new shares**

Need to know!

Financing through issuing straight bonds with warrants attached is, in essence, the same as financing through issuing convertible bonds.

In both cases the company expects to avoid having to find new long term finance to redeem the capital. The debt is, in both cases, 'converted' into equity capital.

Leasing

Long term leasing of assets is a very useful form of financing for certain types of assets. Property, for example, is often leased on a long term basis, avoiding the need for a significant capital outlay when the asset is 'acquired'.

Comparison of leasing with borrowing to buy an asset was covered in chapter 6.

OTHER SOURCES OF FINANCE

There are a number of other sources of long term finance that a well-prepared student should be prepared to discuss.

Small company financing

Financing possibilities for smaller unquoted companies are significantly more limited than those available to large quoted companies. The key issue for smaller, unquoted companies is the difficulty that investors face in seeking to realise their investments. The lack of a secondary market for trading equity or debt makes it much more difficult for smaller, unquoted companies to attract new investors.

What are the main financing possibilities for small companies?

1   Bank term loan/overdraft

Bank lending is a prime source of financing for small companies. This may take the form of a term loan, or, often small companies use overdraft facilities as medium to long term financing.

2 Retained earnings

Many small businesses rely significantly on using retained earnings for financing rather than paying a dividend.

3 Business angels and venture capital funding

Smaller private companies with ambitious growth plans can raise new finance from business angels or venture capital funding. How does this work?

Finance terminology explained

Venture capital funding

Venture capital organisations specialise is providing capital to high potential growth, but riskier, private companies e.g. high technology, or research and development companies. In order to obtain a high return they will normally demand a significant equity stake in return for finance.

As the type of company raising venture capital finance is unlikely to be able to pay a dividend in the short term, the venture capital organisation will look for an exit route from their investment in the medium term e.g. through flotation of a company on a stock market, or through the sale of a company to a larger quoted company.

Finance terminology explained

Business angels

The term business angel refers to a wealthy individual, or group of individuals, who are willing to invest in smaller businesses. Like venture capital organisations they would normally take a significant equity stake. Business angels tend, however, to be prepared to invest at an earlier stage than venture capital organisations, and are often prepared to invest for a longer period of time.

Syndicated loan and securitisation

There are two more finance terms that it is important to be ware of and understand. They are a syndicated loan and securitisation.

Finance terminology explained

Syndicated loan

Sometimes the amount of bank term loan finance required by a company is so significant that no one individual bank would be prepared to provide the full amount of the finance, or bear the full amount of the risk that is involved.

A syndicated loan is where a group or syndicate of banks agree to provide the full amount of finance between them. One bank acts as a lead bank in the syndicate, and arranges to raise the required amount of finance from a number of banks. The pooled funds are then lent to the company. In this way the exposure, and hence risk to the bank, is diversified.

Finance terminology explained

Securitisation

This is a way in which a financial institution can use its assets to raise new finance. How does it work?

1   Suppose a bank provides a range of mortgages to customers. The mortgages would be secured assets as far as the bank is concerned i.e. the mortgages will generate income each year in the form of interest receivable, and when the mortgage is repaid the asset is converted into cash. If the customer defaults the bank could dispose of the property providing the security.

2   A range of mortgages could be turned into a financial instrument – this is the process of securitisation. That instrument could be sold (normally to other financial institutions) to provide cash to finance future expansion.

3   The buyer of the financial instrument would effectively be buying the future mortgage receipts i.e. the interest receipts and the lump sum on repayment of the mortgage.

4   One of the significant problems faced by investors in securitised financial instruments is in understanding the level of risk involved. During 2008 and 2009, many banks who had purchased securitised mortgages found that the quality of mortgages used as security was significantly less (and hence the risk of the mortgages holders defaulting on the loan was significantly higher) than they had been led to believe when purchasing the financial instrument.

The securitisation process

Chapter 8
key points summary

- Equity finance – finance provided by the ordinary shareholders – three types:

    - using retained earnings (or profits generated)

    - rights issue of shares

    - new issue of shares to new investors – results in dilution of control.

- Rights issue – significance of TERP – if actual share price after the rights issue is equal to the TERP – an investor taking up the rights or selling the rights is in a no gain/no loss position.

- Preference share finance – investor receives a fixed return each year in the form of a dividend.

- Debt finance – investor receives a fixed return each year in the form of an interest payment (in most cases but there are exceptions e.g. zero coupon bond).

    - Interest payments must be made by company before dividends to preference or ordinary shareholders.

    - Interest payments are tax allowable to a company.

    - Many different types of debt finance.

- Convertible bonds and straight bond with warrants

    - both allow investor to receive a fixed amount of interest each year

    - both allow the investor to benefit from share price growth.

THE COST OF CAPITAL

Introduction
what is this chapter about?

When investors provide finance to a company they will want a return on their investment. This return will need to compensate them for the risk that they perceive in their investment and the company must provide this return in order to keep their investors satisfied. It is effectively a 'charge' by investors for the use of their funds and therefore represents a cost to the company (which is commonly known as the cost of capital).

Many important finance decisions are based on estimating accurately this cost of capital. In this chapter we explore how a company's finance director can estimate the cost of each of the various sources of capital and how this can be combined to form a weighted average cost of capital for the company.

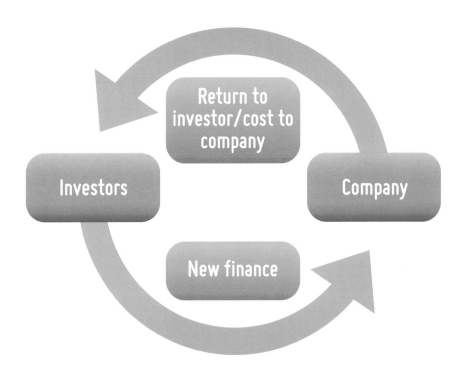

Key areas of the chapter are ....

1 **Cost of equity capital** – when equity finance is raised what returns do shareholders want and what, therefore, is the cost to the company of raising this type of capital?

2 **Cost of debt capital** – what return do investors who provide debt capital require and why is there a difference between the cost of debt to the company and the return that the providers of debt capital require?

3 **Cost of convertible debt** – estimating the cost of convertible debt presents some extra challenges!

4 **Weighted average cost of capital** – what is the overall cost of capital to a company if it is financed by a mixture of equity and debt?

COST OF EQUITY CAPITAL

As we've seen in chapter 8 equity capital refers to the ordinary share capital of a company. Equity providers (shareholders) receive their return in the form of dividends and appreciation in the market value of their shares. The level of return that they require will depend upon how risky they perceive their investment to be. The greater the risk the higher the return will need to be.

What is the link between the return that an investor in equity requires and the cost to the company?

Students of finance often become confused between the return that investors require and the cost to the company.

The good news is that for equity capital they are one and the same thing.

Need to know!

Return required by an equity investor = Cost of equity to the company

Suppose, for example, that a shareholder requires a return of 18% from an investment of $1m in the shares of a company. It follows that the company in question will need to provide a long term return of 18% to satisfy the investor. If the return is less than this then the investor will not be happy and may sell their shares which might cause the share price to fall. The 18% return that the investor requires is therefore also the cost of equity capital to the company. They are really just two ways of looking at the same thing.

How do we determine the return that an investor in equity, or ordinary shareholder, requires?

There are two key approaches that are used in finance:

1 **The dividend valuation model**. This approach is based on a knowledge of the share price and the way in which shares are valued. From knowing the value of a share we can work out the return that shareholders require.

2 **The capital asset pricing model**. This alternative approach is based on an assessment of risk. A fundamental principle of finance is that the return and risk are interrelated. Where there is greater risk attached to an investment, investors will demand higher returns.

If we could therefore measure how much risk is attached to an investment in equity then we should be able to measure the return that investors will then be looking for.

This approach is covered in a later chapter.

The Dividend Valuation Model (DVM) – introduction

This is a theoretical model that allows us to predict the value of a share.

Need to know!

The DVM is based on the idea that the price of a share is equal to the present value of future dividends discounted at the shareholders required rate of return.

In other words – if you buy a share in a company and don't ever plan to sell that share – the only return that you would get from it is the future dividend income that will be paid out by the company.

The time value of money (that we saw in an earlier chapter on investment appraisal) is important here i.e. a dividend of 10c, for example, received by an investor today, would be worth more than the same dividend received in a year's time, because the earlier that it is received the earlier it can be reinvested.

How do we use this model?

We could use this model to estimate:

(a) **the value of a share**. If we know the return that a shareholder requires we could estimate a 'correct' value for a share. In chapter 24 we will see in more detail how the model is used to value a share.

or

(b) **the cost of equity**. If we assume that a share is correctly valued by the stock market we can work backwards and use the model to determine the return that shareholders seem to require and hence the cost of equity.

DVM assuming a constant dividend

Let's assume that a company pays a constant dividend (D) starting in one years' time and continuing up to some infinite date in the future.

An investor buying a share will then receive a constant annual cashflow from time 1 to infinity. This is an example of a perpetuity that we saw earlier in the section on investment appraisal. We can therefore apply the formula for a perpetuity that we saw earlier to this situation and if we also assume that:

Po = the share price now or at time 0
ke = the cost of equity (or shareholders required rate of return)

then:

 Need to know!

$$Po = \frac{D}{ke}$$

Or

$$ke = \frac{D}{Po}$$

Example 1

A company pays a constant dividend of 20c per share. The shareholders required rate of return is 12%. What is the share price?

Solution 1

In this case we are using the DVM to estimate the value of a share. Remember that the shareholders required rate of return is the same as the cost of equity (ke). This needs to go into the formula as a decimal.

$$Po = \frac{D}{Ke}$$

$$Po = \frac{20c}{0.12} = 166.67c$$

Example 2

A company pays a constant dividend of 30c per share. The company's shares are quoted on the stock market and the current share price is 150c per share. What is the cost of equity?

Solution 2

In this case we use the DVM formula to work out the cost of equity rather than the share price.

$$ke = \frac{D}{Po}$$

$$ke = \frac{30c}{150c} = 0.20 \text{ or } 20\%$$

Dividend Valuation Model assuming constant growth in dividends

The basic dividend valuation model assumes a constant dividend. This is not particularly realistic as most companies, and shareholders in those companies, expect dividends to grow in the future.

A variation of the model that all students need to be aware of is where we assume that instead of a constant dividend being paid each year, dividends will **grow at a constant rate each year** from time 1 to infinity.

We can again use a model, either to value a share if we know the shareholders required rate of return, or to estimate the cost of equity (shareholders required rate of return) if we know the share price.

If we assume that:

Po = the share price now or at time 0
ke = the cost of equity (or shareholders required rate of return)
Do = dividend payable now or at time 0
g = constant annual growth rate in dividends expressed as a decimal

then, using a bit of algebra, we end up with this formula:

Need to know!

$$Po = \frac{Do(1 + g)}{ke - g}$$

or

$$ke = \frac{Do(1 + g)}{Po} + g$$

Example 3

The latest dividend paid by James is 15c per share. Dividends are expected to grow in the future at 5% per annum. It is known that shareholders require a return of 18% per annum. What is the value of the shares?

Solution 3

In this case we are using the model to value the shares of a company and therefore need to use the first version of the formula.

$$Po = \frac{Do(1 + g)}{ke - g}$$

$$Po = \frac{15c(1 + 0.05)}{0.18 - 0.05} = 121.15c$$

Example 4

Sam is a quoted company with a current share price of $2.00. Sam has just paid a dividend of 20c to its shareholders who expect dividends, in the future, to grow at 3% per annum on average. What is the cost of equity of Sam?

Solution 4

In this example we are using the model to work out the cost of equity. Be careful – for the formula to work both the share price and dividend need to be expressed in dollars, or they both need to be expressed in cents.

$$ke = \frac{Do(1+g)}{Po} + g$$

$$ke = \frac{20c(1 + 0.03)}{200c} + 0.03 = 0.1330 \text{ or } 13.30\%$$

Ex-div and cum-div

The DVM assumes that if you buy a share at the quoted price, the first dividend receivable would be in 1 year's time. A share price quoted on this basis is termed an ex-div share price.

If the first dividend is receivable immediately then the share price is termed cum-div. In this case the share price would need to be adjusted to convert it to an ex-div basis as follows:

Share price cum-div – latest dividend = Share price ex-div.

Example 5

Spike has in issue 5 million shares quoted at $2.40. A dividend of 20c is due immediately. A growth rate of 4% per annum in future dividends is expected.

What is the cost of equity?

The first step in this case is to work out the ex-div share price. This is the Po value that should go into the DVM formula.

Po = 240c − 20c = 220c

We can then work out the cost of equity as before:

$$ke = \frac{20c(1 + 0.04)}{220c} + 0.04 = 0.1345 \text{ or } 13.45\%$$

How do we estimate future growth?

In order to be able to use the DVM with growth we need some way of estimating future growth in dividends.

There are two acceptable approaches:

1 past average dividend growth

2 Gordon's growth model (earnings retention model).

Past average dividend growth

Using this method we assume that the average growth in past dividends is a good indicator, or predictor of the likely future growth in dividends. The approach is therefore to calculate the average compound growth in dividends in the past, over a reasonable number of years, and assume that dividends will continue to grow in the future at this rate.

Example 6

Greg has paid the following dividends over the last 4 years:

Y/e 31/12/20X1	30c
Y/e 31/12/20X2	34c
Y/e 31/12/20X3	37c
Y/e 31/12/20X4	39c

What is the average rate of growth in dividends achieved in the past?

Solution 6

In order to establish g, we need to take the dividend for two separate years, which will usually be the most recent dividend and the oldest dividend. The number of periods of growth then needs to be established. You need to be careful when assessing this though, as although there are 4 dividends in the example, there are only 3 periods of growth.

If we express the compound growth as g we can say that:

Div 20X1 $(1+g)^3$ = Div 20X4

$30c (1+g)^3 = 39c$

$$(1+g)^3 = \frac{39c}{30c}$$

$$(1+g) = \sqrt[3]{\frac{39c}{30c}}$$

$1 + g = 1.0914$

$g = 0.0914$ or 9.14%

Gordon's growth model

This is an alternative way of estimating future growth. It is based on the assumption that if a company retains earnings, these can then be reinvested each year to generate future growth in earnings and hence dividends.

Growth is therefore based on the following formula:

Need to know!

$g = rb$

Where:

r = the return that the company can obtain when earnings are reinvested and

b = the proportion of earnings retained

The accounting rate of return is sometimes used in questions as an approximation of the return on reinvested funds. If this is not given, or if there is no reasonable way of calculating this, any reasonable assumption would be acceptable.

Example 7

Jack has 10 million ordinary shares in issue, and a market value per share of $1.50 ex dividend on 31 December 20X1.

The latest dividend is 30c. Dividends are, on average, around 20% of the company's earnings. Jack can consistently generate an accounting rate of return on reinvested earnings of 12%.

What is Jack's cost of equity?

The first thing that we need to do is estimate future dividend growth using Gordon's growth model

r = 12% or 0.12
b = 80% or 0.80

Note - as the dividend represents 20% of the company's earnings the proportion retained must be 80%.

g = rb
g = 0.12 x 0.80
g = 0.096 or 9.6%

We can then use the DVM to determine the cost of equity

$$ke = \frac{Do(1 + g)}{Po} + g$$

$$ke = \frac{30c(1 + 0.096)}{150c} + 0.096$$

ke = 0.3152 or 31.52%

COST OF DEBT

In the next section we will consider how a financial manager determines the cost of debt capital.

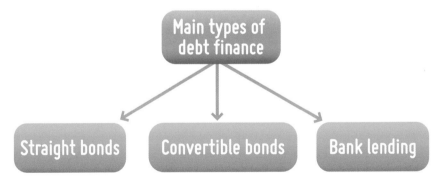

There are three main types of debt finance as shown above. Students need to be able to estimate the cost to the company of each type of debt finance. We will consider each in turn.

In chapter 8 we covered some terminology relating to bonds. Remember that the terms bond, loan stock, marketable debt, debentures all essentially mean the same thing. An examiner could use any of these terms in an exam question.

Straight bonds

A straight bond is essentially a block of debt that is issued by a company. The purchaser of the bond will receive a fixed amount of interest each year. An investor who buys the bond can subsequently sell the bond on a stock market in exactly the same way as shares are sold on the stock market.

This ability to subsequently sell the bond makes this debt a very attractive investment to investors and, as a result, a significant amount of debt finance raised by large companies is of this type.

Before consider the cost of a straight bond in more detail – time for some terminology.

Finance terminology explained

Coupon rate

The interest paid on the debt is always stated as a percentage of nominal value and is fixed for the life of the debt. This is known as the coupon rate. If, for example a bond had a coupon rate of 9% - this would mean that someone owning an amount of debt with a nominal value of $100 would receive interest of $100 x 9% = $9 of interest every year.

Exam tip – Coupon rate and the true return on debt

Don't confuse the coupon rate on debt with the true return on the debt. The coupon rate is the nominal return i.e. the return that an investor would receive on a nominal amount of the debt.

The true return on the debt is based on the cash amount paid to buy a nominal amount of debt and the cash return. We will consider this in more detail below.

How is the price of a straight bond quoted?

The **price of a bond** is always quoted **per $100** nominal value. If, for example, a price of $95 is quoted – this would be the market value of a block of debt that has a nominal value of $100. All calculations relating to bonds are therefore based on a block of debt which has a nominal value of $100.

> Bond
> nominal
> value $100
>
> Coupon rate
> 9%

The market value of this block of debt with a nominal value of $100 could be any amount e.g. $95

What are the different types of straight bond?

There are two main types of straight bond.

1 **Irredeemable** – when this debt is issued it will never be redeemed. An investor who purchases this debt would continue to receive interest on the debt to infinity, or until the debt is sold to another investor.

2 **Redeemable** – this debt would be redeemed by the issuer at some future date. An investor who purchases this debt would receive interest on the debt for a certain number of years and then the debt would be redeemed for a certain amount of cash.

Irredeemable fixed rate bonds – the investors required return

If we assume that an investor who purchases this debt intends to keep the debt for an infinite period of time then the only return that the investor would receive would be a fixed amount of interest from time 1 to infinity.

Need to know!

The market value of the debt is assumed to be equal to the present value of the future interest payments discounted at the debt providers required rate of return. (NOTE – this is the same valuation principle used in the DVM).

In other words, we assume that an investor would be prepared to pay an amount for the debt which equals the present value of the future cashflows that the investor would receive.

If the investor receives a fixed amount of interest from time 1 to infinity then this is another example of a perpetuity. We can therefore apply the perpetuity formula to find the market value of the bond.

If we assume that:

Po = the market value of the bond today
I = annual interest payable
r = investors required rate of return

then applying the formula for the perpetuity

$$Po = \frac{I}{r} \quad Or \quad r = \frac{I}{Po}$$

Example 8

Lewis has in issue a 10% irredeemable bond quoted at $95 ex-interest. What is the return required by the debt providers?

Solution 8

The market value of the bond quoted is per $100 nominal value.

The annual interest payable per $100 nominal value is therefore $100 x 10% = $10

$$r = \frac{I}{Po} \quad \text{therefore} \quad r = \frac{\$10}{\$95}$$

= 0.1053 or 10.53%

Required return, yield and pre-tax cost of debt

Need to know!

The terms:

- investors required rate of return on debt.
- yield on debt.
- pre-tax cost of debt.

all mean the same thing. This considers the return from an investors' point of view. The term yield is often used instead of return when considering debt finance.

We saw with equity that the investors required rate of return was the same as the company's cost of equity. With debt this is not, unfortunately, the case as we need to take into account the impact of corporate taxes.

The term pre-tax cost of debt means the same thing as the investors required rate of return on debt, or yield on debt. This is not, however, the same as the post-tax cost of debt to the company.

Post-tax cost of debt

What is the post-tax cost of debt to a company and how is it different to the pre-tax cost of debt (or yield)?

A company pays dividends to shareholders and interest to the providers of debt. A crucial difference between the two types of payment is that dividends are distributed from post-tax profits whereas interest payments are distributed from pre-tax profits i.e. interest payments are tax allowable. Whenever a company makes an interest payment it will save tax that it would otherwise pay if the company were, alternatively, all-equity financed.

To estimate the true cost to the company of debt finance an adjustment should be made to take the tax relief on interest payments into account.

If a company makes an interest payment of $10, for example, and the corporate tax rate is 30%, then $10 x 0.30 = $3 of tax, which would otherwise be payable, would be saved. The post – tax interest payment is therefore $7 ($10 - $3) = $7.

Irredeemable fixed rate bonds — the post-tax cost

If we assume that:

Po	=	the market value of the bond today
I	=	annual interest payable
kd_{AT}	=	the post-tax cost of debt
t	=	corporate tax rate

then we have a revised version of the formula used to determine the post-tax cost of debt which is:

$$kd_{AT} = \frac{I(1 - t)}{Po}$$

Example 9

Lewis has in issue a 10% irredeemable bond quoted at $95 ex-interest. The rate of corporate tax is 30%. What is the post-tax cost to the company?

 Solution 9

This is the same example as example 8. The only difference is that is this case we are given the corporate tax rate and need to determine the post-tax cost to the company.

Po = $95
I = $10
t = 30% or 0.30

P_0

The annual interest payable per $100 nominal value is therefore $100 x 10% = $10

$$kd_{AT} = \frac{I(1 - t)}{Po} \quad \text{Therefore} \quad kd_{AT} = \frac{\$10(1-0.3)}{\$95}$$

= 0.0737 or 7.37%

If Lewis sought to raise new debt finance it would therefore need to offer a return to the investors 10.53% (which is the pre-tax cost to the company). The equivalent post-tax cost to the company, however, is only 7.37%.

Exam tip – Pre-tax or post-tax cost of debt?

Students often confuse the pre-tax cost and post-tax cost in exam questions. If asked to calculate an overall cost of capital (WACC) then an examiner would want you to calculate the **post-tax** cost of capital. This is the important figure to use when a WACC is being calculated.

If asked for the yield, or the return that an investor would require, then it would be the **pre-tax** cost that would need to be calculated.

Redeemable fixed rate bonds – the investors required return

As with irredeemable bonds, in order to estimate the investors required return (which is the same as the pre-tax cost of debt) we again need to assume that the market value of the bond is equal to the present value of future cashflows associated with that bond discounted at the debt provider's required rate of return.

In this case, however, the cashflows that the investor will receive will be interest payments up to the redemption date and then the redemption value on redemption.

In the case of irredeemable bonds we were able to use a formula to find the investors required return (pre-tax cost of debt). This was because the interest payments to the investor, conveniently, were a perpetuity. Unfortunately, in the case of redeemable debt, we need to go back to first principles of discounting.

The investors required return (pre-tax cost of redeemable debt) is the **Internal Rate of Return (IRR)** of the cashflows. In other words an investor who buys some debt today (cash outflow) will then receive interest for a certain number of years (cash inflows) and then a lump sum on redemption (cash inflow) at a certain date in the future. The 'return' that the investor receives will be the IRR of the cashflows, or the rate at which the present value of these cashflows will equal zero.

To calculate the IRR we use trial and error and then linear interpolation. In other words, we calculate two NPV's at two different discount rates and then use the linear interpolation formula.

The formula for determining the IRR is:

$$IRR = L + \frac{N_L}{N_L - N_H} (H - L)$$

Where:

L = lower discount rate
H = higher discount rate
N_L = NPV at the lower discount rate
N_H = NPV at the higher discount rate

Example 10

Oliver has in issue 12% redeemable bonds which have a further 5 years to go before they are redeemed. Redemption is at par value or nominal value. The bonds are currently trading at $92 ex-interest.

What is the current investors required rate of return (**pre-tax cost**) on the bonds?

Solution 10

Po (current market value)	=	$92 per $100 nominal value
I (annual interest)	=	12% x $100 = $12
RV (Redemption Value)	=	$100

To calculate the current cost of the debt we therefore discount at two different discount rates e.g. 5% and 15%

Time	Cashflow ($)	DF @ 5%	NPV ($) @ 5%	DF @ 15%	NPV ($) @ 15%
T0	(92)	1.000	(92)	1.000	(92)
T1 – T5	12	4.329	51.95	3.352	40.22
T5	100	0.784	78.40	0.497	49.70
			38.35		**(2.08)**

To calculate the IRR:

$$IRR = 5\% + \frac{38.35}{38.35 + 2.08} (15\% - 5\%)$$

IRR = 14.49%

The investors required return (pre-tax cost of debt) is therefore 14.49%. As with irredeemable debt this is the same as the yield. In the case of the yield on redeemable debt this is called the **yield to redemption**, or sometimes, **the gross yield to redemption**.

Redeemable fixed rate bonds – the post- tax cost

This is calculated in exactly the same way as the investors required return (pre-tax cost) on redeemable debt. The post-tax cost is the internal rate of return of the cashflows. In this case, however, we assume that the interest payments on the debt are tax allowable.

Example 11

Oliver has in issue 12% redeemable bonds which have a further 5 years to go before they are redeemed. Redemption is at par value or nominal value. The bonds are currently trading at $92 ex-interest. The rate of corporation tax is 30%.

What is the current **post-tax cost** of the bonds?

This is exactly the same scenario as example 10. All the information is the same apart from the fact that we are given the corporation tax rate and we need to estimate the post-tax cost of the bond instead of the pre-tax cost.

Po (current market value)	=	$92 per $100 nominal value
I (annual interest)	=	12% x $100 = $12
RV (Redemption Value)	=	$100
Corporate tax rate	=	0.30

To calculate the cost of debt we need to discount at two different discount rates e.g. 5% and 15%

Time	Cashflow ($)	DF @ 5%	NPV ($) @ 5%	DF @ 15%	NPV ($) @ 15%
T0	(92)	1.000	(92)	1.000	(92)
T1 – T5	12 (1-0.3)	4.329	36.36	3.352	28.16
T5	100	0.784	78.40	0.497	49.70
			22.76		**(14.14)**

To calculate the IRR:

$$IRR = 5\% + \frac{22.76}{22.76 + 14.14} (15\% - 5\%)$$

$IRR = 11.17\%$ therefore $kd_{AT} = 11.17\%$

The post-tax cost of debt is therefore 11.17%.

Note – tax relief is only available on the interest payments made by the company and not on the redemption value at the end.

Convertible bonds

These are bonds which offer the holder the right to convert the bonds into ordinary shares at some future date. The holder of the convertible bond can alternatively redeem the bond for cash rather than convert into shares.

How do we estimate the cost to the company of a convertible bond?

This is done in two stages.

(a) Firstly we estimate the likely market value of the company's ordinary shares on the date of conversion in the future. From this information we then predict whether the investor will convert into shares or, alternatively, take the cash on redemption. Investors will want to exercise the right to convert into shares if the value of the shares on conversion is greater than the redemption value.

(b) Using the result from a) we calculate the cost of the convertible bond in exactly the same way as we calculate the cost of a redeemable bond i.e. by determining the internal rate of return.

Example 12

Lois has in issue 9% convertible bonds. On 1/1/20X1 the bonds are trading at $96. Conversion into ordinary shares can take place in seven years' time at a rate of 40 shares per $100 debt. The alternative is that the bond can be redeemed at par value. The current share price of Lois is $2.00 per share. It is estimated that the share price will grow at 4% per annum for the foreseeable future. Corporate tax is at a rate of 30%.

What is the post-tax cost of the convertible bond?

Solution 12

Part (a)

The first step is to determine whether or not the investor is likely to convert into shares in the future or, alternatively, take the cash on redemption.

If shares are expected to grow at 4% per annum the estimated share price in 7 years' time will be:

$2.00 \times (1+0.04)^7 = $2.63 per share

An investor who owns $100 nominal value of debt will receive 40 shares on conversion. Per $100 nominal value of debt the value of the shares will therefore be:

40 shares x $2.63 = $105.20

In 7 years' time, given that this value is greater than the value of cash on redemption ($100) the investor is likely to exercise the option to convert into shares.

Part (b)

We now calculate the IRR of the following cashflows:

Po (current market value)   = $96 per $100 nominal value
I (annual interest)   =   9% x $100 = $9
CV (Conversion Value)   = $105.20
Corporate tax rate   =   0.30

To calculate the cost of debt we need to discount at two different discount rates e.g. 5% and 15%

This is the higher of the estimated conversion value and the redemption value from part (a)

Time	Cashflow ($)	DF @ 5%	NPV ($) @ 5%	DF @ 15%	NPV ($) @ 15%
T0	(96)	1.000	(92)	1.000	(92)
T1 – T5	9(1-0.3)	4.329	27.27	3.352	21.12
T5	105.20	0.784	82.48	0.497	52.28
			17.75		**(18.60)**

To calculate the IRR:

$$IRR = 5\% + \frac{17.75}{17.75 + 18.60} (15\% - 5\%)$$

IRR = 9.88%   therefore kd_{AT} = 9.88%

In this example we have been asked to calculate the post-tax cost of debt. We therefore adjusted each interest payment to take into account the tax saving that would arise.

Pre-tax and post-tax cost of convertible bonds

To calculate the pre-tax cost of debt, or the yield, we approach in exactly the same way as we have done in example 12. The only difference would be that we would not adjust the interest payment for the tax saving.

Finance terminology explained

Conversion premium

This is the difference between the market value of the bond on a given date, and the market value of the shares if conversion were to take place on the same date.

Example 13

Let's look again at the example Lois in example 12. What is the conversion premium on 1/1/20X1?

 ## Solution 13

On 1/1/20X1:

The market value of the bond is $96 per $100 nominal value

Each share is worth $2.00, therefore 40 shares would be worth: 40 x $2.00 = $80

The conversion premium would be: $96 - $80 = $16

or as a percentage of the current market value of the bond = $16/$96 = 0.1667 i.e. 16.67%

The bond is currently therefore worth 16.67% more as debt that it would be worth if it was converted into shares on 1/1/20X1.

The cost of bank lending

Bank lending is normally at a variable or floating rate of interest. The cost of bank lending is therefore very straightforward to determine compared to the cost of straight bonds or convertible bonds.

Pre-tax cost of bank lending

This will simply be the current coupon rate on the bank loan.

Post-tax cost of bank lending

This will be the coupon rate adjusted for the corporation tax saving i.e.
kd_{AT} = coupon rate (1-t)

Example 14

Becca has raised a significant amount of debt finance via bank borrowing at a floating rate of interest. The current rate charged by the bank is 8%. Corporate tax is 30%. What is the current post-tax cost of Becca's debt?

 ## Solution 14

kd_{AT} = coupon rate (1-t)

kd_{AT} = 8% (1-0.30)

kd_{AT} = 5.6%

WEIGHTED AVERAGE COST OF CAPITAL (WACC)

The WACC is the overall cost of a company's capital. To determine the WACC we weight the costs of each individual type of finance according to proportions. The proportions should be based on market values.

Approach to calculating a company's WACC

The way we would calculate the company's WACC is as follows:

1   calculate the cost of each individual type of finance. This could comprise equity, preference share capital and a number of different types of debt capital

2   calculate the total market value of each type of finance

3   weight the costs according to proportions in market value terms.

Example 15

Ian has the following capital in issue:

10m shares, each currently trading at $1.50 ex div. The cost of equity has already been calculated using the DVM and is estimated to be 15%.

$5m nominal value of redeemable bonds, currently trading at $90 per $100 nominal value. The post-tax cost of the bonds has been estimated at 9%.

$4m of bank lending. The post-tax cost of the bank loan is 8%.

Determine the WACC of the company.

Solution 15

In this example the costs of each individual type of finance has already been estimated. We can therefore move on to the next step which is to determine the market value of each type of finance:

Type of finance			Market value ($)
Equity	10m shares x $1.50	=	15,000k
Bonds	$5m x 90/100	=	4,500k
Bank lending			4,000k
Total market value			23,500k

We can then work out the WACC by weighting the individual costs according to proportions.

The WACC is therefore

$$= \left(15\% \times \frac{15,000K}{23,500K}\right) + \left(9\% \times \frac{4,500K}{23,500K}\right) + \left(8\% \times \frac{4,000K}{23,500K}\right) = 12.66\%$$

$$= 12.66\%$$

Use of the WACC

The WACC can be used to help make a number of financial decisions, some of which we will see in later chapters. Perhaps the most significant use in finance is as a discount rate for appraising new projects, or investments, using discounted cashflow techniques.

In example 15 above – if we are confident that the current WACC of Ian is 12.66% and Ian is considering a major new investment, we could calculate the investment's NPV using 12.66% as the discount rate. A positive NPV at this rate tells us that the investment will generate a greater level of future cash inflows than are needed to pay interest and dividends to the providers of the company's capital at the levels demanded by investors.

Undertaking such an investment should, therefore, improve shareholder wealth.

What assumptions are being made when we use the WACC as a discount rate for appraising new projects/investments?

 Need to know!

In using the WACC as a discount rate to appraise long term investments we make the following key assumptions:

	Assumption	Meaning
1	That the long term gearing or capital structure of the company will not change.	The WACC is based on the current weighted average of the different types of finance. Any change in the proportions of each type of finance could alter the WACC.
2	That the new project/investment has the same level of risk as the existing projects/investments of the company.	The cost of equity, used as part of the WACC calculation, reflects shareholders perceptions of the risk of the existing business activities of the company. If we apply this to new projects/investments then we must be assuming that the new projects/investments have the same level of risk as existing projects/investments.

Chapter 9
key points summary

- Cost of equity = shareholders required rate of return

  - DVM used to estimate cost of equity.

    - Assuming constant dividend. $ke = \dfrac{D}{Po}$

    - Assuming constant growth in dividends $ke = \dfrac{Do(1 + g)}{Po} + g$

  - Growth estimated by:

    - using past average growth

    - Gordon's growth model $g = rb$

- Cost of debt

  - Return to investor = yield = pre-tax cost of debt.

  - Post-tax cost of debt (after adjusting for corporate tax saving): $kd_{AT} = \dfrac{I(1 - t)}{Po}$

    - irredeemable debt

    - redeemable debt – IRR of post-tax cashflows.

- WACC – overall cost of capital – costs weighted according to proportions in market value terms.

Introduction
what is this chapter about?

In chapter 8 we considered how a company could raise long term finance and analysed some of the key differences between raising debt or, alternatively, equity finance. In chapter 9 we looked at ways in which we could determine the cost of each type of finance (or capital) and the overall cost of capital for a company that is financed by a mixture of different types of capital.

This chapter builds on the previous two chapters (and so if you didn't enjoy the previous two chapters you are probably not going to enjoy this one!) by considering whether a change in the way in which a company is financed would alter the company's overall cost of capital. This is an important question for a finance manager to consider – if the overall cost of a company's capital changes it may have implications for shareholder wealth.

Key areas of the chapter are ....

1. **Traditional theory of gearing** – How traditionally or historically has a change in the gearing of a company been felt to influence the cost of capital and shareholder wealth?

2. **Modigliani and Miller's theory of gearing** – In 1958 Modigliani and Miller published an alternative view of gearing based on perfect market assumptions. How do Modigliani and Miller's conclusions differ from the traditional view?

TRADITIONAL THEORY OF GEARING

Before we consider the traditional theory of gearing in detail we need to clarify some terminology.

Finance terminology explained

What is meant by gearing and how can it be measured?

Gearing is the proportion of debt capital in relation to equity capital in a company's capital structure. The more debt capital that there is – the more highly geared a company is considered to be.

Gearing can be measured from the point of view of the statement of financial position by using either of these two ratios:

$$\frac{\text{Debt}}{\text{Equity}} \quad \text{or} \quad \frac{\text{Debt}}{\text{Debt \& Equity}}$$

Either book values or market values can be used to measure gearing in this way. Using market values generally gives more meaningful information, and **finance theory is always based on market values**.

Gearing can also be measured from the point of view of the income statement by using the interest cover ratio as follows:

$$\frac{\text{Profit before interest and tax}}{\text{Interest payable}}$$

The term **leverage** is sometimes used instead of the term gearing. Increased leverage just means increased gearing.

Finance terminology explained

What is financial risk?

If one company has a higher level of gearing than another – does that matter? The key problem with higher levels of gearing is financial risk and so what does this term mean?

Financial risk is the risk to a shareholder, or a provider of equity capital of a business having debt in its capital structure. A higher level of gearing means a greater level of financial risk to a shareholder.

Why is this the case?

Risk in finance is all about the variability of returns to an investor. When a company raises debt finance, the interest payments to the provider of debt capital must be made on the due date irrespective of how the company is performing. In other words the company has a commitment to pay the interest.

Debt financing increases the volatility in the earnings that a shareholder will receive. The more debt finance that a company raises the greater the volatility of earnings to a shareholder.

The significance of an increase in gearing

If a company increases the proportion of debt in its capital structure there are two key effects of this that you need to be aware of.

1 Benefit = debt is a cheaper form of financing than equity

As interest is a fixed commitment and dividends are not, an investor in debt receives a much more certain, or a much less volatile return than an investor in equity. The return that an investor in debt demands is therefore going to be lower than the return that an investor in equity will demand. The cost to the company of debt finance will therefore be less than the cost of equity finance.

Interest payments made by a company to a provider of debt capital also qualify for tax relief which will reduce the cost of debt further compared to the cost of equity.

More debt **more of the cheaper finance**

2 Drawback = greater levels of debt capital means greater financial risk to a shareholder

The more debt that a company has in issue, the greater the volatility of returns to the shareholders as larger interest payments have to be made by the company. As the proportion of debt in the capital structure increases so does the financial risk faced by shareholders and, as we know, increased risk means that shareholders will require a higher return which in turn leads to a higher cost of equity.

More debt **greater financial risk** **higher cost of equity**

Optimum level of gearing

Before we go further it is important to know how the optimum, or ideal level of gearing would be defined.

The optimum level of gearing is that which would result in the maximisation of shareholder wealth.

This would be the level of gearing which **maximises the value of the company**. If we assume that the value of the company is the present value of future cashflows discounted at the cost of capital (we will see more on this in chapter 25) then the optimum level of gearing is also the level of gearing that **minimises the company's overall cost of capital (WACC)**. The lower the WACC, or the discount rate, the greater the present value of future cashflows.

How does the traditional theory work?

This can be illustrated graphically as follows:

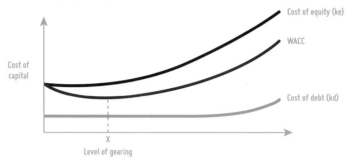

The traditional theory of gearing is based on the interaction of the two effects of an increase in gearing that we saw above.

The key to understanding how this works is to focus on the cost of equity line. It was outlined above that a rise in gearing would increase the level of financial risk and therefore increase the cost of equity. That is true but the way in which the cost of equity rises is also important. The rise isn't linear – it is exponential. This means that at low levels of gearing the rise in the cost of equity as gearing rises is quite small, but, as the level of gearing increases so the rise in the cost of equity gets bigger and bigger.

How does this affect the WACC? Well, initially, at lower levels of gearing, it is felt that if more debt is raised by a company, the benefit of the cheaper finance significantly outweighs the drawback of a (small) rise in financial risk and the cost of equity. The result is that the WACC will fall initially as debt is introduced into a company's capital structure.

Beyond a certain level of gearing, however, it is felt that as more debt finance is raised the (bigger) rise in financial risk, and the cost of equity, will outweigh the benefit the cheaper finance. As a result the WACC would start to rise.

You may also have noticed from the graph that at high levels of gearing the cost of debt will start to rise. This is because at high levels of gearing the providers of debt capital may start to feel that there is a risk that the company will default on interest payments and therefore they will demand a return to compensate for this. The effect of this would be that the WACC would increase further at higher levels of gearing.

 Need to know!

Traditional theory conclusion

(a) There is an optimum level of gearing where the **WACC is minimised**. This is the point marked X on the diagram.

(b) At this point the **value of the company is maximised**.

(c) Under the traditional theory, whilst the relationship between a change in gearing and the WACC follows this pattern for all companies, we cannot conclude that the optimum level will be at exactly the same point for all companies. The specific point will differ from one company to another and can only be found through trial and error.

(d) A company should seek to raise finance so as to find and then maintain this level of gearing.

MODIGLIANI AND MILLER'S THEORY.

In 1958 two American academics Franco Modigliani and Merton Miller (who both became Nobel Prizewinners) produced an alternative theory of gearing which was based on certain assumptions about the way in which markets and investors behave. These assumptions are listed and commented upon in a later section of this chapter.

How does their theory work?

Modigliani and Miller (M&M) without tax – 1958 model

M&M produced their first model in 1958. This can be illustrated graphically as follows:

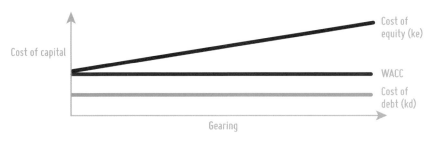

M&M proved their theories of gearing using a process known as arbitrage and assuming, amongst other things that the stock market was perfectly efficient. Arbitrage is the process of buying and selling shares in order to make a riskless gain. The mathematical proof of this theory is outside the scope of this book and is rarely examined.

This first model ignored completely the impact of both corporate and personal taxation.

M&M drew three conclusions, or made three propositions which are as follows.

1 **Proposition 1** – The **total market value** of the debt and equity in a geared company would always be **equal** to the market value of the equity of an equivalent but ungeared company. Gearing therefore has no effect on the value of a company.

2 **Proposition 2** – The cost of equity rises so as to exactly compensate for, or cancel out the benefit of the lower cost debt capital. The result of this is that the **WACC** of a geared company would always **equal** the WACC of an equivalent but ungeared company. When debt is raised, the gains from accessing cheaper finance will be perfectly offset by the rise in financial risk and the cost of equity.

3 **Proposition 3** – The conclusion about company financing in proposition 2 can be extended to a project, or an investment that a company is considering. Whether the project is financed by debt or equity is irrelevant. The value of the project would be the same either way.

Need to know!

M&M – no tax – key conclusions

- Total value of a geared company = Total value of an equivalent ungeared company.

- WACC of a geared company = WACC of an equivalent ungeared company.

- Shareholder wealth is therefore unaffected by a company's gearing. To increase shareholder value finance managers need to focus on assets and future earnings. Seeking to increase shareholder value by focussing on capital structure is a waste of time!

M&M and pizza

Merton Miller was once asked to explain his theory in a simple way to someone who had no understanding of economics.

He said, "I have a simple explanation (for the first proposition). It's after the ball game (a baseball game) and the pizza man comes up to Yogi Berra (a famous baseball player) and he says, 'Yogi, how do you want me to cut this pizza, into quarters?' Yogi says, 'No, cut it into eight pieces, I'm feeling hungry tonight."

He also said "Now when I tell that story the usual reaction is, 'And you mean to say that they gave you a (Nobel) prize for that?'"

A fair point perhaps! The analogy is nevertheless a very good way to understand their theory. Just as the size of a pizza doesn't depend on the number of pieces into which it is cut, so the value of a company doesn't depend upon the way in which it is financed. If a company is financed by a mixture of debt and equity the value of the company is split between two groups of investors. If the company is all equity financed the value of the company all goes to one group of investors – the shareholders.

Modigliani and Miller (M&M) – with corporate tax – 1963 model

In 1963 M&M revised their theory to take into account the impact of corporate taxes. Personal tax was still ignored. The 1963 model can be illustrated graphically as follows:

In this case there is an **additional benefit of debt financing** compared to the M&M no tax model. The extra benefit is that interest payments to the providers of debt capital are tax allowable. The **more debt finance** that is raised the **greater the tax relief** on interest payments. This lowers the WACC and the lower the WACC, the greater the total market value of the company and the greater the wealth of shareholders!

Need to know!

M&M – with tax – key conclusions

- The more debt finance the greater the value of the company and the greater the wealth of shareholders (revised proposition 1).

- The more debt finance the lower the WACC (revised proposition 2).

- The ideal level of gearing in theory would therefore be 99.9% debt finance!

Need to know!

M&M Formulae

M&M revised their propositions to reflect the impact of corporate tax. The first two propositions can be expressed as equations that are often used in examinations. They are:

From proposition 1

$$Vg = Vu + Dt$$

Where:

Vg   =   total market value of a geared company (debt & equity)
Vu   =   market value of an equivalent ungeared company
D   =   market value of debt in a geared company
t   =   corporate tax rate

From proposition 2

and

$$WACCg = Keu \times (1 - \frac{Dt}{D + E})$$

Where
WACCg = WACC of the geared company
Keu = cost of equity of an ungeared company (which must, if a company is ungeared be the same as the WACC of an ungeared company)
D = market value of debt in a geared company
E = market value of equity in a geared company
t = corporate tax rate

Finance terminology explained

Tax shield

Dt from the formula in proposition 1 is sometimes called the tax shield. This is because it represents the extra value arising because some of the company's earnings are 'shielded' from tax when they are distributed to the providers of debt capital as interest payments.

Example 1

Durham is an all equity financed company. It has 10 million ordinary shares in issue which are currently trading at $1.00 per share. The cost of equity is 12%.

The corporate tax rate is 30%.

The company's directors are considering raising $3 million of debt capital. They will use the amount raised to buy back some of the company's share capital at the current market price. This means that 3 million shares will be repurchased (at $1.00) per share – or that the company will repurchase, at market value, 3 shares out of every 10 that are currently owned. The new debt capital has a coupon rate of 7%.

Requirements

(a) What will be the impact of the proposal on the total market value of the company, the market value of the equity, and on the wealth of a shareholder who currently owns 10 shares in Durham?

(b) What will be the impact of the new issue on the company's WACC?

Solution 1

Part (a)

This example is purely focussing on how the company is financed. The $3 million of debt finance that is raised will be used to buy back the company's shares at market value. This means that because the $3 million is not invested in a new project, the value of the company's assets, and the PBIT are not expected to change. The company is therefore the same before and after the new debt issue apart from the way in which it is financed.

We can use M&M's formula to find the total market value of the geared company after the new finance has been raised.

The market value of the geared company = Vg

$Vg = Vu + Dt$

Where:

Vu = 10 million shares x $1 = $10m
D   = $3m (if the new finance is raised by issuing debt)
t   = 0.30
Vg = $10 million + $3 million x 0.30
Vg = $10.9 million

Vg is the total market value of the geared company – meaning that it is the market value of both the equity and the debt in the geared company. The value of the debt raised is $3 million and therefore the value of the equity must be:

Value of equity = $10.9 million - $3 million = $7.9 million

Change in shareholder wealth

If the value of the equity in this case is only $7.9 million whereas it was $10million before the new debt finance was raised does this mean that shareholders are worse off in this case?

No!

A shareholder who owned 10 shares in the company before the issue would have a wealth of 10 shares x $1 = $10.

After the issue there will be (10 million – 3 million) = 7 million remaining shares. Each share would therefore have a market value of $7.9 million/7 million = $1.13 (rounded).

A shareholder who owned 10 shares in the company before the issue would only own 7 shares after the debt is issued but would have received (3 shares x $1) = $3 of cash when the shares were redeemed (and it's easy to forget about this).

The wealth of the shareholder afterwards would therefore be ($3 + $7.91) = $10.91. This is an increase of ($10.91 - $10) = $0.91 in wealth.

Exam tip – M&M & change in shareholder wealth

Raising debt finance under M&M with corporate tax will always increase shareholder wealth (remember that the optimum level of gearing is 99.9% debt finance!)

Your calculations should always support this conclusion - if not - you have made a mistake somewhere.

Part (b)

In this case we need to use the M&M formula from proposition 2 to determine how the WACC changes. We also need to use the results for the value of debt (D) and the value of equity (E) in the geared company that were obtained in part (a) above.

$$WACCg = Keu \times (1 - \frac{Dt}{D + E})$$

Where:

Keu	=	12% or 0.12
t	=	0.30
D	=	$3m
E	=	$7.9m

Therefore:

$$WACCg = 0.12 \times (1 - \frac{3m \times 0.30}{3m + 7.9m})$$

WACCg = 0.1101 or 11.01%

Originally the company was all equity financed. For an all equity financed company the WACC is equal to the cost of equity.

The impact of financing by debt is therefore to reduce the WACC from 12% to 11.01%.

Assumptions of M&M

The main assumptions of M&M are as follows.

Assumption	Meaning & significance
Markets are perfectly efficient	This is covered in detail in chapter 14. It means that all investors get exactly the same information about a company at the same time and they all read it and understand it in the same way.
There are no transaction costs	The proof of the theories is based on arbitrage i.e. buying and selling to make gains. The proof assumes that no fees are incurred when shares are bought or sold.
All investors act rationally	This means that if an investor could make a riskless gain by buying shares in one company and selling in another then the investor would do this. The investor is economically rational.
Investors are indifferent between personal and corporate gearing	This means that an individual can borrow up to the same proportion as a company in relation to assets owned and the individual will pay the same rate of interest as a company.

Modigliani and Miller also ignored the following real life problems associated with higher levels of gearing:

1 Bankruptcy risk

As gearing increases then so does the possibility of a company defaulting on debt repayments and hence there is an increased risk of bankruptcy. The increased risk of bankruptcy will result in investors in both equity and debt demanding higher returns to compensate for this. As a result the cost of equity and cost of debt may both increase at higher levels of gearing.

2 Tax exhaustion

M&M's theories assume that all interest payments on additional debt finance will result in relief of tax which would otherwise be paid. In practice, at higher levels of gearing a company may find that interest payments exceed the operating profits being generated – in which case it may not be able to claim tax relief on further interest payments from further debt finance.

3 Borrowing/Debt capacity

In practice there are often severe restrictions on the ability of companies to borrow. This may be because of restrictions placed in the articles of association by the providers of existing debt capital. It may therefore not be possible to achieve very high levels of gearing.

Chapter 10
key points summary

- If gearing increases:

  - a company benefits from having more of the lower cost debt finance which tends to reduce the WACC

  - there is greater financial risk to shareholders which will increase the cost of equity which tends to increase the WACC.

- Under the traditional theory of gearing:

  - some debt financing is beneficial

  - there is an optimum level of gearing at which shareholder wealth is maximised.

- Modigliani and Miller without tax

  - The market value of a geared company is equal to the market value of an equivalent ungeared company.

  - The WACC of a geared company is equal to the WACC of an equivalent ungeared company.

- Modigliani and Miller with corporate tax

  - There are two important formulae to be understood.

    - $Vg = Vu + Dt$

    - $WACCg = Keu \times (1 - \dfrac{Dt}{D + E})$

  - As gearing increases, the value of a company will increase and the WACC will fall.

  - The optimum level of gearing is, in theory, 99.9% debt finance!

PORTFOLIO THEORY & CAPM

Introduction
what is this chapter about?

The capital asset pricing model was developed in the 1960s as a way of pricing assets, such as shares, by considering the level of risk associated with investing in those assets. In this chapter we explore how the capital asset pricing model was developed and how it can be used to make finance and investment decisions.

Key areas of the chapter are ....

1 **Portfolio theory** – a key principle of finance is that where there is a greater level of risk investors will demand higher returns. Can the risk facing an investor be reduced by investing in a portfolio of investments?

2 **Capital asset pricing model** – one of the most important development in modern finance has been the capital asset pricing model. What is this model and how can it be used to help a finance manager make investment decisions?

PORTFOLIO THEORY

The principle behind portfolio theory is very simple. It suggests that when investors diversify their investment (that is they undertake a number of investments rather than just one), the overall risk that they face can be reduced for a given level of return. In other words it is the principle of "not putting all of your eggs in one basket".

Let's see how this principle works. Suppose you were given a bonus by your employer of $10,000 for passing your last set of exams (unlikely I hear you say - who is that employer & can I work for them!). Let's assume that you don't want to spend the money straight away but instead plan to invest it. How would you go about this?

What are the possible investment opportunities available to the investor?

There are three main possibilities when we consider the combination of risk and return. They are as follows.

1   Avoid risk altogether

If you want to avoid risk altogether but still want to generate a return you could invest in what is called a risk free asset. This is basically an investment in an asset where there is no risk whatsoever. Short term government securities are often used as an example of a possible risk free investment. If you invested your $10,000 in this asset you would earn a rate of interest but the rate of interest would be very low, perhaps no more than 2%-3%.

2   Invest in a single risky investment

You might think that investing the $10,000 bonus in a risk free asset is rather 'boring' and safe – especially given the hard work that you would have put in to achieving exam success! An alternative to this would be to purchase $10,000 worth of equity in a company whose shares are traded on a stock market. This investment would have a much higher potential return than the first investment but also a much higher level of risk. If the company went into liquidation soon after you have made your investment you could lose everything.

3   Invest in a portfolio of risky investments

Rather than invest the $10,000 in a single risky investment, another alternative would be to invest this amount in a portfolio of risky investments, for example, invest $500 in each of 20 companies spread across different sectors of the stock market.

In this way it would be possible to reduce the risk of investing in risky investments without adversely affecting the potential return. It would be possible to expect to receive a similar potential return to that which would be possible from investing in a single share, **but** the risk would be significantly less.

How would a risk averse investor invest the $10,000?

In the first chapter we considered the investors attitude to risk and return, and defined what was meant by an investor being risk averse.

A quick recap – being risk averse means that an investor will demand a higher potential return for a given level of risk. It does not mean that an investor will always avoid risk – that depends on an individual's attitude to the combination of risk and return.

It is reasonable to assume that all investors are risk averse and we could therefore generalise as follows:

- If an investor wishes to **avoid risk** ➡ invest in a **risk free asset** such as treasury bills

- If an investor is willing to **accept more risk** ➡ invest in a **portfolio of risky investments**

Risk averse investors would not invest in a single risky investment because by investing in a portfolio of investments the investor could achieve the same potential return for less risk.

Of course – there will always be exceptions to this approach in real life. An investor may take a 'gamble' and put the full $10,000 into one risky company because the investor may feel that that one company is going to be a star performer and deliver returns which are well above the stock market average over the next few years.

In the long term, however, a serious investor who invests consistently year after year, is likely to do better by investing in a portfolio of companies rather than a single company.

Why does risk reduce when an investor invests in a portfolio of risky investments?

A good question – and just imagine – if you had been the first person to come up with the answer to this you could have won a Nobel prize!

The idea that there is less risk when an investment is spread across a portfolio of risky investments is a common sense idea. Instinct would tell us that the less dependent we are on a single investment, or a single company, the less risk that there is.

The first person to analyse this mathematically and to understand how risk reduction occurred when investing in portfolios of investments was Harry Markowitz.

Harry Markowitz

Harry Markowitz is an American economist who produced a series of pioneering works on portfolio selection in the 1950s. Prior to Markowitz it had been understood that the value of an investment in the stock market, or the value of a share, was based on the present value of future cashflows (which we saw in chapter 9). Markowitz was the first to relate, in a mathematical way, the return that an investor required to the level of risk attached to the investment. He explored the correlation between investments, how diversification reduced risk, and how to find the most efficient portfolio of investments.

The capital asset pricing model is based on a development of Markowitz's work.

Correlation between investments

The term correlation sounds very mathematical but don't worry – you should be able to understand the principles without going into the mathematics. Most examiners focus on the principles behind portfolio theory and the correlation coefficient, rather than the mathematics and therefore this is what we focus on in this book.

Markowitz suggested that risk reduced when investing in a portfolio of investments because of the correlation between the investments. Correlation is a statistical technique that measures the way in which the returns from one investment change in relation to the returns from another investment. It can have any value between +1 and -1.

Negative correlation **this means that as the returns from one investment increase, the returns from another investment will fall**

Positive correlation **this means that as the returns from one investment increase, the returns from another investment will also increase**

Suppose, for example, that a government announces a very significant increase in carbon tax rates payable by airlines on flights to other destinations within the same country. All airline companies are likely to be adversely affected by this change, and therefore there would be positive correlation between one airline company and another (the potential returns to investors in both companies would fall) in response to this announcement. A train operator, however, may well benefit from this announcement if more passengers chose to travel by train instead of by air. We could therefore conclude that there would be negative correlation between an airline company and a train operator in relation to this announcement.

Need to know!

Markowitz concluded that the more negative the correlation between the investments within a portfolio of investments the less risk there would be. He also concluded that the risk of a portfolio of investments could be reduced to below the risk of any individual investment because of negative correlation.

Diversification

The key to achieving as much negative correlation between investments as possible is diversification. This means spreading the investment into as many different companies and market sectors as possible.

Let's go back to the example of the $10,000 bonus that we considered earlier (you are probably still thinking about that possibility!). Suppose you invest the $10,000 in ten different airline companies. Whilst there would be some risk reduction the effect would not be as great as would be the case if you invest in ten different types of company in totally different market sectors. Rather than invest in 10 different airline companies it would be better to invest in one airline company, one train operating company, one retailer etc. There would be more negative correlation between the investments in this type of portfolio and hence it would have lower risk.

Need to know!

Diversification reduces risk. The more that an investor diversifies the greater the risk reduction effect.

How diversified can a portfolio be?

If Markowitz concluded that the more an investor diversifies the greater the risk reduction effect, then the question arises, how much diversification is it possible to achieve?

If we take a single stock market such as the New York Stock Exchange, the most diversified an investor on the stock market could be would be to buy shares in every single company on that stock market. This achieves the greatest possible spread of investments and hence the greatest risk reduction effect.

Finance terminology explained

The efficient (or market) portfolio

Markowitz concluded that the most efficient portfolio of investments that a stock market investor could achieve in terms of reducing risk would be the market portfolio. This is achieved by buying shares in every company on the stock market in proportion to their market size. The investor's portfolio becomes a mini version of the stock market as a whole.

In practice it is much easier for investors to 'buy' the market portfolio, and achieve this maximum risk reduction effect than the theory suggests. An investment company, with enormous amounts of money available to invest could quickly build up a portfolio resembling the market portfolio. An individual investor with a small amount of money available to invest on the stock market could then buy shares in that investment company and achieve the same risk reduction effect.

THE CAPITAL ASSET PRICING MODEL

The capital asset pricing model was developed from portfolio theory by William Sharpe in the 1960s. The model is widely used (honestly!) to find a return that diversified investors would require from a single investment, and to value investments.

William Sharpe

William Sharpe is an American Professor of Finance who published a paper in 1964 on the capital asset pricing model. The paper was based on a doctoral thesis written under the supervision of Harry Markowitz.

The model develops the conclusions drawn from portfolio theory and provides a direct relationship between the risk of a single investment and the return that a well-diversified investor would require from a single investment.

In 1990 Sharpe, Markowitz and Merton Miller (and I'm sure that you remember Merton Miller from chapter 10) jointly won the Nobel prize for economics.

A well-diversified investor

The capital asset pricing model starts with the concept of a well-diversified investor. The term refers to an investor who owns the market portfolio, or an efficient portfolio, under the principles of portfolio theory.

Given that most of the shares of companies quoted on a stock market are owned by institutional investors, such as pension funds, investment companies, and life assurance companies, it is reasonable to assume that most investors on a stock market own well-diversified portfolios.

Systematic and unsystematic risk

When analysing investment risk, Sharpe suggested that the risk which affects an investment in an individual share can be neatly categorised into two different types of risk - systematic risk and unsystematic risk.

Systematic risk

This is the risk of returns from an investment varying from period to period because of market-wide or systematic factors. These factors affect every single company, whose shares are quoted on the stock market, to some extent. Examples of systematic risk factors are:

- a significant rise in interest rates

- a significant change in corporate and personal tax rates

- a natural disaster affecting the economy as a whole.

If, for example, there was a rise in interest rates, many companies would be directly affected by this. A company with significant floating rate debt finance would find that its cost of borrowing would rise significantly. Many other companies would be indirectly affected by the rise. Personal borrowing costs would rise and there would be fewer consumers spending which would affect the level of economic activity.

Systematic risk does not mean that the factors affect all companies to the same extent. It just means that all companies are affected to some extent. A rise in interest rates would, for example, affect companies that have high gearing, or companies that sell luxury goods, more than companies with low gearing, or that sell essential goods such as food.

Exam tip – Systematic risk

A common mistake when discussing systematic risk is to say that this is risk that affects all companies to the same extent. It is not.

Whilst systematic risk affects all companies, the degree to which it affects each company will vary from company to company and is measured by the beta factor (which we will see later).

Unsystematic risk

This is the risk that is unique to a company or the industry within which a company operates. Unsystematic risk factors will not affect every company on the stock market. Examples of unsystematic risk factors are:

- a poor management decision, for example, about a new product launch

- the risk of a new competitor setting up in the market place and taking market share

- a major crisis affecting a company, for example, the outbreak of salmonella in a food manufacturing company.

Diversification and risk reduction

Need to know!

Suppose an investor, for example, invested in the shares of one airline company. The returns from that investment would vary from period to period because of both systematic and unsystematic factors. If the investors started to diversify the investment, and, for example, combined an investment in an airline company with investments in other airlines, and in other forms of transportation such as train operating companies, we find that the impact of unsystematic risk is reduced, or is diversified away. If all of the planes from one airline are grounded because of a safety problem, passengers wishing to travel would use other airlines or other modes of transport. The impact of the safety problem on the investor is therefore reduced.

Need to know!

This effect can be shown graphically as follows:

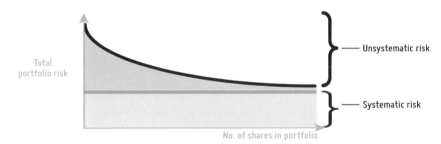

Now it was mentioned earlier that whilst in theory we need to invest in every share on the stock market to eliminate unsystematic risk completely – the good news is that in practice the full risk reduction effect of diversification can be more or less achieved by investing in a portfolio of as few as 15-20 shares, provided that these are carefully selected and spread well across a stock market. Even with your $10,000 bonus therefore, if you selected your investments carefully, you could achieve the full risk reduction effect.

The risk of a single investment

If an investor owns a well-diversified portfolio of investments this has important implications for any single investment within that portfolio, or any single new investment that an investor is considering undertaking.

We have seen already that the return that an investor would expect to receive from any investment will relate to the risk of that investment. Where there is greater risk an investor would expect to receive a higher return.

For an investor who owns a well-diversified portfolio of investments this relationship needs to be amended. Now we can say that any unsystematic risk of an investment can be ignored as this has been diversified away.

 # Need to know!

The return required by a well-diversified investor will only need to compensate for the systematic risk of the investment.

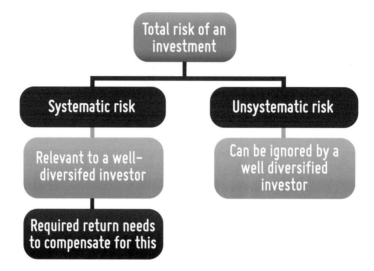

Measuring systematic risk — the beta factor

Systematic risk is market risk, or the risk due to factors that affect all investments on the stock market. If is much more useful to measure systematic risk relative to the stock market as a whole than it is to measure systematic risk in absolute terms.

Beta factor

Systematic risk is measured by using the beta factor (β). This is defined as follows:

$$\beta = \frac{\text{systematic risk of an individual investment}}{\text{risk of the market as a whole}}$$

The risk of the market as a whole is the systematic risk of the market. If we are looking at a portfolio which represents the whole stock market, or the market portfolio, unsystematic risk will have been diversified away, leaving only systematic risk. This, by definition, will represent the average systematic risk of all of the investments in the market.

How do we interpret a beta factor?

The beta factor for the market as a whole, the market portfolio, is defined as 1. If the risk of a market is an average of the systematic risk of the investments in a market, then by definition some investments must have a level of systematic risk which is above the average and others below the average. This means that the beta factor for some investments must be greater than 1 and for other investments less than 1.

For an individual investment:

If β = 1 ➡ this means that the investment has exactly the same systematic risk as the market (sometimes called **risk neutral** investments)

If β > 1 ➡ this means that the investment has a greater level of systematic risk than the market (sometimes called **aggressive** investments)

If β < 1 ➡ this means that an investment has less systematic risk than the market (sometimes called **defensive** investments)

The beta factor therefore tells an investor how the return from an investment is expected to change if there is a given change in the return from the stock market as a whole. If the return from the stock market fell by 20% in a given period, for example, the returns from an investment in a company with a beta of greater than 1 would be expected to fall by more than 20% and the returns from an investment with a beta of less than 1 would be expected to fall by less than 20%.

The beta factor for individual investments can be established via regression analysis which is outside the scope of this book.

Investing in aggressive and defensive shares

From the above it follows that if an investor expects a **bull** market, where shares are expected to rise significantly, the investor should invest in aggressive shares rather than defensive shares. If the returns from the stock market as a whole increase, the returns from aggressive shares should increase by more than the market.

Similarly, if an investor expects a **bear** market where shares are expected to fall significantly, the investor should switch into defensive shares. This will protect the investor from the impact of the fall in the stock market.

OK – now if you have got this far through the chapter without taking a break – well done – perhaps now would be a good time to have a break before you tackle the next bit!

The CAPM equation and security market line

If the beta factor for an investment can be measured, then the return that a well-diversified investor requires from the investment can be found by using the security market line, or the equation of the security market line – the CAPM equation. What is the security market line?

The security market line can be shown graphically as follows:

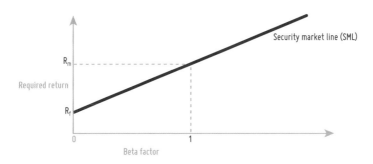

The security market line (SML) measures the relationship between the beta factor and the return that a well-diversified investor would require from a single investment.

If an investment had a beta factor of 1, this means that an investment has the same systematic risk as the market as a whole and therefore an investor would require the same return as that which would be expected when investing in the market portfolio. If an investment had a beta of zero it would mean that it has no systematic risk, and given that unsystematic risk is diversified away it is effectively risk free. In this case the return that an investor would require would be the risk free rate of return. There is then a linear relationship between these two points which also extends above a beta of 1.

Given that the relationship between the risk of an investment (measured by beta) and the required return is linear then we can derive an equation for the security market line, which is also known as the CAPM equation.

Need to know!

Required return for an investment = Rf + β (Rm - Rf)

Where:

Rf = The risk free rate of return
Rm = The return from the market portfolio
β = The beta factor for the investment in question

Rf and Rm will usually be given to you in questions – you will not need to derive them.

CAPM and the cost of equity

In chapter 9 we saw that the return that an investor in equity required was exactly the same as the cost of equity to the company. This means that the CAPM equation can be used to estimate the cost of equity for investment undertaken by a well-diversified investor.

If Ke is the cost of equity the CAPM equation is shown as:

$$Ke = Rf + β (Rm - Rf)$$

Equity risk premium

In the CAPM equation, (Rm - Rf) is sometimes referred to as the 'equity risk premium'. This is because it represents the extra amount, or premium, that is added to a risk free investment when investing in the market portfolio of risky investments.

An examiner may give you the equity risk premium in a question instead of both Rm and Rf. If this is the case the CAPM equation becomes:

$$Ke = Rf + β (equity\ risk\ premium)$$

Example 1

If the risk free rate is 5%, the equity risk premium 3% and a company has a beta factor of 1.20, what is the company's cost of equity?

Rf = 5% or 0.05

Equity risk premium = 3% or 0.03

Therefore

Ke = 0.05 + 1.20 x 0.03 = 0.0860 or 8.60%

The alpha value and asset pricing

We have already considered the beta – now the alpha – does that mean that we are going to go through the whole Greek alphabet? – thankfully not – it is just the alpha and beta – at least in this chapter!

The CAPM equation allows us to estimate the return that shareholders **require** from a new investment based upon the level of risk of that investment. This might not be the same as the actual return or indeed the expected return from that investment in the short term because of market inefficiencies.

If a well-diversified investor calculates the **required return** for a new investment, he or she can compare this to its **expected return**. The difference between the two is called the alpha value.

Alpha value = expected return from an investment – required return from an investment

What is the significance of an alpha value?

If the **alpha value is positive** it means that a new investment is worthwhile. The expected return exceeds the return that an investor requires to compensate for the systematic risk of the investment and it should therefore be undertaken.

A positive alpha value also means that the investment is undervalued. If the investment is in shares on a stock market, and the market is perfectly efficient (which we will cover in detail in chapter 14), through arbitrage (which we saw in chapter 10) the share price will rise, and the expected return will fall. This process will continue until the expected return equals the required return, or the alpha is zero.

positive alpha means... → expected return > required return → excess demand for the investment at the current price → price will rise and expected return will fall until... → expected return = required return

Conversely, if the alpha value is negative it means that the new investment is not worthwhile. The expected return is less than the return that the investor requires and should not be undertaken.

In this case the share is overvalued. In a perfectly efficient market the share price should fall, and expected return should rise, until it equates with the required return, or the alpha is zero.

The model therefore provides a means of pricing investments (or capital assets) in a perfectly efficient market. The investment should be priced so that the expected return from the investment is equal to the required rate of return.

Example 2

Rosie's Bakes is seeking a listing on a stock market. The shares have been offered for sale at 200c per share. An investor paying this amount for a share would expect a return of 13% per annum based on forecasts of future dividends.

A well-diversified investor is considering purchasing some of these shares when the listing takes place. The investor has obtained the following information:

The beta of Rosie's Bakes is 0.80, the risk free rate is 6% and the equity risk premium is 7%.

Should the investor purchase the new shares at this price?

Solution 2

The first step is to calculate the required return for the share using the CAPM equation

Rf = 6% or 0.06

Equity risk premium = 7% or 0.07

Therefore

Required return= 0.06 + 0.80 x 0.07 = 0.1160 or 11.60%

We can then calculate the alpha value

Alpha value = 13% - 11.60% = 1.4%

As the expected return exceeds the required return, and the alpha value is positive, it means that the share is undervalued. The investor should therefore purchase the shares at 200c per share.

Application of CAPM

The principles behind CAPM can be used to determine the return that investors require from a variety of investments including:

1 **A potential investment in new shares or bonds**. Suppose a company floats on a stock market and a well-diversified investor is considering purchasing shares in the company. CAPM can be used to work out the required return, which could then be compared to the expected return based on the proposed issue price of the shares. If the expected return exceeds the required return the investment should be undertaken. A potential investment in new risky bonds can be assessed in a similar way.

2 **A potential investment in a new project**. Suppose a company, owned by well diversified investors, is considering undertaking a new project. The beta factor of the project could be determined, and a required return from the new project could be calculated, using CAPM. This could then be compared to the expected return (which would be the IRR for a project). If the expected return exceeds the required return then the project should be undertaken.

In the next chapter we will consider in more detail how CAPM can be used to appraise new potential projects.

Assumptions behind CAPM

The capital asset pricing model is based on a number of important assumptions including the following:

Assumptions	Meaning & significance
The risk factors affecting an investment are either systematic or unsystematic.	The real world isn't quite as neat as that. It could be argued that some risk factors are somewhere between the two.
The return required by a well-diversified investor will only reflect systematic risk.	In the real world there is some evidence to suggest that sometimes even well-diversified investors take unsystematic risk into account when assessing the return that they require.
The stock market is perfectly efficient.	This is covered in more detail in chapter 14. The significance here is that shares are only priced correctly by CAPM if all investors have perfect information about a company.
CAPM is a single period model.	This means that the result of the calculation of the cost of equity using the CAPM equation is only valid for one time period. If any of the variables change, for example, the risk free rate of interest, we are into a new time period, and the cost of equity needs to be recalculated.
The CAPM is an 'ex-ante' model but uses 'ex-post' data.	This means that the variables used in the CAPM equation, such as the calculation of the beta factor, are based on historical information (ex-post). The model is used, however, to estimate future returns that are required (ex-ante).
CAPM only considers the level of return and not how the return is received by the provider of finance.	CAPM does not distinguish between a return to an investor in shares in the form of dividends, or a capital gain. In real life the way in which an investor receives a return can have an impact on a share price as we will see in chapter 15 on dividend policy.

Congratulations – you have reached the end of one of the most difficult chapters in the book. If you didn't get a bonus for passing your last set of exams then you certainly deserve one for getting to the end of this chapter!

Chapter 11
key points summary

- Portfolio theory

    - Diversification reduces the risk of an investment.

    - The more negative the correlation the greater the risk reduction effect.

    - The most efficient portfolio of risky shares is the market portfolio.

- Capital asset pricing model

    - Can only use if we assume that investors are well-diversified.

    - Two types of risk:

        - unsystematic risk – unique to a company or industry – diversified away in a well-diversified portfolio

        - systematic risk – risk due to market wide factors – cannot be diversified away.

- CAPM equation - Required return = Rf + β (Rm-Rf)

    - Beta measures systematic risk – the higher the beta factor the greater the level of systematic risk.

    - The required return for a shareholder = cost of equity. CAPM therefore provides another way of determining the cost of equity to the DVM.

- Alpha value = expected return – required return

    - If positive – investment is worthwhile.

    - If negative – investment is not worthwhile.

PROJECT COST OF CAPITAL AND APV

12

Introduction
what is this chapter about?

In the previous chapter we looked at the capital asset pricing model (CAPM) and saw that for any investment in securities we could establish a required rate of return for that investment based upon its beta factor. We also saw that the beta factor measured the systematic risk of an investment.

In this chapter we will consider how the capital asset pricing model can be used to help perform NPV calculations in more complex situations, and where using the company's WACC (do you remember that!) might not be an appropriate discount rate.

Key areas of the chapter are ....

1 **Adjusting the beta factor** – the beta factor measures systematic risk. The beta factor may, however, need to be adjusted in certain situations. When and how might the beta factor be adjusted?

2 **Project cost of capital** – a new project or investment may have a different level of risk compared to the existing activities of the company. If this is the case how can CAPM and the beta factor be used to find a cost of capital that reflects the risk of the project?

3 **Adjusted present value** – the adjusted present value technique is an alternative way of appraising a new investment, and the way in which the new investment is financed. What is the adjusted present value technique and how can it be used to appraise a new investment?

ADJUSTING THE BETA FACTOR

The beta factor measures systematic risk. That is true – but the systematic risk of what? It really measures the systematic risk of a business, or of an investment that the business undertakes. The beta of car manufacturer, for example, measures the systematic risk of the business of making cars.

OK – so how and why might the beta factor need to be adjusted?

There are two ways in which a beta factor may need to be adjusted in exam questions (only two – so not too bad is it!) before it is used to accurately find a cost of equity. These are:

1   weighted average beta factor

2   beta factor and financial risk.

Need to know!
Weighted average beta factor

A beta factor for a company is a weighted average of the beta factors of the individual investments that the company has undertaken. Weighting is according to proportions based on market values.

What does this mean? Well - the way to look at a company is that it may be focused purely on one business area, for example, making cars, or it may have a number of different and relatively distinct businesses, for example, a division that makes cars and another division that makes washing machines. If the latter – each business will have its own beta, and therefore the company beta is a weighted average of the beta factors applicable to each business.

This principle can be used in a number of different ways by an examiner in exam questions. Let's consider this through a couple of examples.

Example 1

Hereford is a company that is made up of two quite separate and distinct businesses. The first business involves producing cider from locally grown apples. It is known that the beta of this business is 0.90. The second business involves operating a chain of restaurants. It is known that the beta of this second business is 1.30.

If the cider production business represents approximately 30% of the company's total market value, what will be the overall company beta for Hereford?

Solution 1

The beta of Hereford will be a weighted average of the beta's applicable to each of the two businesses that Hereford operates. If cider production is 30% of the company then the restaurant chain must be 70% of the company.

The beta of Hereford = (beta of the cider business x proportion) + (beta of the restaurant business x proportion)

The beta of Hereford = (0.9 x 30%) + (1.3 x 70%)

The beta of Hereford = 1.18

And now a slightly more complex example.

Example 2

Farnham is a quoted company that has a beta factor of 1.50. There are two divisions within the company. The first division offers sailing holidays in Greece. The second division sells financial service products such as pensions and investment portfolios. It is known that the beta of the division selling financial services is 1.20, and that this division represents approximately 60% of the company's value.

What is the beta of the division operating sailing holidays in Greece?

Solution 2

In this case we need to work backwards to find the beta of a division from a knowledge of the company's overall beta.

The beta of Farnham = (beta of the sailing holidays division x proportion) + (beta of the financial services division x proportion)

1.50 = (beta of the sailing holidays division x 40%) + (1.2 x 60%)

1.50 = (beta of the sailing holidays division x 40%) + 0.72

(1.50 – 0.72) = (beta of the sailing holidays division x 40%)

0.78 = (beta of the sailing holidays division x 40%)

$\dfrac{0.78}{0.40}$ = beta of the sailing holidays division

beta of the sailing holidays division = 1.95

The sailing holidays division has a significantly higher beta than financial services and is therefore a much more risky business (in terms of systematic risk) than financial services.

Beta factor and financial risk

In chapter 11 we saw that business risk is made up of systematic risk and unsystematic risk, and that unsystematic risk could be diversified away.

A complication that we now need to consider is that if a company is geared, as we saw in chapter 10, a shareholder will also face financial risk.

Time for a quick reminder – financial risk is the risk to a shareholder because of the need to pay interest to the providers of debt capital before the shareholders receive a return.

Financial risk has an impact on the beta factor. To consider how this impacts on the beta factor we need to introduce two new terms.

Finance terminology explained

Asset beta (βa)

This is the beta which reflects only systematic risk. It is the beta relevant to the asset, or the investment itself. If a company was all equity financed, and there was, therefore, no financial risk, it would also be the beta relevant to the investment in shares in the company.

Finance terminology explained

Equity beta (βe)

This is the beta which reflects both systematic and financial risk. It is the beta applicable to an investment in the equity or shares of a company. When a company is geared this beta will reflect the financial risk to a shareholder as well as the systematic risk.

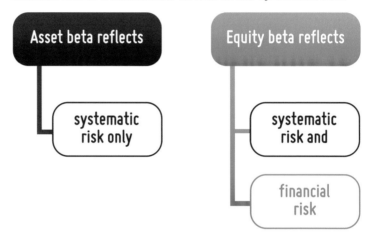

If a company was all equity financed the asset beta and equity beta would be the same. In an all equity financed company there is no financial risk, and therefore the beta of the investment that the company makes in its assets is the same as the beta of an investment in the company's shares.

If a company is geared, the asset and equity beta will not be the same. The equity beta will always be greater than the asset beta because of the additional financial risk.

Need to know!

The asset/equity beta formula

Modigliani and Miller produced the following formula which relates an asset beta to an equity beta:

$$\beta a = \beta e \times \frac{Ve}{Ve + Vd\,(1\text{-}t)} + \beta d \times \frac{Vd\,(1\text{-}t)}{Ve + Vd\,(1\text{-}t)}$$

We have already defined βa and βe. The other terms are defined as follows:

βd = **Debt beta**. This is the beta applicable to risky debt. If debt has some risk we can use this beta to determine the returns that a potential investor in risky debt would require

Ve = The market value of equity in the geared company

Vd = The market value of debt in the geared company

Often in exam questions the debt beta is assumed to be zero when using the formula. If this is the case then the formula becomes:

$$\beta a = \beta e \times \frac{Ve}{Ve + Vd\,(1\text{-}t)}$$

This abbreviated version is a bit more manageable – and thankfully it is this version that is normally used in exam questions!

This relationship can be used in a number of different ways by an examiner, for example it could be used to estimate the impact of a change in gearing on a company's cost of equity. Let's see an example of this.

Example 3

Anfield is an all equity financed company. It manufactures sports equipment that is sold to wholesalers and retailers. The beta of its investments (or its assets) has been estimated to be 1.2. We also know that the risk free rate is 4% and that the equity risk premium is 8%.

Anfield's finance director is considering issuing some debt capital (in the form of marketable bonds) and will use the proceeds to buy back some of the company's shares at market value. Following this issue of new debt capital it is estimated that Anfield's gearing will be 30% debt by market value.

Assume that all debt is risk free and that βd is zero. Corporate tax is 30%.

Requirements

(a) What is Anfield's current cost of equity?
(b) What will Anfield's new cost of equity be after it has changed its gearing?

Part (a)

The current cost of equity can be found by using the CAPM formula that we saw in chapter 11. When we use the CAPM formula the beta in the formula could be an asset beta or an equity beta depending on whether or not the company is geared. In this case the company is not currently geared and therefore the relevant beta would be the asset beta.

$Ke = Rf + \beta$ (equity risk premium)

Where

$Rf = 4\%$ or 0.04
$\beta a = 1.2$
Equity risk premium = 8% or 0.08

Therefore

$Ke = 0.04 + 1.2 \times 0.08$
$Ke = 0.01360$ or 13.60%

Part (b)

After the company has issued some debt capital and therefore become a geared company, the asset beta and equity beta will not be the same. The asset beta needs to be 'geared up' into an equity beta to reflect the financial risk as well as the systematic risk.

The beta factor can be 'geared up' (that is increased because of the financial risk that a shareholder now faces) by using Modigliani and Miller's formula.

$$\beta a = \beta e \times \frac{Ve}{Ve + Vd (1-t)}$$

Where:

$Vd = 30\%$ - therefore we will assume 30
$Ve = 70\%$ - therefore we will assume 70
$t = 30\%$ or 0.3
$\beta a = 1.2$

Therefore:

$$1.2 = \beta e \times \frac{70}{(70 + 30(1-0.3)}$$

$1.2 = \beta e \times 0.769$

$$\beta e = \frac{1.2}{0.769} = 1.56$$

This beta reflects the systematic risk of investing in manufacturing sports equipment, and the financial risk of a 30% level of gearing (market value debt/total market value).

The new cost of equity can then be found by using the same CAPM equation:

Ke = 0.04 + 1.56 x 0.08

Ke = 0.1648 or 16.48%

The cost of equity would therefore have risen from 13.60% to 16.48% because of the increased financial risk to the shareholder.

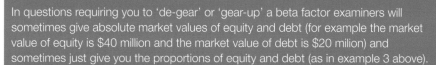

Exam tip – 'De-gearing' and 'gearing-up' betas

In questions requiring you to 'de-gear' or 'gear-up' a beta factor examiners will sometimes give absolute market values of equity and debt (for example the market value of equity is $40 million and the market value of debt is $20 milion) and sometimes just give you the proportions of equity and debt (as in example 3 above).

If given the proportions make an assumption about the market value of equity and the market value of debt for use in the formula. In the solution to example 3 we assumed a market value of debt of 30, and a market value of equity of 70. We could alternatively have assumed a market value of debt of 3, and a market value of equity of 7. As long as the relative proportions are correct we would, of course, get the same answer.

Weighted average beta factor and financial risk

OK – now a great deal of pleasure can be gained from using these two relationships on their own but applying them together to a scenario is even more enjoyable(!!).

Let's see how this works through an example.

Example 4

Penarth is an all equity financed company. It has two divisions. One division is a retailer of cricket equipment through specialist outlets at cricket grounds throughout the country. The other division provides cricket coaching courses to junior cricketers. The retail division represents approximately 45% of the value of the company.

Penarth is a privately owned company and as a result does not have a quoted beta factor. Its shareholders are, however, well-diversified and therefore the finance director of Penarth, Rhys Evans, wishes to use the principles of CAPM to find a cost of equity for the company.

The approach adopted is to use industry average information. It is known that the average asset beta for cricket retailers is 1.10. The only information available, however, relating to suppliers of cricket coaching courses is that the average equity beta is 1.80 and the average gearing is 40% debt to total market value.

Assume that all debt is risk free. Corporate tax rate is 30%.

Requirement

What is a suitable beta factor to use to find a cost of equity for Penarth?

Working 1 – 'de-gear' the average cricket coaching course equity beta

Because we are only given the equity beta for suppliers of cricket coaching courses, and not the asset beta, the first thing to do is to 'de-gear' this beta (that is, we need to find an equivalent asset beta).

Vd = 40% - therefore we will assume 40

Ve = 60% - therefore we will assume 60

t   = 30% or 0.3

βe = 1.80

Therefore

$$\beta a = 1.80 \times \frac{60}{(60 + 40(1-0.3))}$$

βa = 1.80 x 0.682

βa = 1.23

Working 2 – weighted average asset beta

We can now find a weighted average asset beta for Penarth's investments or assets. 45% of the business is cricket retailing and 55% is providing coaching courses.

Penarth asset beta = (asset beta of cricket retailing x proportion) + (asset beta of coaching courses x proportion)

Penarth asset beta = (1.10 x 45%) + (1.23 x 55%)

Penarth asset beta = 1.17

Given that Penarth is an all equity financed company, this beta is a suitable beta to use in the CAPM equation to find a cost of equity for Penarth.

Note – if Penarth had been geared, we could have then 'geared-up' the asset beta to find a suitable equity beta for Penarth which could then have been used in the CAPM equation.

PROJECT COST OF CAPITAL

In chapter 9 we worked out how to calculate the WACC of a company. This WACC could be used as a discount rate when appraising new investments using discounted cashflow techniques.

In using the WACC of a company in this way it was noted in chapter 9 that two very important assumptions were being made. They were:

1	That the long term gearing or capital structure of the company will not change.
2	That the new project/investment has the same level of risk as the existing projects/investments of the company.

Now – let's think for a minute about the second of these two assumptions. How realistic or relevant is this to real world investments?

The problem is that in real life **all new projects are unique** to one degree or another and therefore have different levels of risk. In many cases we can ignore the differences because a new project is so similar to the existing activities of the company that using the WACC as a discount rate would reasonably and adequately reflect the risk of the project. If, for example, an airline operator is considering investing in a new aircraft model that has just come onto the market, whilst the new project is not quite the same as the existing business, it is similar enough to mean that it would be reasonable to use the current WACC of the company to calculate a project NPV.

Diversification

What if, however, a new project under consideration involves significant diversification such that the risk of the new project is significantly different to the risk of the existing activities of the company?

In this case using the WACC of the company as a discount rate for the project would give a misleading result because the WACC would not adequately reflect the risk of the project.

How do we, in such a situation, find a suitable discount rate, or cost of capital?

Need to know!

Finding a project cost of capital

It is possible to find a project cost of capital when a company diversifies in this way:

Step 1 – find a proxy company beta

The first task is to find a beta factor for a proxy company to the new project. A proxy company means another company which operates a similar type of business to the new project. If the proxy company is quoted then its beta factor should be readily available. This proxy company should have the same systematic risk as the new project.

Step 2 - 'de-gear' the proxy company beta to find an asset beta

Whilst a proxy company beta will have the same systematic risk as the new project, it will, however, reflect the financial risk, or gearing of the proxy company, and not the gearing of the new project. The next step therefore is to remove this financial risk. This would give us the equivalent asset beta of the proxy company.

Step 3 - 'gear up' the proxy company asset beta

If the project, or company undertaking the project, is geared there will be financial risk to the shareholders. To reflect this, the relevant asset beta needs to be 'geared up' using the gearing level for the project – that is to reflect the way in which the project will be financed.

Step 4 - find a project cost of equity

We can then use the CAPM equation to find a project cost of equity.

Step 5 - find a project cost of capital

If the project is geared, and therefore partly financed by debt capital, the cost of debt needs to be found, and then an overall project cost of capital. This is found by weighting the costs of capital according to proportions.

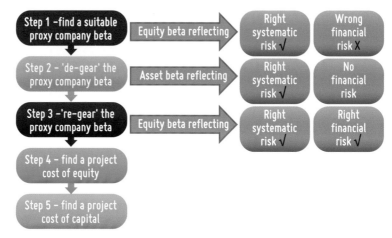

Example 5

Falmouth Air is a low cost airline business that operates scheduled flights throughout Europe. The company is 40% debt financed and its equity beta is 1.30.

The chief executive of Falmouth Air, Jack Forbes, feels that the time is right for the company to diversify into different business areas. One possibility is the package holiday business. Jack feels that whilst investing in the package holiday business involves significant diversification away from the company's current activities, the company can obtain considerable benefits from using its existing airlines on chartered package holiday flights.

The finance director of Falmouth Air has obtained some information about a leading package holiday company called Dreamtours. The equity beta of Dreamtours is 1.80 and Dreamtours is 30% debt financed.

It is also known that the post-tax cost of debt of Falmouth Air is 7%, that the risk free rate is 5% and that the equity risk premium is 4%. The new investment will be financed using the same proportion of debt and equity as is currently used by the company, that is 40% debt financing. Corporate tax is payable at 30%.

Requirement

Determine a suitable discount rate to use for appraising the new investment in the package holiday business.

When using Modigliani and Miller's formula you may assume that all debt is risk free.

Step 1 – find a proxy company beta

A suitable proxy company for the new investment is Dreamtours. Its equity beta is 1.80.

Step 2 - 'de-gear' the proxy company beta to find an asset beta

We need to remove the current financial risk of Dreamtours from the beta factor. Dreamtours is 30% debt financed.

V_d = 30% - therefore we will assume 30
V_e = 70% - therefore we will assume 70
t = 30% or 0.3

$$\beta_a = 1.80 \times \frac{70}{(70 + 30(1-0.3))}$$

$\beta_a = 1.38$

Step 3 - 'gear up' the proxy company asset beta

The project will be financed by 40% debt. We will therefore 'gear-up' using this gearing ratio.

V_d = 40% - therefore we will assume 40
V_e = 60% - therefore we will assume 60

Therefore:

$$1.38 = \beta_e \times \frac{60}{(60 + 40(1-0.3))}$$

$1.38 = \beta_e \times 0.681$

$$\beta_e = \frac{1.38}{0.681} = 2.03$$

Step 4 - find a project cost of equity

$K_e = R_f + \beta$ (equity risk premium)

Where

R_f = 5% or 0.05
β_e = 2.03

Equity risk premium = 4% or 0.04

Therefore

K_e = 0.05 + 2.03 x 0.04
K_e = 0.01312 or 13.12%

Step 5 - find a project cost of capital

This is simply the weighted average of the project cost of equity and the project cost of debt. The post-tax cost of debt is given in the question as 7%.

$$\text{Project cost of capital} = \left(13.12\% \; x \; \frac{60}{(60 + 40)}\right) + \left(7\% \; x \; \frac{40}{(60 + 40)}\right)$$

Project cost of capital = 10.67%

ADJUSTED PRESENT VALUE (APV)

What is this?

A company WACC, or a project cost of capital, both build the effect of financing into the discount rate which is then used to calculate an NPV. The project cost of capital in example 5 above reflects the benefits of debt financing (cost of debt at 7% is lower than the cost of equity, which pulls down the final cost of capital) and the drawback of debt financing (equity beta is higher than asset beta which results in a higher cost of equity).

The APV approach looks at the impact of financing in a different way. Instead of building the impact of financing into the discount rate the impact of financing is considered totally separately to the investment itself.

How does the adjusted present value approach work?

The approach involves two distinct steps.

Step 1 – the project NPV

The project NPV is calculated by using the **cost of equity** based on an **asset beta** as a discount rate. This is often referred to as the base case NPV.

The discount rate used to determine the project NPV therefore completely ignores any debt financing implications. It doesn't matter whether the company or the new project is financed by debt – for this part of the analysis we ignore debt completely.

Step 2 – the present value of the financing effects of the project

We then focus on the way in which the project itself is financed. The present value of any net financing effects are then calculated. The discount rate used for determining the present value of the financing effects is normally either the yield on the debt, or the risk free rate. Cashflows relating to the financing of a project are less risky that the cashflows of the project itself and therefore a different discount rate is used.

The APV approach is based on Modigliani and Miller's theories of gearing. Under this theory, if corporate tax is ignored, the benefits and drawbacks of financing by debt as opposed to equity cancel each other out. When using the APV technique we therefore only focus on the net effects of financing that do not cancel out under Modigliani and Miller's theories. The typical effects seen in a question are:

(a) **issue costs** associated with an issue of shares or bonds

(b) interest savings from a special **subsidised loan** available because the particular investment is undertaken

(c) **tax relief** on interest payments on debt – often called the **'tax shield'**

Step 3 – the adjusted present value

This is found by adding the results from steps 1 and 2.

Decisions are then based on the total APV for a project.

Example 6

Zagreb is a company that manufactures engines for the aerospace industry. 50% of the company financing is debt, and the equity beta of Zagreb is 1.42.

Zagreb wishes to diversify its business operations. It is considering setting up a new division of the company which will involve manufacturing equipment for the telecommunications industry. The investment will cost $20 million and is expected to produce post-tax cashflows of $6 million per annum for the next five years.

The equity beta of a proxy company that manufactures equipment for the telecommunications industry is 1.58. The proxy company is 45% debt financed by market value.

The new project is to be financed by a bond issue which will need to raise a net amount of $20 million. The bond will be repayable at the end of the project's life. Issue costs of 5% of the gross amount of the bonds issued will be charged by the company's issuing bank. The government is prepared to subsidise the interest payable on the bond to the extent of reimbursing 3% of any interest paid by Zagreb in respect of the financing for this project. This is part of its strategy of encouraging investment in the telecommunications industry.

The corporate tax rate is 30% with tax payable in the same year as the cashflows. The risk free rate is 8% and the equity risk premium is 5%. The company's debt is assumed to be risk free and therefore the yield on the company's debt can be assumed to be 8% – the same as the risk free rate.

Requirement

What is the adjusted present value of the new investment? Should the company go ahead with the new investment?

Step 1 – the project NPV

To find the project NPV we need to discount at a cost of equity using an asset beta. Because the company is diversifying, the relevant asset beta will be the asset beta of the proxy company. The equity beta of the proxy company therefore needs to be 'de-geared'.

For the proxy company

Vd = 45% - therefore we will assume 45

Ve = 55% - therefore we will assume 55

t = 30% or 0.3

$$\beta a = 1.58 \times \frac{55}{(55 + 45(1 - 0.3))}$$

$\beta a = 1.00$

Note – we do not 'gear up' this beta when using the APV technique. The relevant beta to use when calculating the project NPV is always the asset beta.

We can then find the project cost of equity by using the CAPM equation

Rf = 8% or 0.08

$\beta a = 1.00$

Equity risk premium = 5% or 0.05

Therefore

Ke(ungeared) = 0.08 + 1.00 x 0.05

Ke(ungeared) = 0.13 or 13%

The **project NPV** is then found as follows:

Time	Narrative	Cashflow $	Discount factor @ 13%	Present value $
T0	Initial Cost	(20,000,000)	1.000	(20,000,000)
T1 – T5	Post-tax cashflow	6,000,000	3.517	21,102,000
	NPV			**1,102,000**

The project therefore has a positive NPV of $1,102,000 when discounted at the cost of equity based on an asset beta.

Even if the project NPV had been negative – using the APV technique the investment may still be worthwhile when we consider the financial effects. Let's now consider these.

Step 2 – the present value of the financing effects of the project

(a) issue costs

The issue costs are 5% of the gross amount of bonds issued. This means that the net amount of finance raised must be 95% of the gross amount of bonds issued.

The gross amount of the bonds issued is therefore $\dfrac{\$20,000,000}{0.95} = \$21,052,632$

The issue costs are therefore $21,052,632 x 5% = $1,052,632

Issue costs on debt are normally assumed to be tax allowable whereas issue costs on equity are normally not assumed to be tax allowable. Tax is payable in the same year as the cashflow therefore the post-tax issue costs would be:

$1,052,632 x (1 – 0.30) = $736,842

Given that these issue costs are payable immediately there is no need to discount as these costs are already at their present value.

(b) interest savings from the subsidised loan

There is a saving of 3% interest compared to the rate that Zagreb would normally pay if debt finance is raised. If interest payments are, however, assumed to be tax allowable, this means that when interest is saved, the company loses tax relief that it would otherwise receive. The true saving is therefore the interest saved adjusted for corporate tax.

The gross loan issued was $21,052,632 (from part (a)).

The annual post-tax interest saved because of the subsidy is therefore:

$21,052,632 x 3% x (1 – 0.30) = $442,105

The bond has a life of 5 years and therefore the present value of the interest savings when discounted at the yield (8%) would be:

Time	Narrative	Cashflow $	Discount factor @ 8%	Present value $
T1 – T5	Subsidised interest	442,105	3.993	1,765,325

(c) the present value of the 'tax shield'

If there is a subsidy of 3% interest, this means that the company will still need to pay interest on the bond at 8% - 3% = 5%. The interest payments that are made at this rate will qualify for tax relief at 30%.

Annual tax relief on interest payments on debt = $21,052,632 x 5% x 30% = $315,789

The bond has a life of 5 years and therefore the present value of the tax shield when discounted at the yield of 8% would be:

Time	Narrative	Cashflow ($)	Discount factor @ 8%	Present value ($)
T1 – T5	Tax shield	315,789	3.993	1,260,945

Step 3 – the adjusted present value

This is found as follows:

Narrative	Present value ($)
Project NPV	1,102,000
Financing effects:	
Issue costs	(736,842)
Subsidised loan	1,765,325
Tax shield	1,260,945
Adjusted present value	**3,391,428**

The project and the way in which it is financed therefore has a total present value of $3,391,428. If Zagreb goes ahead with this project and finances the project in the way proposed, shareholder wealth should increase by this amount.

Exam tip – APV and debt capacity

Questions on APV sometimes refer to an increase in the debt capacity of the company. The debt capacity is the 'extra' amount of debt that a company is able to raise because of a decision to undertake a particular investment.

The '**tax shield**' financing effect should always be based on the **debt capacity** even if this is different to the actual amount of debt finance raised by the company in the scenario. This will reflect the potential benefit available as a result of undertaking the investment.

Other financing effects, however, such as a subsidised loan, or issue costs should be based in the **actual amount** of new finance raised.

When do we use the APV technique?

The APV is an alternative investment appraisal technique to calculating the NPV of a project at a company WACC or a project WACC. It is just a different way of evaluating the cashflows that would arise from both the investment and financing decisions. As a result it could, in theory, be used as an alternative investment appraisal technique in any investment appraisal situation.

Where the technique is, however, particularly useful is when **the financing of the investment is different to the current company financing**, that is, when a company's gearing will change as a result of undertaking the new investment. Incorporating the financing changes into a WACC is extremely difficult (there are a lot of problems and issues to consider) – with APV we do not need to worry about this because the financing effects are evaluated separately.

Need to know!

NPV and financing — a summary of when we use each of the techniques

The best approach to take can be summarised by using the following table:

	Project does not involve diversification	Project involves diversification into a new business area
Project financing is the same as the company financing	Project NPV using the company WACC as the discount rate	Project NPV using the project WACC as a discount rate
Project financing is different to the company financing	APV technique: • Project NPV @ Ke using the **company asset beta** • Financing effects @ the yield	APV technique: • Project NPV @ Ke using the **project asset beta** • Financing effects @ the yield

Whenever the project financing is different to the company financing APV is the best approach to take. If the project involves diversification the discount rate needs to reflect the risk of the new business area and will therefore be based on the beta of a proxy company.

Chapter 12
key points summary

- Adjusting the beta factor.

  - Weighted average beta - the beta of a company = (beta of 1st division x proportion) + (beta 2nd division x proportion) etc.

  - Asset/Equity beta relationship - $\beta a = \beta e \times \dfrac{Ve}{(Ve + Vd(1\text{-}t)} + \beta d \times \dfrac{Vd\,(1\text{-}t)}{(Ve + Vd(1\text{-}t)}$

    - Asset beta – measures risk of the asset – ignores gearing/financial risk.

    - Equity beta – measures risk of equity – includes gearing/financial risk.

- Project cost of capital.

  - Appropriate where diversification but no change in gearing.

  - Approach:

    - find proxy company for new project

    - 'de-gear' proxy company beta

    - 'gear up' proxy company beta

    - find project cost of equity

    - find project WACC.

- Adjusted present value (APV).

  - Appropriate if project financing is different to company financing.

  - Approach

    - project NPV @ Ke based on asset beta

    - present value of financing effects discounted at yield.

DEBT YIELDS

Introduction
what is this chapter about?

The yield on debt is the return that investors in debt capital require. In this chapter we explore the relationship between the yield and the period of time until the debt matures, and look at alternative ways of determining the yield.

Key areas of the chapter are ....

1   **Yield curve** – This measures the relationship between the yield from debt and the period of time until the debt matures. What factors determine the yield curve and how can the yield curve be used by a finance manager?

2   **Estimating the yield** – what are the alternative methods for determining the yield that the providers of debt require? How can these alternatives be used to estimate a post-tax cost of debt to a company?

YIELD CURVE

A quick reminder about the term 'yield'. This is the term given to the pre-tax return that a provider of debt capital requires. We are therefore looking at the return from the investors' point of view rather than the post-tax cost to a company. An investor may, for example expect to receive a return of 8% when investing in the debt – if so – this is the 'yield' from the debt.

Finance terminology explained

What is the yield curve?

The yield curve measures the relationship between the yield from debt and the period of time until the debt matures. If we take two different blocks of debt capital that are identical in all respects except for the period of time until the debt matures, we find that the yield demanded by investors will be different for each block of debt.

A typical yield curve will be 'upward sloping' as follows:

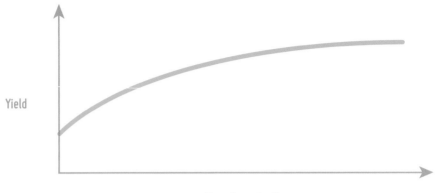

Yield

Term to maturity

The graph is showing us that the longer to maturity the higher the annual yield that an investor would expect to receive. If we take government bonds, for example, a bond maturing in 2 years' time might offer an investor a yield of 4% per annum, whereas the same government bond maturing in 5 years' time might offer an investor a yield of 5% per annum.

What determines the shape of the yield curve?

There are three main factors that determine the shape of the yield curve. They are:

1   Liquidity preference theory

This explains why the yield curve is normally upward sloping. Investors have a preference for 'liquid' investments as opposed to less liquid investments. Liquidity is the ability to convert the investment into cash. The shorter the period of time until the investment matures then the more liquid the investment is. Investors who are prepared to invest in debt which has longer until maturity and is therefore less liquid will require a premium on their return to compensate for this. The longer to maturity the higher the yield.

2   Expectations theory

When investors invest in medium and long term debt, the return, or yield that they will require will take into account the way in which they think short term yields will change in the medium to long term. An investor who invests in debt which matures in 5 years' time, for example, will take into account the expectation of the change in the 1 year yield over the next 5 years.

If the 1 year yield is expected to rise significantly over the next 5 years from the current level, an investor in 5 year debt will require a higher yield than would otherwise be the case to compensate. Similarly if the 1 year yield is expected to fall significantly over the next 5 years from the current level, an investor in 5 year debt will accept a lower yield than would otherwise be the case. The lower 5 year yield would still be at a premium to the expected average short term yield though, to reflect liquidity preference.

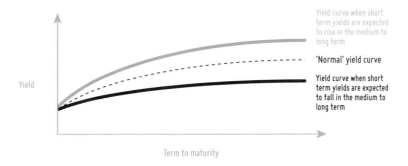

3   Segmented markets theory

This is a very grand term for a very straightforward idea. It simply means that there are different groups of investors who invest in shorter term debt compared to medium and longer term debt. As a result there is a different supply/demand relationship for short term debt compared to long term debt and therefore a different yield will arise on short term debt compared to long term debt. If there is very little demand for short term debt, for example, but a lot of supply, the suppliers of debt (those who want to borrow) will have to offer higher yields to increase demand.

This 'theory' doesn't tell us whether the yield on short term debt is higher or lower than the long term debt – it could be either at any point in time. All that this theory tells us is that there will be a difference between the yields.

How could a finance manager use the yield curve?

There are many potential uses of the yield curve. One possibility would be if a finance manager uses a lot of short term debt finance which is periodically 'rolled over'. Suppose a finance manager uses a 6 month $2 million loan. This is replaced every 6 months by a new loan and the interest is fixed for the 6 month duration of the loan. Every time a new loan is issued the interest rate charged by the provider of the finance will reflect the market rate for short term finance.

If the finance manager saw that a published yield curve was very strongly upward sloping, it would tell the finance manager that (based on the expectations theory) the market expects short term yields to rise in the medium to long term. This may prompt the finance manager to hedge the exposure to potential rises in interest rates by using one of the techniques covered in chapter 22.

ESTIMATING THE YIELD

In chapter 9 we looked at how the yield on debt, or return that an investor in debt requires could be determined. We based the yield on an assumption that the market value of a bond (marketable debt) was equal to the present value of the future cashflows that the investor would receive discounted at the investors required rate of return. From this relationship we could determine the investors required rate of return when the market value of the bond is known.

This is sometimes called the **DVM (dividend valuation model) approach** to determining the yield because it is the same as the approach used to value shares which was also covered in chapter 9. (Note: don't be confused by the fact that it is called the dividend valuation model – think of it simply as a method of valuing a stream of cash flows). For irredeemable bonds we then used a formula to calculate the yield and for redeemable debt we calculated the IRR of the cashflows.

One problem with the DVM approach is that it tells us what the yield would be on marketable bonds, but it **doesn't tell us why** an investor would require that particular yield. We could, for example use the DVM approach to determine that an investor in a particular bond requires a yield of 7% compared to a yield on a risk free investment of say 3% but we will not know why the required yield is 7%.

The reason for different yields on different types of debt capital is, of course risk. This takes us right back to chapter 1 – the greater the level of risk attached to a bond the greater the yield demanded by an investor to compensate for that risk.

Need to know!

Yield and the cost of debt

In chapter 9 we also looked at the relationship between a yield that an investor requires and the post-tax cost of debt to the company.

In general we can say that:

Yield (1-t) = Post-tax cost of debt

Where t = corporate tax rate

If the yield was 10%, for example, and the corporate tax rate was 30%, then the post-tax cost of debt would be 10% x (1-0.30) = 7%.

This relationship isn't perfectly true for all types of debt. Because the redemption value of a redeemable bond is not tax allowable, for example, the post tax cost isn't quite the yield multiplied by (1-t). The relationship is, however, close enough to make it acceptable to use in most situations.

Alternative approaches to determining the yield

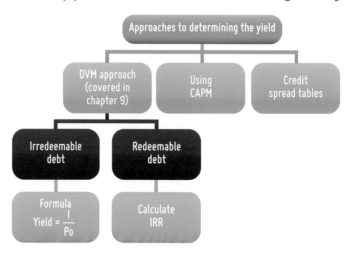

There are two alternatives to using the DVM that we need to consider in this chapter. Let's look at each of these in turn.

Using CAPM to determine the yield

In chapter 11 we saw how the capital asset pricing model could be used to determine the return that investors in equity would require from an investment. We can use the same model to determine the return that an investor in risky debt would require from the investment. To use the model we need to be able to estimate the variables including the beta of the risky debt.

The CAPM formula applied to risky debt is:

Required return = Rf + βd (Rm - Rf)

Where:

Rf = The risk free rate of return

Rm= The return from the market portfolio

βd = The beta factor of the risky debt

Note: the beta of debt will always be low compared to an equity beta. This is because investing in debt is less risky than investing in equity.

Example 1

A company has a marketable bond in issue. The bond has a beta of 0.30, the risk free rate of return is 5% and the return from the market portfolio is 12%.

What is the return required by the investor in this bond?

Solution 1

Rf = 5% or 0.05

Rm= 12% or 0.12

βd = 0.30

Required return = 0.05 + 0.3 (0.12 - 0.05) = 0.0710 or 7.10%

Using credit spread tables to determine the yield

Finance terminology explained

Credit spread

The credit spread is the amount added to a risk free rate for a particular bond to reflect the risk attached to the debt. It is sometimes called the 'default risk premium' because, the risk to an investor in debt is the risk of the borrower defaulting on interest payments or on the repayment of the debt on the redemption date.

Credit rating agencies produce and publish credit spread tables which can be used in conjunction with a knowledge of the risk free rate of return to determine the yield on a particular bond. The tables are based on a measurement of the 'quality' of the bond and the term to maturity.

Different rating agencies categorise the quality of the bond in slightly different ways but they all use similar terminology and a similar approach.

A typical extract from a credit spread table is shown below:

Rating	1 year	2 year	3 year	4 year	5 year
AAA	6	9	14	20	24
AA	12	21	28	34	40
A	36	48	60	82	96
BBB	66	89	104	132	156
BB	102	128	156	194	232

The table shows the default risk premium in basis points. 1 basis point is equal to 0.01%.

The rating shows the 'quality' of the bond. Triple 'A' rated bonds are the best quality and the risk of the borrower defaulting on these bonds is very low. As the rating falls the risk of default rises. The yield curve also has an impact – the longer the term to maturity the higher the yield.

How are the tables used?

The table tells us the default risk premium, or the amount that needs to be added to the relevant risk free rate of return to determine the yield, or investors required return.

Required return = Risk free rate + default risk premium.

Example 2

Using the tables shown above, determine the yield that an investor would require on BBB rated bonds with 4 years to maturity. The risk free rate for 4 year debt is 4%.

If the corporate tax rate is 30% what would the post-tax cost of debt be for these bonds?

Solution 2

From the tables the relevant default risk premium is 132 basis points (the intersection of the BBB row and the 4 year column). This is 1.32%.

The yield required by the investor would therefore be (4% + 1.32%) = 5.32%

The post-tax cost of debt can therefore be estimated at 5.32% (1 - 0.30) = 3.72%

Chapter 13
key points summary

- Yield curve.

  - Relationship between the yield and the term to maturity.

  - Three factors influence the yield curve.

  - Liquidity preference theory – the longer to maturity the less liquid the investment therefore the higher the yield demanded by investors.

  - Expectations theory – interest rates expected to rise – more strongly upward sloping yield curve.

  - Market segmentation theory – different investors for long and short term debt.

- Estimating the yield.

  - Use DVM approach (see chapter 9).

  - CAPM – yield is found by using CAPM equation.

  - Use credit spread tables.

- Post tax cost of debt = yield (1-t).

MARKET EFFICIENCY

Introduction
what is this chapter about?

In chapter 8 we considered how companies can raise long term finance. We saw how important the role of the capital markets were in this process. In order to issue share capital, or issue bonds, a company needs to be listed on a stock market.

In this chapter we explore how efficient a stock market is at communicating information to investors, and the significance to both investors and companies of different levels of efficiency.

Key areas of the chapter are ....

1 **Market efficiency** – how efficient are stock markets at communicating information about a company into the share price?

2 **Implications for analysts of market efficiency** – what are the implications for analysts and financial managers of different degrees of efficiency?

MARKET EFFICIENCY

Finance terminology explained

What is market efficiency?

An efficient capital market is one in which the share price, at any given time, fully and accurately reflects the available relevant information.

Investors buy and sell shares on a stock market. The market price of a share is determined by supply and demand. If demand for shares in a particular company increases but the supply of shares stays the same, investors will be prepared to pay more for those shares and hence the share price will rise. Conversely if the demand falls but supply stays the same, this will lead to an oversupply of shares and hence the share price will fall.

Through this process new information about a company is reflected in the share price. If, investors, for example, become aware of new information about a company that indicates that future dividends are likely to be a lot higher than previously forecast, this is likely to increase demand for the share and result in a rise in the share price. The share price will therefore reflect this new information.

In an efficient market, any information that is relevant to the company, and is available to investors, would be fully and accurately reflected in the share price.

The level of efficiency of any particular stock market has a significant impact on a number of aspects of finance. Analysts often, for example, refer to shares as being undervalued (and therefore a good 'buy') or overvalued (time to sell). In an efficient market any shares quoted on the market should always be 'correctly' priced.

Efficient market hypothesis

The efficient market hypothesis defines market efficiency at three different levels. In other words, if we assume that a capital market is efficient at communicating information into the share price, this theory suggests that there are three different levels, or speeds at which that information is reflected in the share price.

They are:

1   weak form efficient
2   semi-strong form efficient
3   strong form efficient.

Finance terminology explained

Weak form efficient

The weak form of the efficient market hypothesis states that the current share price fully and accurately reflects all information contained in past share price movements.

The best way to think of this statement is that in this type of market the share price at any given time always reflects relevant information, but that the information sometimes takes a little bit of time following a public announcement to be reflected in the share price.

Suppose that the directors of a manufacturing company discover a major fault with one of their products which will mean that a product recall is necessary. The product recall is likely to result in a fall in sales and profit over the next three years.

An announcement of the product recall is likely to reduce demand for the share and result in a fall in the share price. In a weak form efficient market, however, the response to the announcement is quite slow. It will take some time for the share price to settle at a new level, although, after a period of time, the share price will fully reflect the impact of this information.

Finance terminology explained

Semi-strong form efficient

The semi-strong form of the efficient market hypothesis states that the current share price fully and accurately reflects all publicly available information.

The difference between the weak form and semi-strong form market is really the speed, following a public announcement, with which information about a company is reflected in the share price.

Let's take the example of the product recall that we saw above. In a semi-strong form, efficient market investors will instantly absorb the new information, demand will instantly change and the share price will fall to a new level. The share price will therefore instantly respond to the public announcement.

Finance terminology explained

Strong form efficient

In a strong form efficient market the share price reflects all information about a company, whether this is publicly available or not.

In this type of market, as soon as the directors themselves become aware of the product recall the share price will change to fully and accurately reflect this information.

In a strong form efficient market there is, in essence no such thing as non-private information – all information is assumed to be in the public domain.

The three levels of efficiency – summary

The three levels of efficiency really build upon each other. In other words, if a market is semi-strong form it must also be weak form, and if a market is strong form it must also be semi-strong and weak form. A market that, for example, perfectly and accurately reflects all information about a company must, by definition, reflect all publicly available information about a company.

Random walk

If a market is efficient, of any type, even if just weak form, share prices are said to follow a random walk. This means that if we were to study past share price movements for a company, for example Marks and Spencer, the movement would be totally random in an efficient market.

If a share price perfectly and accurately reflects information about a company, that information will be randomly good or bad. It therefore follows that the share price movement will be random. This means that in an efficient market we will not see any trends or patterns that repeat – if we do think that there is a trend or a pattern – then that is not a real trend or pattern – it is just our imagination!

IMPLICATIONS FOR ANALYSTS OF MARKET EFFICIENCY

Types of analyst

Analysts spend significant time and effort studying past share price movements and information about a company in order to predict future share price movements and recommend whether to buy, sell, or hold shares.

What approach do analysts take?

There are two main approaches:

- chartist approach and

- fundamental analysis.

Chartist approach

A chartist (sometimes called a technical analyst) is a type of analyst who looks for trends and patterns in past share price movements and expect these to repeat in the future. There are many patterns or trends that are looked for. An example is a 'head and shoulders' pattern shown below.

This type of chart is explained by investor behavior in an imperfect world. If for example, a share appears to be on a rising trend, as is the case in weeks 1 and 2, when the share price reaches a certain level (e.g. 250p) that may act as a 'trigger' for some investors to take the profit that they have made. The share prices dips as these investors' cash in. The share the quickly resumes the rising trend. By then end of week 4, there may be a perception in the market that the share price has peaked, in which case a lot of investors will seek to sell their shares at this peak. The share price drops very suddenly because of excess supply, but then bounces back up as the market corrects.

If an analyst can see the beginning of the repetition of this pattern it enables the analyst to predict future share price movements.

Need to know!

Market efficiency and chartist analysis

If a stock market is efficient then the share price, as explained earlier, follows a random walk. The implication of this is that repetitive patterns do not exist – share price movements are always random. An analyst taking a chartist approach would not, in an efficient market be able to make any statistically significant gains.

Fundamental analysis

Analysts who use fundamental analysis to predict share price movements seek to obtain as much information as they possibly can about a company, and then value the shares using a model such as the DVM (dividend valuation model) on the basis of this information.

The success of this approach depends on the type of efficiency that exists in the market.

Need to know!

Weak form market

In a weak form market, the share price reacts slowly to new information that is publicly announced. In such a market any analyst who obtains publicly available information quickly has an opportunity to beat the market.

Need to know!

Semi-strong form market

In a semi-strong form market all publicly available information is reflected in the share price. The only way for an analyst to beat the market would be to aim to get hold of non-publicly available information e.g. through insider trading! As this is illegal – there would clearly be severe consequences of aiming to do this!

Need to know!

Strong form market

In this case, as the share price reflects all information about a company it would not be possible to beat the market through seeking to obtain and use information.

Real life illustration – insider trading

Ivan Boesky was a Wall Street analyst, who ran his own arbitrage firm between 1975 and the mid 1980s. He looked for companies that were potential takeover targets. He would then buy shares in those companies just before a public announcement of the takeover. As soon as the announcement was made he would then sell the shares for a profit.

Boesky was incredibly successful with this strategy and built up a multi- billion dollar business. A significant part of the success, however, was a result of insider trading. Boesky would pay significant amounts to contacts within companies for advanced information about imminent takeovers.

In 1986 he was convicted of insider trading. As a result of his actions Congress passed the Insider Trading Act of 1988 which increased penalties for insider trading and provided incentives and rewards to whistle-blowers.

Boesky's actions were only possible because the stock market was not strong form efficient.

How efficient are established stock markets in the real world?

Most research indicates that established stock markets are, on the whole, efficient at communicating information about a company into the share price, and that, in terms of the level of efficiency, they most closely resemble semi-strong form.

The implications of this are:

1   there is little long term benefit from seeking to analyse trends in share price movements using charts

2   share prices are unlikely to be significantly over or under priced by the market. The current share price should, reasonably accurately, reflect publicly available information about that company at the time

3   it is possible to beat the market consistently but only through obtaining non-publicly available information i.e. insider trading

4   directors of companies will often have access to important information that has not yet been made public. Directors need to exercise great care in deciding how and when this information is to be made public because of the impact that the public announcement will have on the share price and on shareholder wealth.

Finance terminology explained

Information asymmetry

When directors or managers in a company have access to information that has not yet been made public this is known as information asymmetry. Whenever information asymmetry arises there is always a risk that managers can manipulate a share price.

Chapter 14
key points summary

- What is market efficiency?

    - The share price fully and accurately reflects information about a company.

    - Share prices follow a random walk.

- Types of efficiency:

    - weak form – past information reflected in the share price

    - semi-strong form – share price reflects all publicly available information

    - strong form – share price reflects all information whether publicly available or not.

- Implications for analysts of market efficiency.

    - In a weak form market analysts can gain by using publicly available or non-publicly available information.

    - In a semi-strong form market analysts can gain by using non-publicly available information.

    - In a strong form market – analysts cannot beat the market.

DIVIDEND POLICY

Introduction
what is this chapter about?

When a company generates profits, or earnings, a key decision for the board to make is how much of the profit should be distributed to shareholders as a dividend, and how much should be retained and reinvested within the company. This chapter explores the factors that need to be taken into account when making that decision, and also explores common dividend policies in practice.

Key areas of the chapter are ....

1 **Dividend policy and shareholder wealth** – how does dividend policy influence shareholder wealth?

2 **Dividend policy in the real world** – how do companies in the real world decide on the level of dividends to pay out?

3 **Scrip dividends and share buybacks** – what are the alternatives to paying a cash dividend?

DIVIDEND POLICY AND SHAREHOLDER WEALTH

How does dividend policy influence shareholder wealth?

Shareholder wealth – we have already seen in earlier chapters how important it is to consider shareholder wealth when making finance decisions. Dividend policy is no exception. The key question to ask when assessing dividend policy is therefore – how does dividend policy influence shareholder wealth?

Shareholders should, at least in theory, benefit to some extent whatever decision is made. If dividends are paid out to shareholders they could reinvest those dividends elsewhere. If dividends are not paid out, but instead earnings are retained and reinvested (wisely) this should lead to growth in future earnings, and therefore dividends.

Exam tip – Dividend policy and shareholder wealth

A common error made by students, when discussing dividend policy is to state that shareholders will not benefit unless the profits are distributed as a dividend.

Always make the point that shareholders should benefit whether profits are paid out as a dividend, or retained and reinvested. The key question is which policy will benefit the shareholders the most?

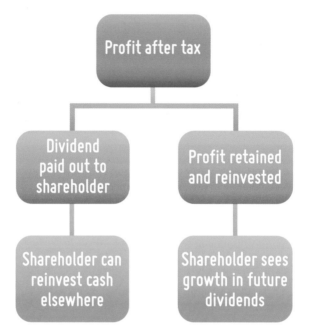

If shareholders benefit either way can we draw any conclusions about which has the greater effect on shareholder wealth – paying profits (or earnings) out as a dividend or retaining and reinvesting those profits?

Modigliani and Miller's hypothesis (or theory)

Modigliani and Miller (M&M) suggested that, in a perfect capital market, dividend policy becomes irrelevant.

Need to know!

According to Modigliani and Miller – in a perfect capital market (this is defined later in the chapter) shareholder wealth is unaffected by the dividend decision i.e. shareholder wealth is the same whether earnings are paid out as dividends, or, alternatively, earnings are retained and reinvested within the company.

How does this theory work?

1   Suppose a company is all equity financed and the shareholders required rate of return (or cost of equity) is 15%. If **positive NPV projects** are available at a 15% discount rate then the company **should retain and reinvest earnings** in these projects. The return from reinvesting earnings will be greater than the return that shareholders could get elsewhere for the same level of risk.

2   In a perfect capital market, because of arbitrage, other companies would be attracted to set up similar projects to those that have a positive NPV. This would reduce the value of those projects and, eventually, **only nil NPV projects** at best would be available.

3   At this point **dividend policy becomes irrelevant to shareholder wealth**.

   a.   Suppose a company generates profits after tax of say $1m in an accounting period. This could be paid out to shareholders as a dividend or, alternatively, the company could retain and reinvest $1m in a nil NPV project.

   b.   If the project has a nil NPV the present value of the future cash inflows must be equal to the amount retained and reinvested in the project i.e. $1m. In theory the company's value should equal the present value of its future cashflows (we will see this in more detail in a later chapter), and therefore the company's value should rise by $1m – exactly the same amount as the dividend foregone.

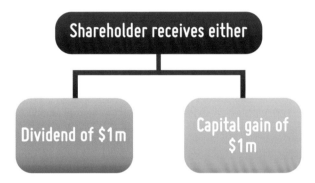

4   The shareholder could therefore either receive a dividend of $1m or make a capital gain of exactly the same amount. If earnings are retained and reinvested rather than paid out as a dividend, and an investor wants cash, the investor could sell some of the higher value shares to 'simulate' a dividend.

5   Of course, this doesn't happen in the real world because M&M's assumptions about a perfect capital market do not hold true.

What assumptions underlie M&M's dividend theory?

A perfect capital market, which underlies M&M's theory, is based on the following assumptions:

Assumptions	Meaning & significance
All investors have equal access to the same information.	One investor would not be able to obtain 'better' information than another investor and therefore benefit at the expense of other investors.
All investors act rationally.	If an investor could make a gain without any risk by doing something then we can assume that the investor would always do this.
Taxation is ignored.	If there are different tax implications for dividends and capital gains this will affect the investors 'indifference' between receiving a dividend and a capital gain.
No transaction costs or stockbrokers fees.	Any fees charged for buying and selling shares would mean that an investor selling shares to obtain cash would not get quite as much as the dividend foregone.
Dividend decisions are not used to convey information.	Shareholders will not 'read' into the dividend anything 'wider' about the company's future prospects.

DIVIDEND POLICY IN PRACTICE

Why does dividend policy influence shareholder wealth in the real world?

Research suggests that in the real world dividend policy can and does have a significant impact on shareholder wealth. There are a number of reasons for this, some of which are based on areas where Modigliani and Miller's assumptions do not hold true. The main reasons are:

1   Dividend signalling

Shareholders tend to see the dividend declared by a company as a 'signal' or indication of how well a company is doing and of how much confidence the managers in the company have about its future prospects. If a dividend is cut, shareholders tend to see this as an indication of problems e.g. lack of cashflow. As a result a cut in a dividend, for whatever reason, often leads to a drop in the share price of a company.

2   Clientele 'effect'

Shareholders may well have invested in the company in the past partly because of the dividend policy that the company had adopted.

A company, for example, that has consistently retained a high proportion of its earnings is likely to have shareholders who were seeking high share price growth rather than significant cash dividends. If the company suddenly changed its dividend policy, the current shareholders may decide to sell their shares and the share price may fall.

The current shareholders are the 'clientele' of the company. They are likely, therefore, to be unhappy with any deviation away from the current dividend policy.

3   **Taxation**

Modigliani and Miller ignored taxation. In reality tax implications of dividends and capital gains for both individual investors and institutions, like pensions funds, will have a significant impact on their preference for a dividend or a capital gain.

4   **Agency theory**

The board of directors will make the dividend decision. This decision should be based on the directors' perception of what is best for the shareholders of the company (agency theory). In reality, the decision may be based on their own personal interests.

Managers in a manufacturing business may, for example, feel that the best policy for long term shareholder wealth might be to retain earnings and use the funds to finance major new investment in research and development needed for long term growth. They may, however, decide to increase the dividend instead, despite the long term consequences, because of a fear that shareholders will remove the board if dividends are not increased.

5   **Cash and profit**

Modigliani and Miller's theory assumes that all of the profit could be distributed as a dividend, or alternatively retained and reinvested within the company.

In practice there may be very significant differences between the levels of profit and the amount of cash that is generated. A company may, therefore, face significant liquidity problems if it seeks to pay out more than a certain proportion of its profits as a dividend.

Common dividend policies

Ok – if we now accept that, in the real world, dividend policy does have an influence on shareholder wealth then what are the more common dividend policies pursued by companies in the real world?

1   **Constant dividend or constant growth in dividends**

The **most common dividend** policy is to increase the dividend by a predictable amount each year e.g. 5%. Ideally this increase will be above the rate of inflation so that shareholders see a real increase in the dividends that they receive from year to year.

Real life illustration – Tesco

Over a 10 year period, between 2000 and 2010, Tesco increased its dividend by an average of 11.32% a year - an impressive performance!

What is also notable about Tesco's dividend history is how consistent the growth rate has been from year to year. The lowest rate of growth was 9.1% (in 2010) whilst the highest was 14.5% (in 2006).

This type of policy leads to **share price stability** as investors can predict future dividend income more accurately, and with more certainty i.e. there is less risk to shareholders.

The initial dividend paid should be set well below the earnings level to allow dividends to grow significantly whilst at the same time ensuring that there is significant retention and reinvestment of earnings.

A major difficulty with this type of policy is that companies may **struggle to maintain growth** in dividends when earnings are flat, or are falling, and may be forced into a change of policy. If they do seek to maintain the dividend growth rate when earnings are flat, this could create significant liquidity problems and may also result in a significant reduction in long term investment which would impact on future growth rates.

2   Constant payout ratio

An alternative to constant dividends or constant growth in dividends would be for companies to **pay a constant percentage of earnings out as a dividend,** for example, approximately 40% of earnings are paid out as a dividend each year.

This policy has the advantage of ensuring that the company continues to retain earnings, and hence reinvest in the business, even if earnings fall. It overcomes the difficulties created when companies seek to pay an unrealistically high dividend in order to maintain a growth trend in dividends.

A major problem with this type of policy is that as earnings can be quite volatile, **dividends may also be quite volatile**, and difficult to predict, which may have an adverse effect on the share price.

3   Residual dividend

In this case a company **pays a dividend** to shareholders **only if the earnings cannot be reinvested** in positive NPV projects within the company.

The major benefit of this type of policy is that the company is able to take advantage of good investment opportunities, and finance these in the simplest way possible (retained earnings). The company is in theory acting in the best interests of their shareholders by doing this i.e. providing them with a return which is greater than the return that they could get elsewhere themselves.

This type of policy could only work in the real world if the shareholders (clientele) are looking for high share price growth rather than dividend income.

SCRIP DIVIDEND AND SHARE BUY-BACK

Finance terminology explained

Scrip or bonus dividend

This is an alternative to a cash dividend. In this case a dividend is 'declared' by the company but instead of being paid out to shareholders as cash the dividend is 'converted' into share capital and share premium. This is in essence exactly the same as a dividend paid followed immediately afterwards by a rights issue.

The advantage of this is that it gives the 'impression' that a dividend is being paid out (which is important if a trend such as the Tesco dividends above is being analysed) whilst at the same time retaining the cash within the company (and therefore avoiding liquidity problems).

The double entry (so that accountants feel at home!) would be:

Dr Dividend   X

Cr Share capital/share premium   X

Finance terminology explained

Share buy-back

A share buy-back is an alternative way of returning cash to shareholders to paying a cash dividend. If a company has built up significant earnings and cash that it does not wish to invest in projects it could return this cash to shareholders by declaring and paying a very significant one-off dividend. This would, however, disturb the normal pattern of dividends.

A more sensible way of returning the cash to shareholders would be to 'buy back' some of the share capital.

The double entry for this would be:

Dr Share capital/reserves   X

Cr Cash   X

An individual shareholder would own the same proportion of the company before and after the buy-back (the shares would be bought back in proportion to the original shareholding). The effect on the investors' wealth is therefore exactly the same as if a dividend had been paid.

Students often confuse a scrip dividend with a share buy-back. They are very different.

Need to know!

A scrip dividend means that cash is retained within the company whereas a share buy-back means that cash is returned to shareholders. Both are an alternative to a cash dividend but they have quite different impacts on a business.

Chapter 15
key points summary

- Modigliani and Miller's theory:

    – earnings should be retained and reinvested in positive NPV projects

    – if only nil NPV projects available shareholder wealth is the same whether earnings paid out as a dividend or retained and reinvested

    – based on perfect market assumption.

- Dividend policy in the real world influenced by:

    – signalling effect

    – clientele effect

    – taxation

    – agency theory

    – cash and profit.

- Common dividend policies:

    – constant dividend or constant growth in dividends

    – constant payout ratio

    – residual dividend.

"What are long term investments?
They are short term investments gone
wrong!"

Anon

WORKING CAPITAL MANAGEMENT

16

GENERAL WORKING CAPITAL MANAGEMENT

Introduction
what is this chapter about?

A certain level of working capital, or net current assets, is needed by all businesses to survive and prosper. A business therefore needs to invest in working capital in the same way as it would invest in non-current assets. In this chapter we consider how a business decides on the level of working capital investment needed, and also on how that investment should be financed.

Key areas of the chapter are ....

1   **Working capital investment** – what is working capital, and how does a finance manager make a decision about the level of working capital investment needed?

2   **Cash operating cycle** – this is an important series of ratios that is often used to measure the efficiency of working capital management. What is the cash operating cycle and what does a change in the length of this cycle tell us?

3   **Working capital financing** – after deciding on the level of working capital needed a finance manager will then need to consider how this working capital should be financed. Would it be better to finance the working capital needed by using long term or short term finance?

WORKING CAPITAL INVESTMENT

OK - before we can consider how much a business should invest in working capital we need to define the term.

Finance terminology explained

What is working capital?

There are a number of different definitions of working capital (just to confuse matters) but the most widely accepted is that it represents current assets less current liabilities. Current assets include cash, inventory, receivables, short term investments and prepayments. Current liabilities include payables, short term bank loans and overdrafts.

An alternative term for working capital is therefore net current assets.

Need to know!

Working capital = Net current assets

What is working capital management?

This refers to the process within the business of managing the elements that make up working capital, and managing working capital as a whole. A decision by managers to, for example, operate a just-in-time policy for inventory management, may reduce the average level of inventory within the business, and as a result reduce the overall level of working capital, or the overall net current assets.

The status of short term bank loans and overdrafts

When discussing policies for the management of working capital, or how working capital should be financed, a point of confusion is how to treat short term bank loans and overdrafts.

Short term bank loans and overdrafts are current liabilities. In the standard definition (used in accounting) of working capital they are netted off against current assets (alongside other current liabilities) to give us the net working capital figure. Short term bank loans and overdrafts are also, however, a way of financing current assets – an increase in inventory could, for example, be financed by increasing a bank overdraft.

When making decisions about working capital levels, and how these should be financed, this anomaly needs to be resolved.

The normal approach adopted for financial management is to consider **short term loans and overdrafts as a means of financing working capital** rather than part of working capital itself.

Often, therefore, when analysing working capital, the standard definition of net current assets that we saw above is amended to exclude short term loans and overdrafts.

A Statement of Financial Position is often effectively rearranged and analysed in this way in order to analyse working capital levels, and the way in which an investment in working capital should be financed:

	$'000	$'000
Non-current assets		120
Inventory	40	
Receivables	30	
Cash	20	
Payables	(35)	
Net current assets/working capital		**55**
Total		175
Share capital		50
Retained earnings		35
Long term liabilities		60
Short term bank loans and overdraft		30
Total		175

Net current assets (working capital)

Equity financing

Long term debt financing

short term debt financing

Exam tip – What does an examiner mean by net current assets?

In answering an exam question on working capital management, or working capital financing, it is essential to be absolutely clear about what an examiner means when referring to working capital or net current assets. Does this include or exclude short term bank loans and an overdraft? Different examiners will approach this in different ways therefore a careful reading of the question information is essential.

How much should a business invest in working capital?

Working capital is necessary for a company to continue in business. The ideal amount, or level, of working capital will vary considerably from business to business and will depend on many factors including:

- **The nature of the industry**. Manufacturing and heavy industrial companies will require significantly more working capital than companies involved in retailing, or service based industries. A large manufacturing company, for example, a car manufacturer, will typically have a long production cycle with significant amounts of raw material, work-in-progress and finished goods, hence a high level of inventory. It will probably also offer a long credit period to customers and will therefore have a significant level of receivables as well. A retailer on the other hand will turn over inventory quickly and sales will often be mainly cash sales, resulting in much lower levels of inventory and receivables.

- **Growth level**. Fast growing companies will typically require significantly more working capital that slower growth companies. The faster the rate of growth the more inventory and receivables will be needed to sustain that growth.

- **Credit periods offered and taken**. The credit period that a business needs to offer to customers to generate the required level of sales will dictate the level of receivables. If competitors increase the credit period offered to customers a business may feel compelled to do the same to maintain market share. Similarly, the ability of a business to take credit from suppliers will dictate the level of payables.

- **Access to cash**. A business with an ability to access cash quickly, perhaps because it turns over a significant amount of cash on a daily basis (for example a supermarket) or because it has significant overdraft facilities, could generally operate with a lower level of working capital than a business that does not have the same access to cash.

Profitability and liquidity

When considering how much working capital is needed for a particular business, the two most important factors to take into account are the impact that the level of working capital will have on profitability, and the impact that it will have on liquidity.

Impact on profitability

In general a **lower level** of working capital is likely to **improve profitability**. This is because of the need to finance working capital. If, for example a manufacturing company was able to reduce its inventory levels through more efficient inventory management, and reduce receivables through implementing a more efficient receivables management system, the major benefit of this is that it could reduce its financing levels, and hence its' financing costs. A reduction in average working capital of $1 million, could, for example, result in a reduction in a short term bank loan of $1 million. If interest was payable at 8% per annum this would result in an interest saving of $1 million x 8% = $80,000 per annum before tax.

Unfortunately the relationship between working capital levels and profitability is not always as simple as this (if only it was!).

- If a business reduces the credit period offered to customers in order to reduce the level of receivables and hence the level of working capital, this could result in a significant loss of sales. The loss of sales revenue may outweigh the finance cost savings and hence profitability may fall.

- If a manufacturing business seeks to hold less finished goods to reduce the level of inventory and hence the level of working capital, the business may not be able to meet a sudden increase in demand for a product and hence may lose sales.

Impact on liquidity

Liquidity is a company's ability to meet its' cash obligations. In general a **higher level** of working capital is likely to **improve liquidity**. This is because the more working capital a business has the less likely it is to face liquidity problems such as an inability to pay suppliers or employees. All current assets can, in theory, be turned into cash in a short time frame, and therefore the higher the level of working capital the more liquid a business is felt to be.

As with profitability, however, the relationship between the level of working capital and liquidity is not as simple as this.

- The mix between the elements of working capital has a big impact on liquidity. One business may have a high level of working capital but a very significant part of this may be inventory rather than cash. Another business in the same industry may have a lower overall level of working capital but higher levels of cash and receivables. Despite having a lower level of working capital this business may be considered to be more liquid.

- The access to cash at short notice also has a big influence on liquidity. A business with a very low level of working capital but with a significant unused overdraft facility may be considered to be very liquid.

There is not, therefore, a simple relationship between the level of working capital and liquidity and profitability. In an exam you should be prepared to discuss the relationship in a sensible way.

Overtrading

This is a term that is often used when discussing working capital – so what does it mean?

The term refers to a situation where a growing business, often with healthy profitability, does not have sufficient finance or capital to fund the increase in working capital that is needed. The result is that the business may not be able to pay its payables on time, or it may run out of inventory, or may face other serious liquidity problems which may threaten the ability of the business to continue.

Overtrading often arises in businesses that are expanding and growing too quickly, or where there is a failure to plan and manage its working capital levels or to raise sufficient long term finance or capital.

CASH OPERATING CYCLE

The operating cycle is a useful tool to analyse how efficiently working capital is being managed.

Finance terminology explained

What is the cash operating cycle?

For a business this is the length of time taken between paying for raw materials and receiving the cash from the sale of the related finished goods.

The length of the cash operating cycle is therefore a measurement of how quickly cash spent on raw materials can be recovered by the business when the finished goods that are produced are eventually sold.

The operating cycle can be measured in days, weeks or months. It is most commonly measured in days.

How can the cash operating cycle be measured?

It is measured by calculating a series of ratios. The process is different when measuring the cycle for a manufacturing company compared to a retail or wholesale company because of the different stages of inventory in a manufacturing company.

Need to know!

Operating cycle for a manufacturing company

The cycle is normally measured in the following way:

		Days
Raw material days	$\dfrac{\text{Average raw material inventory}}{\text{Credit purchases}} \times 365 =$	X
Work-in-progress (WIP) days	$\dfrac{\text{Average WIP inventory}}{\text{Cost of sales}} \times 365 =$	X
Finished goods days	$\dfrac{\text{Average finished goods inventory}}{\text{Cost of sales}} \times 365 =$	X
Receivables days	$\dfrac{\text{Average receivables}}{\text{Credit sales}} \times 365 =$	X
Less - Payables days	$\dfrac{\text{Average payables}}{\text{Credit purchases}} \times 365 =$	(X)
Length of operating cycle		**X**

A few points to note

- Each element of the cycle measures the relevant length of time. The raw materials days, for example, measures how many days' worth of raw material is in inventory at any point in time. This is also, therefore, the number of days, on average, that each unit of raw material takes to pass through this phase of the manufacturing process.

- The relevant days are added together, except for the payables days which are deducted. This is because the **payables days reduce the cash operating cycle** – in other words, the longer a business takes to pay its payables the better in terms of cashflow (although this creates other problems as we will see in chapter 18).

- If the operating cycle is measured in weeks, each ratio is multiplied by 52 instead of 365. If measured in months each ratio is multiplied by 12 instead of 365.

- Strictly the ratios should be based on average asset amounts as shown (for example average raw material, average WIP etc.) but often year end asset amounts, from a published set of accounts, are used instead.

Operating cycle for a retail or wholesale company

The cycle is measured as follows:

		Days
Inventory days	$\dfrac{\text{Average inventory}}{\text{Cost of sales}} \times 365 =$	X
Receivables days	$\dfrac{\text{Average receivables}}{\text{Credit sales}} \times 365 =$	X
Less - Payables days	$\dfrac{\text{Average payables}}{\text{Credit purchases}} \times 365 =$	(X)
Length of operating cycle		X

The difference in a retail or wholesale business is that there is only one type of inventory – goods are bought by a retailer or wholesaler and then sold – they are not converted from one format into another.

Note on the measurement of the cycle — modern approach!

Traditionally the cash operating cycle has been measured by using credit sales for the receivables days and credit purchases for the payables days as outlined above, and the vast majority of text books on the subject follow this approach. There is, however, a strong argument (which is a relatively modern approach) for using total sales instead of credit sales and total purchases instead of credit purchases. If the focus of the cycle is on how quickly cash is generated it could be argued that cash sales and cash purchases are relevant when we consider the average length of time that it takes for cash to be generated.

Exam tip - Operating cycle

Make sure that you read the question carefully to determine how the examiner wants receivables days and payables days to be calculated – are they based on credit sales and purchases or total sales and purchases?. If the question doesn't state how this is calculated you could take either approach – but state your assumptions.

Interpreting the results of a cash operating cycle calculation

The cash operating cycle is a series of ratios. Like all ratios they need to be analysed on a **comparative** basis. Measuring the length of the cycle for one company, for one year, does not provide a finance manager with a lot of information. Comparing the change in the cycle from one year to the next does, however, allow managers to focus on the areas where the business is becoming more or less efficient at managing working capital.

The alternative comparison could be with other companies in the same industry or with an industry average. The length of the cycle will vary significantly from industry to industry but benchmarking the company against competitors in the same industry provides a manager with useful information.

Whilst the cash operating cycle focuses on the speed with which cash is turned over within the business, by looking at this cycle a manager also obtains useful information about the management of inventory, payables and receivables.

Example 1

The following information is available for a manufacturing company, Sion, for the last two years.

Extracts from the Statement of Financial Position:

	20X2	20X1
Raw materials inventory	200,000	160,000
WIP inventory	330,000	220,000
Finished goods inventory	340,000	350,000
Receivables	600,000	620,000
Payables	500,000	320,000

Extracts from the Income Statement:

		20X2		20X1
Revenue		2,800,000		2,700,000
Cost of sales:				
Opening inventory	730,000		700,000	
Purchases	2,000,000		1,900,000	
Closing inventory	(870,000)		(730,000)	
		(1,860,000)		(1,870,000)
Gross profit		940,000		830,000

Requirement

Determine the length of the cash operating cycle for 20X1 and 20X2.

The operating cycle for each of the two years can be determined as follows (based upon year end balances rather than averages):

	20X2 Days			20X1 Days	
Raw material days	$\dfrac{200,000}{2,000,000}$ × 365 =	37	$\dfrac{160,000}{1,900,000}$ × 365 =	31
Work-in-progress (WIP) days	$\dfrac{330,000}{1,860,000}$ × 365 =	65	$\dfrac{220,000}{1,870,000}$ × 365 =	43
Finished goods days	$\dfrac{340,000}{1,860,000}$ × 365 =	67	$\dfrac{350,000}{1,870,000}$ × 365 =	68
Receivables days	$\dfrac{600,000}{2,800,000}$ × 365 =	78	$\dfrac{620,000}{2,700,000}$ × 365 =	84
Less – Payables days	$\dfrac{500,000}{2,000,000}$ × 365 =	(91)	$\dfrac{320,000}{1,900,000}$ × 365 =	(61)
Length of operating cycle		**156**		**165**

In this example we were only asked to calculate the length of the cycle – which we have done. What if we were asked to comment on the changes that we see? Well – these are the types of points that could be made.

- The cash operating cycle has fallen by 9 days between 20X1 and 20X2. This indicates an improvement in the speed with which cash is recycled within the business.

- The WIP days has, however, increased significantly from 43 to 65 days. This may indicate a problem in the management of WIP, or in the management of the production process within the business. This would need to be investigated and the reasons for the change ascertained.

- The payables days has also increased significantly from 61 to 91 days. This increase has counterbalanced the increase in WIP days and is the reason why the overall cash operating cycle has fallen. This significant rise in payables days may be a result of suppliers offering more generous credit terms, or, alternatively, it may be that the company is delaying payment to payables because of cashflow issues. As with WIP, the reasons for the change need to be investigated.

FINANCING WORKING CAPITAL

When a business has decided on the level of working capital needed it then needs to consider how this working capital should be financed.

In assessing how to finance working capital – to recap – we consider working capital, or net current assets, to comprise the net of inventory, receivables and payables. Bank overdrafts or term loans (short, medium long term) are considered to be ways of financing the working capital.

Types of net current assets

To analyse the financing of working capital in more detail we will classify the net current assets into two different types.

Permanent net current assets

This is the minimum level of net current assets that the business is likely to need to continue to operate. At no point in the business cycle is the level of net current assets likely to fall below this.

Given that current assets are by definition – current! – that is – they are expected to be recovered within the current business cycle (normally 12 months) – how can they be permanent?

Of course, each individual receivable is expected to be recovered (meaning that we recover the cash) in the business cycle and each unit of inventory is expected to be sold within the cycle but they will always be replaced by new receivables or inventory. The has the effect of creating a minimum level of current assets – that is, a level that we never expect the current assets to fall below – this is the permanent level of net current assets.

Fluctuating net current assets

In many businesses, for example seasonal businesses, the level of working capital will fluctuate between the minimum (the permanent net current assets) and maximum levels. A games manufacturer, for example, may build up significant levels of inventory in the run up to Christmas, but once these are distributed to retailers the inventory levels will fall back to their minimum levels. This is the fluctuating element of net current assets.

How should working capital be financed?

The choice is between using long term financing (such as a bank loan) and short term financing (such as a bank overdraft). As with many decisions in finance – this decision is based on an analysis of risk and reward (you may have noticed that we always seem to go back to risk and reward! – in fact – if you are struggling for points in any financial management exam it is worth thinking – could I generate any extra points by considering risk and reward?).

The key points to consider are as follows.

- **Finance cost** – the finance cost of long term financing tends to be greater than the finance cost of short term financing. The interest rate payable on a bank loan, for example, is typically greater than the interest rate payable on a bank overdraft. This was covered in chapter 13 when we looked at the yield curve. The longer to maturity the greater the return that the investor will demand.

- **Flexibility** – short term financing offers greater flexibility than long term finance. Overdraft financing of working capital means that the finance needs can be increased or decreased in line with changes in working capital needs. This flexibility is not available for long term financing.

- **Risk** – short term financing is more risky than long term financing. An overdraft, for example, is repayable on demand. A bank could therefore demand repayment of an overdraft at short notice creating serious liquidity problems for the company. A bank term loan will only need to be repaid at the end of the term.

Need to know!

In general – short term financing carries greater risk (repayable on demand) but greater reward (lower cost and greater flexibility).

Working capital financing policies

There are three possible approaches to financing working capital or net current assets which are as follows:

Moderate (or matching) financing policy

In this case the aim is to finance permanent net current assets through long term finance and fluctuating net current assets through short term finance as shown below.

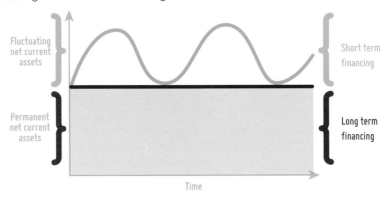

This policy is a balance between risk and reward. Short term financing is used for fluctuating net current assets in order to benefit from lower cost and flexibility but long term financing is used to finance permanent net current assets to avoid risk.

Aggressive financing policy

In this case short term financing is used to finance a proportion of the permanent net current assets as well as the fluctuating net current assets.

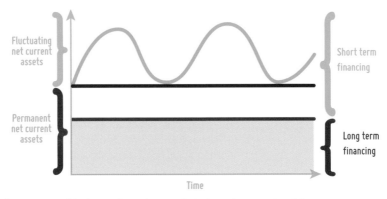

This policy can result in lower financing costs but carries greater risk.

Conservative financing policy

In this case long term financing is used to finance a proportion of the fluctuating net current assets as well as the permanent net current assets.

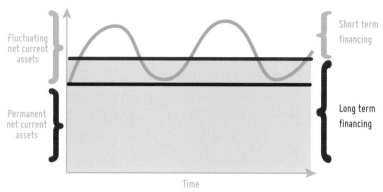

This is a very safe financing policy in terms of avoiding sudden liquidity problems but is a more expensive way of financing net working capital.

Example 2

Zoom is a manufacturer of fireworks. Demand for the product is very seasonal which has resulted in significant fluctuations in working capital levels from month to month. The finance director has, up to now, adopted a very conservative approach to financing its working capital. The approach has been to finance 100% of its permanent net current assets, and 30% of its fluctuating net current assets by means of a long term loan. The remainder of the fluctuating net current assets are financed via an overdraft.

The finance director is concerned about the cost of this policy as long term finance is more expensive than short term finance. Interest payable on a long term loan is at 9% per annum, and on the overdraft is at 7% per annum. The finance director is therefore considering a much more aggressive policy of financing 40% of the permanent net current assets and 100% of the fluctuating net current assets by means of the overdraft, and the remainder of the permanent net current assets by means of the long term loan. It is assumed that the overdraft facility is sufficiently large to allow this.

The following information about working capital levels over the last accounting period is also available:

	Maximum level ($ million)	Minimum level ($ million)
Inventory	5.6	3.9
Receivables	4.2	1.6
Payables	3.4	1.9

Requirements

(a) Determine the permanent level of net current assets (based on inventory, receivables and payables) and the fluctuating level of net current assets.

(b) Based on the current financing policy what is the total annual interest payable on the loan and overdraft if the average fluctuating net current assets is assumed to be halfway between the minimum and maximum levels? Ignore the tax relief available on interest payments.

(c) If the new financing policy is adopted, how much annual interest would the company expect to save?

Part (a)

Be careful about how you interpret maximum and minimum information. The permanent working capital or net current assets (excluding an overdraft) would be the minimum inventory and receivables and the **maximum** payables.

The permanent and fluctuating working capital will be:

	Permanent (minimum) working capital ($million)	Maximum working capital ($million)
Inventory	3.9	5.6
Receivables	1.6	4.2
Payables	(3.4)	(1.9)
Total	2.1	7.9

The working capital levels will therefore fluctuate between a minimum of $2.1 million and a maximum of 7.9 million. The fluctuating element of working capital is therefore ($7.9 million - $2.1 million) = $5.8 million.

Part (b)

To estimate the interest payable we need to use averages. The fluctuating working capital will fluctuate between zero (when the only working capital is permanent working capital) and $5.8 million as calculated above. On average the fluctuating element of working capital will therefore be 50% of this.

The average fluctuating working capital will be 50% x $5.8 million = $2.9 million.

Based on the current conservative financing policy the total interest payable will be:

	Financed by		Interest payable ($)
Permanent net current assets	Loan	$2.1 million x 100% x 9% =	189,000
Fluctuating net current assets	Loan	$2.9 million x 30% x 9% =	78,300
Fluctuating net current assets	Overdraft	$2.9 million x 70% x 7% =	142,100
Total cost			**409,400**

Part (c)

If a more aggressive policy is adopted the total interest payable will be:

	Financed by		Interest payable ($)
Permanent net current assets	Loan	$2.1 million x 60% x 9% =	113,400
Permanent net current assets	Overdraft	$2.1 million x 40% x 9% =	75,600
Fluctuating net current assets	Overdraft	$2.9 million x 100% x 7% =	203,000
Total cost			**392,000**

The more aggressive financing policy would therefore result in an interest saving of ($409,400 – $392,000) = $17,400 per annum.

It should be noted, however, that:

- The result is based on average levels of working capital. If part of the fluctuating net current assets is financed by means of a loan, as is the case with the current policy, it would be useful to know how Zoom uses the surplus cash when the fluctuating level of net current assets falls below the level of loan financing. If the cash is invested and generates interest then this would reduce the overall cost of the current conservative policy.

- Under the more aggressive policy there is more flexibility in terms of the use of finance. When the fluctuating levels of working capital fall, Zoom can reduce the overdraft accordingly.

- The more aggressive policy does, however, carry more risk. The overdraft is repayable on demand and, if called in by the bank, Zoom may face serious liquidity problems.

Chapter 16
key points summary

- Working capital investment is influenced by a number of factors including:

    - profitability – in general less working capital means greater profitability

    - liquidity – in general more working capital means greater liquidity.

- Cash operating cycle – the length of time between paying for raw materials and receiving cash from the sale of the related finished goods – a longer cycle means more money tied up in working capital.

- Working capital financing.

    - Short term financing is cheaper but more risky.

    - An aggressive policy means using short term financing for fluctuating current assets and some permanent current assets.

    - A conservative policy means using long term financing for permanent current assets and some fluctuating current assets.

RECEIVABLES AND PAYABLES MANAGEMENT

17

Introduction
what is this chapter about?

The management of receivables (debtors) and payables (creditors) are key elements of the management of working capital. This chapter considers how these two elements of working capital can best be managed.

Key areas of the chapter are ....

1   **Receivables management** – what are the main costs and benefits associated with receivables. How can receivables be managed more efficiently and what does a debt factoring company do?

2   **Payables management** – are payables a free form of finance? Would a business benefit from accepting a discount for prompt payment offered by suppliers?

RECEIVABLES MANAGEMENT

There are a number of possible policies that a business can pursue in relation to the management of receivables. These include offering discounts for promt payment, invoice discounting, and using the services of a debt factoring company.

When we evaluate the different policies that can be pursued our main focus will be on the impact that they have on a company's profitability. Before we look in greater depth at the different policies that a company could adopt we need to understand the different types of costs that arise in relation to receivables, and the management of receivables.

Costs associated with receivables and the management of receivables

The costs include the following:

(a) Irrecoverable receivables

Irrecoverable receivables represents a direct loss of sales revenue. A business would clearly wish to keep the level of irrecoverable receivables to a minimum and there a number of ways in which this can be done.

(b) Finance cost

I suppose that it is important to try and get the term finance into each chapter of the book! The finance cost is certainly an important cost for receivables management. As we saw in chapter 16, all working capital needs to be financed, for example, by using a bank overdraft. It follows therefore that the greater the level of receivables (and hence working capital) then the greater the finance cost.

(c) Receivables administration

This is the cost of credit control including the cost of setting up and updating a credit control system within a business and employing credit control staff. In order to reduce the level of irrecoverable debts and reduce the average length of time that receivables take to pay, a business may need to increase the amount spent on receivables administration.

(d) Lost sales revenue and contribution

This is a more subtle cost but it is neverless equally relevant to consider. The credit policy of a business (that is the length of time that a business allows customers to pay) could have a significant impact on the level of sales revenue and hence contribution generated. A business that, for example, reduces the credit period offered from say 90 days to 60 days may experience a significant fall in customer demand.

In order to maximise profitability a business will seek to minimise the total costs associated with receivables. Some of the costs, for example, the potential loss of sales revenue from reducing a credit period, are very difficult to estimate and would require significant research and understanding of the customer base. In exam questions assumptions will be given about the impact of a new receivables policy on various costs, for example, a question may suggest that reducing the credit period by 20 days may result in a loss of 5% of sales revenue.

Need to know!

An important relationship for calculations relating to receivables management

Many calculations relating to receivables management are based on averages. This is really the only way to produce calculations to estimate the impact of a new receivables policy on the profitability of a business. In order to deal with these calculations in an exam situation it is important to be comfortable with the relationship between receivables days that we saw in chapter 16 and the average level of receivables.

In chapter 16 we saw (when we considered the cash operating cycle) that receivables days could be measured as follows:

$$\frac{\text{Average receivables}}{\text{Credit sales}} \times 365 = \text{Receivables days}$$

If we know the receivables days and wish to find the average receivables the formula can be rearranged as follows:

$$\frac{\text{Receivables days}}{365} \times \text{Credit sales} = \text{Average receivables}$$

Ok – let's look at how we can use this relationship exam in questions.

Example 1

A company makes credit sales of $15 million per annum. The average level of receivables is currently $3 million.

Requirements

(a) What is the current average length of time that customers take to pay?

(b) If, as a result of introducing better credit control systems, receivables days were reduced to 30 days, what would be the impact on the average level of receivables?

Solution 1

Part (a)

The current average length of time that customers take to pay is as follows:

$$\frac{\$3 \text{ million}}{\$15 \text{ million}} \times 365 = 73 \text{ days}$$

Part (b)

If the average length of time that receivables take to pay was reduced to 30 days the average level of receivables can be calculated as follows:

$$\frac{30}{365} \times \$15 \text{ million} = \$1,232,877$$

The average receivables would therefore fall by ($3,000,000 - $1,232,877) = $1,767,123

What are the main receivables management policies that a business can pursue?

The main policies that you need to be able to evaluate are as follows.

- **Change the amount spent on administration**. It may be appropriate to increase the amount spent on administration (for example by employing more people!), and as a result improve the efficiency of receivables management (at least we hope that this would happen!), reduce the credit period, and possibly the level of irrecoverable receivables. Alternatively a business may consider that a credit control department is overstaffed and that it is possible to cut the amount spent on administration without this adversely affecting receivables management.

- **Change the credit period offered to customers**. A business may increase the credit period offered to customers perhaps in the hope of increasing market share, sales, and hence contribution. Alternatively a business may seek to reduce the credit period offered in order to reduce the average receivable and hence the financing cost of receivables.

- **Offering an early settlement discount**. A common policy in real life is to offer a discount to customers who pay within a certain period of time. A business offering this would hope that the benefits of recovering the receivable earlier would outweigh the loss of revenue.

- **Using the services of a debt factoring company**. This involves using a specialist debt collection company. We will consider their role in more detail later in the chapter.

We will consider how to go about evaluating each of these policies through the following examples:

Example 2

Hook is a company that supplies specialist IT services to telecommunication companies. Hook's customers currently take an average of 90 days to settle invoices and approximately 1% of invoices are irrecoverable. Annual sales are $10 million and Hook's credit control department costs $80,000 per annum.

Hook is considering employing 2 additional credit controllers. It is expected that this new policy would increase credit control department costs to $130,000 per annum, reduce the average length of time that customers take to settle invoices to 70 days and reduce irrecoverable receivables to 0.5% of credit sales.

Working capital is financed by a bank overdraft with an interest rate of 8%.

Requirement

Determine whether the new policy is expected to be beneficial to Hook.

Exam tip – Receivables management calculations

There are many ways in which solutions to receivables management questions could be presented in an exam, including, for example, working out as a single calculation the net change in various costs as a result of the new policy.

The best way to work through and present the calculations, however, is to calculate the total annual cost of the current policy based on the question information, and then separately the total cost of any new policy proposed. This type of presentation should make it less likely that arithmetical errors would arise, make it easier to manage the question information, and, perhaps, most importantly, make it easier for the marker to mark.

We will start by calculating the annual cost of the current receivables management policy.

Cost of the current policy:

		$
Finance cost	$10 million x $\dfrac{90}{365}$ x 8% =	197,260
Administration cost		80,000
Irrecoverable debts	$10 million x 1% =	100,000
Total cost		**377,260**

The average receivable is found by rearranging the receivables days equation as previously shown. In this case the average receivable would be

$$\$10\text{million x} \dfrac{90}{365} = £2,465,753$$

The finance cost is calculated by multiplying the average receiveable by the overdraft interest rate of 8%. The logic of this is that if the average receivable is £2,465,753 we assume that there is a need for an overdraft of a similar level to finance this investment. The annual cost is therefore the average receivable multiplied by the overdraft rate.

We can now consider the cost of the new policy.

Cost of the new policy:

		$
Finance cost	$10 million x $\dfrac{70}{365}$ x 8% =	153,425
Administration cost		130,000
Irrecoverable debts	$10 million x 0.5% =	50,000
Total cost		**333,425**

Under the new policy the company will benefit from a reduction in the finance cost (because the average receivables will fall) and a reduction in irrecoverable debts. The extra administration cost will, however, be offset against this.

The new policy is therefore expected to result in an annual saving of ($377,260 – $333,425) = $43,835.

Early settlement discount

A business may offer a discount to a customer for early settlement of outstanding invoices. This policy can be evaluated in exactly the same way as a policy to change the amount spent on credit control administration – that is by comparing the costs of the new policy with the costs of the current policy.

Example 3

We will use the same information as example 2 and consider a different proposed policy.

To recap from example 2:

Hook is a company that supplies specialist IT services to companies telecommunication companies. Hook's customers currently take an average of 90 days to settle invoices and approximately 1% of invoices are irrecoverable. Annual sales are $10 million and Hook's sales ledger department costs $80,000 per annum.

Working capital is financed by a bank overdraft with an interest rate of 8%.

Additional information

Hook is now considering an alternative new policy. This will involve offering a discount of 2% if customers settle outstanding invoices within 10 days rather than the current average of 90 days. It is expected that 30% of customers will take advantage of the discount. There will be no change in the overall administration cost as a result of the new policy but irrecoverable debts are expected to fall to 0.75% of sales.

Requirement

Determine whether the new policy of offering an early settlement discount is expected to be beneficial to Hook.

Solution 3

The annual cost of the current policy will be exactly the same as the amount calculated in example 2, that is $377,260.

Cost of the new policy:

The approach to take is to firstly work out the average number of days that customers are now expected to take to pay. This will be a weighted average of the 10 days that customers taking the discount will take to pay and the 90 days that the remaining customers are expected to take to pay.

Average number of days = (30% x 10 days) + (70% x 90 days) = 66 days

We can then calculate the cost of the new policy is the same way as before:

		$
Finance cost	$10 million x $\dfrac{66}{365}$ x 8% =	144,658
Discount cost	$10 million x 30% x 2% =	60,000
Administration cost		80,000
Irrecoverable debts	$10 million x 0.75% =	75,000
Total cost		**359,658**

The new policy of offering a discount for prompt payment is therefore expected to result in an annual saving of ($377,260 - $359,658) = $17,602

The policy of offering a discount for early settlement is also therefore expected to provide a greater benefit than the policy of increasing the administration expenditure seen in example 2.

Debt factoring and invoice discounting

These two methods of managing receivables both involve using the services of a specialist receivables collection company.

Finance terminology explained

What is invoice discounting?

Invoice discounting is an advance of funds from a specialist company which is secured against specific outstanding invoices from specific customers. The advance is repaid when the customer settles the outstanding invoice and a finance cost is charged for the advance. The way that this is normally 'charged' is that the specialist company will advance less than the face value of the invoice that is outstanding. The difference between the face value and the amount advanced is the finance cost.

Invoice discounting therefore effectively involves selling selected invoices early to recover a receivable earlier than would otherwise be the case. The arrangement is on an invoice by invoice basis – there is no long term commitment to continue to receive the advance.

Finance terminology explained

What is debt factoring?

Whilst debt factoring services are often provided by the same specialist companies who provide invoice discounting services there are some significant differences between the two arrangements.

A debt factoring arrangement involves using the specialist company to provide the following services.

- Credit control administration. In return for a fee (normally a percentage of the sales revenue) the debt factoring company is able to provide full credit control administration services including invoice production, management of outstanding receivables, processing of receipts and recovery of overdue amounts. As a result, a business using the services of a debt factoring company in this way will avoid having to incur these administration costs.

- Finance advance. The factoring company can advance a percentage of the face value of all outstanding receivables. In practice the advance tends to be to a maximum of 80% of the face value of the outstanding invoices and will be from the date that the invoice is produced until the normal due date. A finance charge will be made for this service.

A business could use the factoring company to provide only the sales ledger administration services or, alternatively, the factoring company could provide both sales ledger adminstration and a finance advance.

The factoring arrangement will be a medium to long term arrangement. It is particularly useful for fast growing businesses where it is difficult to estimate the level of resources that need to be devoted to sales ledger adminstration.

Non-recourse and with recourse factoring

A couple of extra terms for you to be aware of when analysing a debt factoring arrangement. A non-recourse basis means that if an outstanding invoice proves to be irrecoverable the factoring company cannot reclaim any advance made from the company that has used its services (hence the factoring company has no recourse or ability to reclaim the advance). A with recourse arrangement means that the advance could be reclaimed by the factoring company if the receivable defaults.

A non-recourse arrangement therefore reduces the risk to a business using the services of a factoring company **but** it will always be more expensive than a with recourse arrangement.

Example 4

As with example 3, we will again use the same scenario as example 2 (you are probably fed up of this scenario by now – it is, however, useful to compare the different policies by using the same information). To recap:

Hook is a company that supplies specialist IT services to companies telecommunication companies. Hook's customers currently take an average of 90 days to settle invoices and approximately 1% of invoices are irrecoverable. Annual sales are $10 million and Hook's sales ledger department costs $80,000 per annum.

Working capital is financed by a bank overdraft with an interest rate of 8%.

Additional information

Hook is now considering using the services of a debt factoring company. The factoring company will provide full sales ledger administration services for a fee of 1.5% of the annual sales. As a result Hook will avoid most of its sales ledger management costs although an annual amount of $10,000 will still be incurred. The factor will advance 75% of outstanding invoices on a non-recourse basis. The factor will charge 9% per annum for the advance. The non-recourse arrangement means that Hook will avoid all costs of irrecoverable debts. Customers are still expected to take an average of 90 days to settle outstanding invoices.

Requirement

Determine whether the new policy of using the services of a debt factoring company is expected to be beneficial to Hook.

The annual cost of the current policy will be exactly the same as the amount calculated in example 2, that is $377,260.

Cost of the new policy:

The key to dealing with the advance made by the factoring company is to approach this in the same way as the finance cost for receivables – that is on an average basis. Each advance from the factor is for 90 days on average, and therefore the average advance will be 90 days worth of the annual advance.

		$
Finance cost – advance	$10 million x 75% x $\dfrac{90}{365}$ x 9% =	166,438
Finance cost - remainder	$10 million x 25% x $\dfrac{90}{365}$ x 8% =	49,315
Factoring company fee	$10 million x 1.5%	150,000
Administration cost		10,000
Irrecoverable debts		NIL
Total cost		**375,753**

Using the services of the factoring company in this way is therefore only expected to save Hook an amount of ($377,260-$375,753) = $1,507 per annum.

Of the three policies considered in examples 2, 3 and 4 the early settlement discount provides the greatest benefit to Hook.

PAYABLES MANAGEMENT

Obtaining credit from suppliers is effectively a form of 'free' financing for a business. The greater the length of time taken to pay payables, the larger the payables balance, and, as a result, the less financing via interest bearing debt is needed.

Using payables as a form of financing is not, however, without problems.

- **Interest charge**. The supplier may charge interest for late payment or offer a discount for early settlement. This adds a cost to any attempt to use payables as a form of financing current assets.

- **Legal action**. The supplier may take legal action to recover amounts that are outstanding beyond an agreed settlement date. There may be additional costs in defending a business against legal action by a supplier.

- **Loss of goodwill**. There may be a loss of goodwill in terms of a relationship with a supplier. This may result in delayed deliveries in the future or a reduction in quality of the goods or services purchased from the supplier.

- **Withdrawal of credit terms**. A supplier may withdraw credit facilities and only trade on an immediate cash settlement basis.

Despite these problems – using payables as a form of financing, especially when a company is in a strong bargaining position in relation to its suppliers is a very tempting and commonly used method of reducing the need to finance working capital.

Real life illustration – Carlsberg

In August 2009 the Danish beer producer Carlsberg suddenly announced a change in the terms for paying suppliers. The number of days until purchase invoices were to be settled was increased from 30 days following the end of the month in which an invoice was received to 95 days!

Despite significant criticism from small business organisations, the company justified the change by stating that it needed to find a better balance between payments to suppliers and receipts from customers, and improve group cashflow. Carlsberg also stated that it was not alone in the industry in changing the terms of supplier payment.

Discount for early settlement

If a business is offered an early settlement discount by a supplier should the offer be accepted?

The way in which this decision is normally evaluated is by calculating the effective annual cost of not taking the discount, and comparing this to the cost of an alternative method of financing working capital, for example a bank overdraft rate.

Need to know!

Effective annual cost of not accepting a discount

This is calculated by using the formula:

$$\text{Annual cost} = \left(1 + \frac{\text{discount}}{\text{amount to pay}}\right)^{\text{no of periods per annum}} - 1$$

This formula looks horrendous but don't be put off – it is really just a bit of compounding – similar to that which we saw in chapter 2 (if you can remember that far back!)

Example 5

A company is offered a discount of 2% on all purchase invoices that are settled within 30 days. The normal settlement period is 90 days.

Working capital is financed by using a bank overdraft at 8% interest per annum.

Requirement

Should the company accept the discount offered?

Solution 5

The approach to take is to look at the discount as if it was an interest charge for paying on the due date. If we assume that the company was prepared to take the discount and pay on day 30, but then suddenly changed its mind and decided to pay on the normal due date (90 days), it is effectively being charged interest for borrowing money for an extra 60 days.

The approach to take is to look at the discount as if it was an interest charge for paying on the due date. If we assume that the company was prepared to take the discount and pay on day 30, but then suddenly changed its mind and decided to pay on the normal due date (90 days), it is effectively being charged interest for borrowing money for an extra 60 days.

If we take a $100 invoice as an example, a 2% early settlement discount means that the company can either pay £98 on day 30 or $100 on day 90. It is therefore being charged $2 for 'borrowing' $98 for an extra 60 days. To work out the equivalent amount charged per annum we need to compound up by the number of 60 day periods in one year.

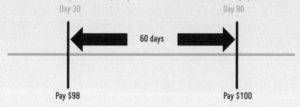

The effective annual cost $= \left(1 + \dfrac{2}{98}\right)^{\frac{365}{60}} -1 = 0.1308$ or 13.08%

This means that if a company 'delays' paying the supplier (does not take the discount) it is effectively being charged 13.08% for 'borrowing' money from the supplier. This is greater than the cost of borrowing from a bank using the overdraft facility.

The company is therefore advised to take the discount and finance working capital by using a bank overdraft rather than using payables.

Chapter 17
key points summary

- Receivables management calculations are often based on calculating an average receivable and multiplying this by the relevant cost of financing e.g. a bank overdraft rate. The average receivable is calculated using this formula.

$$-\ \frac{\text{Receivables days}}{365}\ \times\ \text{Credit sales} = \text{Average receivables}$$

- Main receivables management policies are:

  - change administration expenditure

  - change credit period offered

  - offer an early settlement discount

  - use the services of a debt factoring company – which are:

    - sales ledger administration – fee charged (%age of sales)

    - finance advance – finance cost charged.

- Payables are a 'free' form of financing but delaying payment can cause problems.

- Payables – accept an early settlement discount?

  - To answer need to calculate the effective annual cost of not taking the discount and compare to the normal working capital financing rate

  - Effective Annual cost $= \left(1 + \dfrac{\text{discount}}{\text{amount to pay}}\right)^{\text{no of periods per annum}} - 1$

INVENTORY AND CASH MANAGEMENT

Introduction
what is this chapter about?

In this chapter we will consider how to manage inventory and cash. We will examine the main issues involved and also see how various models can be used to assist in the management of both inventory and cash.

Key areas of the chapter are ....

1   **Inventory (or stock) management** – what are the main considerations when managing inventory and is there an optimum (ideal) level of inventory that minimises the total cost of inventory to a business?

2   **Cash management** – what are the main ways in which cash can be managed? Can cash management models help in the management of cash levels within the business?

INVENTORY MANAGEMENT

How do different levels of inventory impact upon business profitability? As with receivables in chapter 17 the best way to consider this question is to focus on costs, and how these can be kept to a minimum. We can do this by considering the costs of holding high levels of inventory or alternatively of holding low levels of inventory.

Costs of high levels of inventory

- **Finance cost**

  Inventory levels will need to be financed – probably by using a bank overdraft or a long term loan. The higher the inventory level the greater the financing need and the greater the annual cost.

- **Storage/warehousing cost**

  Inventory, whether in the form of raw material, work-in-progress or finished goods, will need to be physically stored for the time that it is within the business. The cost might be a direct cost of warehousing facilities or an opportunity cost in the form of lost potential alternative usage of the facilities used to store the inventory.

- **Obsolescence/damage**

  The higher the levels of inventory within the business the greater the risk of obsolete or damaged goods. Let's take an example of a major retailer of computer equipment. If inventory levels are increased, perhaps to meet seasonal demand, this will increase the risk of being left with equipment that cannot be sold, or can only be sold at below cost price.

Costs of low levels of inventory

- **Lost sales**

  A business that seeks to operate with low levels of inventory faces a risk of losing sales, and hence losing contribution that the sales will generate. Suppose the retailer of computer equipment reduces significantly the amount of inventory held in the store. This will inevitably lead to disappointed customers who will find a much more limited range of products on offer, or that a particularly sought after model is sold out!

- **Increased ordering & delivery costs**

  Operating with lower levels of inventory is likely to result in a business ordering materials from suppliers in lower quantities and on a more frequent basis. This will increase the administration cost of placing the orders, and also increase the delivery costs.

- **Lost quantity (bulk purchase) discounts**

  Buying smaller quantities of inventory on a more frequent basis will mean that the business is unlikely to be able to take advantage of quantity discounts that may be available from a supplier.

The economic order quantity (EOQ)

This is a model which can (in theory) be used to determine the optimum quantity of inventory to order whenever an order for inventory is placed. The model is based on minimising total inventory costs when taking into account the following.

- Finance costs.

- Storage/warehousing costs.

- Ordering and delivery costs.

The model can be amended to take into account the possibility of quantity discounts (which we will see through an example) but the model is too simplistic to allow is to take into account potential lost sales revenue or the possibility of obsolete or damaged inventory, both of which are more subjective and difficult to measure.

How does the EOQ work?

The EOQ is based on the relationship between the number of units of inventory ordered every time an order is placed and the total costs of inventory.

The EOQ treats finance costs and storage/warehousing costs as inventory **holding costs** in the model. These costs will **increase** as the number of units of inventory in each order increase. The more inventory that is ordered whenever an order is placed with a supplier, the greater the average level of inventory held and the greater the annual holding cost for the inventory.

Ordering and delivery costs are called **ordering costs** in the model. These costs will **decrease** as the number of units in each order increase. The greater the number of units ordered each time an order is placed the fewer the number of orders that will be placed in a year and the lower the total ordering costs.

This can be shown graphically as follows:

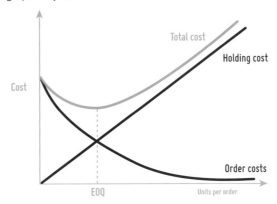

The EOQ is the order quantity that minimises the total inventory costs.

Assumptions of the EOQ

The EOQ assumes the following.

- **Demand for the inventory is constant**. For a retailer this means that we assume that demand from customers is constant. For a manufacturer it means that demand for the raw material used in production is constant. Is this realistic? Possibly – for some types of manufacturing businesses that produce a fairly constant amount of output each month such as a car manufacturer. For a retailer, however, such as a computer retailer, demand will be much more seasonal and subject to change and therefore this assumption is unrealistic.

- **The lead time is constant**. This means that we assume that the time between an order being placed and the delivery of the inventory is exactly the same every time an order is placed. This also means that we can then place an order for a new delivery so that new inventory arrives in the business just as the last inventory from the previous order is being used – and not a moment too early or too late!

- **No buffer inventory is held**. Because demand is constant and the lead time for the delivery of new inventory is constant there is no need for a business to keep a buffer level of inventory – that is, the business does not need to keep a certain amount of inventory just in case the new delivery does not arrive in time.

- **Purchase price is constant**. There is no change in the cost of purchasing new inventory.

These assumptions can be illustrated by using the following graph.

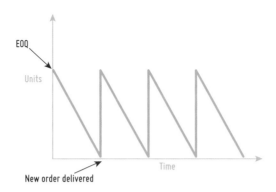

New order delivered

Need to know!

EOQ formula

A formula can be found for determining the EOQ. We saw in an earlier graph that the EOQ is the point at which the total cost curve is minimised – and is therefore the point at which the gradient of the total cost curve is equal to nil. By using differential calculus (don't worry – you are unlikely to have to prove this in any examination!) the following formula can be produced which would allow us to find the EOQ:

$$EOQ = \sqrt{\frac{2\,CoD}{Ch}}$$

Where:

Co = cost per order

Ch = holding cost for one unit of inventory for one year

D = annual demand for the inventory

A good, but perhaps rather irreverent way of remembering the formula for an exam is to remember that the EOQ is the square root of **2 CoD** and **Ch**ips!

Example 1

Holly is a manufacturer of personal computers. As part of its manufacturing process it requires 150,000 identical circuit boards which are all delivered by the same supplier. The cost of ordering and delivering the circuit boards from the supplier is $800 per order placed. The cost of storing the circuit boards within the business before being used in manufacturing is $3 per circuit board per annum. Each circuit board costs $10 to purchase and working capital is financed by a bank overdraft at 8% interest.

Requirement

Using the EOQ model determine how many circuit boards should be ordered every time an order is placed, and determine the total annual cost of the inventory excluding the purchase price.

The holding cost of the inventory will comprise two elements – the direct cost of storage, and the finance cost. The finance cost is the total interest payable each year if one unit is purchased and then kept in the business for one year.

Co = $800

Ch = $3 + ($10 x 8%) = $3.80

D = 150,000 units (circuit boards)

$$EOQ = \sqrt{\frac{2 \times 800 \times 150,000}{3.80}} = 7,947 \text{ units}$$

The company should therefore order the circuit boards in batches of 7,947. This will minimise the total inventory cost.

The total cost excluding the purchase price would be:

		$
Annual order cost	$\dfrac{150,000}{7,947}$ x $800 =	15,100
Annual holding cost	$\dfrac{7,947}{2}$ x $3.80 =	15,100
Total annual cost		**30,200**

The annual holding cost is based on the average number of units held in inventory. Under the EOQ model this is always half the amount of inventory ordered. If the demand for inventory is constant and a new delivery of inventory arrives just at the inventory level reaches nil, the average inventory must be half the amount ordered.

Exam tip – EOQ

At the EOQ order level, the total annual holding cost and the total annual order cost should be the same (apart from some small rounding errors). In example 1 they are both $15,100.

This is a useful check to make sure that your calculation of the EOQ level was correct. If the annual holding cost and order cost are the same, your calculation of the EOQ was correct.

EOQ and quantity discounts

A supplier of inventory may offer a quantity discount, that is, a discount if more than a certain amount of units are ordered every time an order is placed. If this is the case how can the EOQ model be adapted to reflect a quantity discount?

The **approach** to take is as follows.

1   Calculate the EOQ ignoring the possibility of quantity discounts and determine the total inventory cost at the EOQ level.

2   Calculate the total inventory cost assuming that the minimum number of units are ordered that would qualify for a quantity discount.

3   Repeat step 2 for each quantity discount offered.

4   Compare the total cost at the EOQ order level with the total cost at each quantity discount order level to determine whether the discount should be accepted.

This sounds a lot worse than it really is! Best to see how it works through an example.

Example 2

We will use the same information as in example 1.

If the supplier now offered Holly a discount of 1% on the purchase price if 12,000 units or more were ordered every time an order was placed, should Holly increase the size of the order from the EOQ level to 12,000 units?

Solution 2

In this case, as well as the order cost and holding cost we also need to take into account the saving on the purchase price that would arise if the quantity discount was accepted.

The total cost assuming that 10,000 units were ordered would be:

		$
Annual order cost	$\dfrac{150,000}{12,000} \times \$800 =$	10,000
Annual holding cost	$\dfrac{12,000}{2} \times \$3.80 =$	22,800
Purchase price saving	$150,000 \times \$10 \times 1\% =$	(15,000)
Total annual cost		**17,800**

The quantity discount should therefore be accepted and orders placed in batches of 12,000 units. This will reduce the total inventory cost from $30,200 to $17,800.

CASH MANAGEMENT

The most sensible and commonly used cash management technique is cash forecasting and budgeting.

Cash forecasting and budgeting

A cash forecast is the current estimate of future cash receipts and payments taking into account all known variables. A business may, for example forecast the future cash receipts from customers based on forecast market size, market share and average time that customers take to pay following a credit sale.

A cash budget includes cash forecasts and the impact of any action taken on the basis of the cash forecasts. A business may, for example, plan to delay expenditure on replacing equipment following a forecast of cash receipts and payments. The impact of this delay would be taken into account in the cash budget.

Alas – cash forecasting and budgeting are beyond the scope of this book – in fact it would probably take a complete book of a few hundred pages to consider this area in sufficient detail.

We can, however, consider two models that could be used to assist with the management of cash. They are the Baumol model and the Miller-Orr model.

Baumol model

The Baumol cash management model applies the EOQ formula for inventory to the management of cash. How is this possible?

The model in essence treats cash in exactly the same way as inventory and assumes that there is a holding cost and an order cost for cash. The demand for cash (to meet day to day spending needs) is, like the inventory model, assumed to be constant.

The model assumes that when cash is received from sales it is invested in short term investments (yes – I know that this is unrealistic but this assumption allows the inventory model to be adapted to cash).

In order to raise the cash short term investments must be sold. A cost is incurred whenever short term investments are sold (the equivalent of the order cost) and there is an opportunity cost when cash is not invested (the equivalent of the holding cost). This opportunity cost is the interest foregone when cash is not invested in short term investments, but is instead kept as pure cash within the business.

The formula applied to the management of cash is:

$$\text{Cash EOQ} = \sqrt{\frac{2\,\text{CoD}}{\text{Ch}}}$$

Where:

Co = cost of 'ordering' cash (by selling short term investments)

Ch = holding cost for one unit of cash for one year

D = annual demand for cash in units

To use the model for cash management, a decision needs to be made about what constitutes a 'unit' of cash, for example, one unit might be $1.

Example 3

A company wishes to use the Baumol cash management model to minimise the cost of managing cash. All cash receipts are invested in short term investments at no cost to the business. The annual demand for cash is $800,000. The interest rate on short term investments is 9% per annum and the cost of 'ordering' cash through selling short term investments is $300 per order.

Requirement

Using the Baumol model determine the amount of cash to order whenever short term investments are sold.

Solution 3

If we assume that each unit of cash is $1 then:

Co   = $300

Ch   = $1 x 9% = $0.09

D   = $800,000

$$\text{Cash EOQ} = \sqrt{\frac{2 \times 300 \times 800{,}000}{0.09}} = \$73{,}030$$

The company should therefore sell $73,030 worth of short term investments every time an order is placed for cash.

Miller–Orr model

The Baumol cash management model assumes that the demand for cash is constant, that is, exactly the same amount of cash will be needed by the business on each trading day. In reality the pattern of cash demand is not, of course, constant (if it was – there would be less need for accountants – now there's a thought!)

There will be periods, for example, on the day that employees are paid, where there will be a significant cash outflow, and other periods, for example, when a major customer settles an outstanding invoice, where there will be a significant cash inflow.

The Miller-Orr model allows for the possibility of uncertain cash inflows and outflows on each trading day, and to this extent is more realistic than the Baumol model.

The following diagram illustrates how the model works:

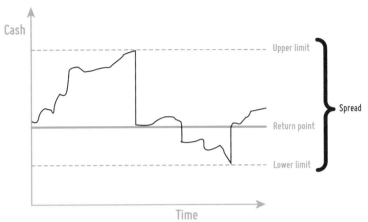

Management set the lower limit of cash. This will be based on the risk of running out of cash and is really a buffer level to meet unforeseen demand for cash.

The cash level is then allowed to move up and down randomly between the lower limit and the upper limit. When the cash balance reaches the lower limit, cash is immediately raised by selling short term investments until the cash balance is at the return point. When the cash balance reaches the upper limit, cash is immediately invested in short term investments until the cash balance is at the return point.

The Miller-Orr model allows us to determine the spread between the upper and lower limit and to also calculate the return point. The following formulae are used:

Need to know!

$$\text{Spread} = 3 \left[\frac{3}{4} \times \frac{\text{transaction cost} \times \text{daily variance of cashflows}}{\text{daily interest rate}} \right]^{\frac{1}{3}}$$

$$\text{Return point} = \text{lower limit} + \left(\frac{1}{3} \times \text{spread} \right)$$

The first formula is not very friendly but with a bit of practice you'll soon be able to use a calculator to find the result.

Example 4

A company has a lower cash limit of $10,000. The cost of buying and selling short term investments is $60 per transaction. The daily cashflow variance (the variance is the standard deviation squared) is $2 million, and the daily interest rate is 0.05% (as a decimal = 0.0005).

Requirements

(a) What is the spread between the upper and lower limits?

(b) What is the upper limit and the return point?

Part (a)

Using the formula the spread is calculated as follows:

$$\text{Spread} = 3 \left[\frac{3}{4} \times \frac{\$60 \times \$2,000,000}{0.0005} \right]^{1/3}$$

Spread = $16,939

Part (b)

The upper limit is the spread added to the lower limit

Upper limit = $16,939 + $10,000

Upper limit = $26,939

We can use the other formula to determine the return point as follows:

$$\$10,000 + (\frac{1}{3} \times \$16,939)$$

Return point = $15,646

Chapter 18
key points summary

- Inventory management.

  - Costs that increase with high inventory levels:

    - finance cost (in EOQ)

    - storage cost (in EOQ)

    - obsolecence (not inEOQ).

  - Costs that increase with low inventory levels:

    - lost sales (not in EOQ)

    - order cost (in EOQ)

    - quantity discount (EOQ adapted to reflect).

  - EOQ formula - $\text{EOQ} = \sqrt{\dfrac{2 \text{ CoD}}{\text{Ch}}}$

- Cash management.

  - Baumol model – applies EOQ to cash – formula - $\text{Cash EOQ} = \sqrt{\dfrac{2 \text{ CoD}}{\text{Ch}}}$

  - Miller Orr model – allows random movement of cash balance

    - $\text{Spread} = 3 \left[\dfrac{3}{4} \times \dfrac{\text{transaction cost} \times \text{daily variance of cashflows}}{\text{daily interest rate}} \right]^{\frac{1}{3}}$

    - Return point = lower limit + $\left(\dfrac{1}{3} \times \text{spread} \right)$

"Derivatives are financial weapons of mass destruction."

Warren Buffett

RISK MANAGEMENT AND DERIVATIVES

FOREIGN CURRENCY RISK MANAGEMENT

19

Introduction
what is this chapter about?

Many businesses have significant foreign currency transactions which typically arise from exporting, importing or investing in different countries. In this chapter we consider the different types of risk faced by such companies resulting from exchange rate movements (known as exchange rate risk), and also consider the ways in which such risk can be reduced and managed.

Key areas of the chapter are ....

1   **Types of foreign currency risk** – what types of currency risk does a business potentially face? Can all types of foreign currency risk be managed?

2   **Exchange rate theory** – exchange rates can be quoted in a number of different ways. There are also a number of theories relating to the way in which exchange rates may change over time. What are the main influences on exchange rates and is it possible to predict accurately how exchange rates will change over time?

3   **Internal hedging techniques** – a number of techniques are available which allow a company to internally hedge its exchange rate risk. What are these techniques and how effective are they at reducing exchange rate risk?

4   **External hedging techniques** – a number of more elaborate techniques for managing exchange rate risk are available by using outside parties. What are these techniques and which are the most effective at reducing risk?

TYPES OF FOREIGN CURRENCY RISK

Before we consider the different types of foreign currency risk faced by a business it is important to understand what this term means. Foreign currency risk can also be called exchange rate risk or forex risk (an abbreviation of foreign exchange risk).

Finance terminology explained

What is foreign currency risk?

This refers to the risk of a change in the value of future cash flows or a change in the value of assets or liabilities that arises solely as a result of exchange rate movements.

Suppose, for example, a UK company whose home currency is the pound, is due to receive $500,000 in 6 months' time. As the exchange rate between the dollar and the pound changes the equivalent value of the receipt in pounds will also change.

Is risk always bad? No – a mistake that students often make when discussing foreign currency risk is to focus only on the downside. It is important to note that there is **both an upside (or favourable) and downside (or adverse) aspect to foreign currency risk**. The equivalent value in pounds of the $500,000 due in 6 months' time could increase or decrease because of an exchange rate change.

When we reduce the risk of an adverse movement in exchange rates it is therefore important to note that **in most cases we also reduce the risk of being able to benefit potentially from favourable movements in exchange rates**. In most cases, this is acceptable because the overriding aim is to reduce the adverse risk.

Strengthening and weakening of currencies

Students often become confused when discussing strengthening and weakening of currencies. What do these terms mean?

Suppose that we have the following scenario:

On 1/1/20X1 the exchange rate is $1.20 for each €1.00

On 31/12/20X1 the exchange rate is $1.50 for each €1.00

During 20X1 we can say that:

1 **The euro (€) has strengthened**, or appreciated. This is because each euro is able to buy more dollars at the end of 20X1 than was the case at the beginning of 20X1.

2 **The dollar ($) has weakened**, or depreciated. This is because it would require more dollars to buy each euro at the end of 20X1 than was the case at the beginning of 20X1.

This, of course, means that as one currency strengthens the other will weaken – therefore make sure that you are very clear about the currency being referred to when you discuss strengthening or weakening.

What are the different types of foreign currency risk?

Foreign currency risk facing a business can be neatly categorized into three different types. They are:

1   transaction risk
2   translation risk
3   economic risk.

Finance terminology explained

Transaction risk

This is the risk of a gain or loss arising from movements in exchange rates when a transaction has taken place which involves a foreign currency.

Examples of transaction risk are:

- **Exporting or importing goods or services – the most common type of transaction risk**

    Suppose a manufacturing company based in France exports goods to a customer based in the United States, and invoices the customer in US dollars. The invoice is for an amount of $200,000. The customer is offered 60 days' credit and is therefore expected to pay this amount to the French company in 60 days' time.

    The exchange rate on the date of the sale is $1.20 per euro.

    If the receipt from the sale could be converted into euro on the date of the sale the French company would receive

    $$\frac{\$200,000}{\$1.20} = €166,667$$

    What if the exchange rate in 60 days' time (that is, on the date that the transaction has to be settled) has change to $1.50 per euro?

    If the receipt from the sale is converted into euro on this date the French company would only receive

    $$\frac{\$200,000}{\$1.50} = €133,333$$

    The receipt in euro is therefore ($166,667 - $133,333) = $33,334 less than expected because of exchange rate changes.

- **Interest payable on an overseas loan**

    Suppose the French company had borrowed a certain amount in US dollars. Interest is payable every six months on the loan in dollars. In this case, transaction risk arises on each six month interest payment. If the interest payments are in US dollars, then the French company will need to buy these dollars at the time the payment is due. Therefore the interest cost in the home currency, the euro, could increase or decrease because of exchange rate movements.

Finance terminology explained

Translation risk

This is the risk of a gain or loss arising in the published financial statements as a result of exchange rate changes.

When the French manufacturing company translates its US $ loan into euro at each year end for presentation in the financial statements, the value in euro may change as a result of exchange rate movements during the accounting period.

Finance terminology explained

Economic risk

This is the change in the present value of future cashflows of the business, and hence in the value of the business because of exchange rate movements.

This sounds a bit technical but is really the long term version of transaction risk.

Suppose the French manufacturing company makes, on average, 30% of its sales to customers in the United States and invoices in dollars. Let's assume that the value of the sales in US dollars is $20,000,000 per annum and that the exchange rate in the first accounting period is $1.20 per euro, in the second accounting period is $1.40, and in the third accounting period is $1.60 per euro. What is the long term impact on the business of this exchange rate change?

The sales in euro when converted at the exchange rate would be:

Year 1 – $\dfrac{\$20,000,000}{\$1.20} = €16,666,667$

Year 2 – $\dfrac{\$20,000,000}{\$1.40} = €14,285,714$

Year 3 – $\dfrac{\$20,000,000}{\$1.60} = €12,500,000$

The key point here is that an exchange rate change like this will have significant long term consequences for the business – the sales revenue in euro will be falling each year even though the selling price in dollars and the sales volume stays the same! Unless the company reduces costs or increases the selling price in dollars (which might make it uncompetitive) it will suffer a fall in profitability.

Impact of strengthening or weakening of a currency on the different types of foreign currency risk

Need to know!

In general we can say that a **strengthening of the home currency**:

- is an **adverse** exchange rate movement when **exporting**. In the examples that we have seen so far the euro has strengthened against the dollar. How did this affect the French company that was exporting? Well – it resulted in adverse transaction and economic risk – that is, the receipts in the euro fell as a result of exchange rate changes. This is the reason why governments around the world often seek to keep their home currency weak (or are often accused of deliberately seeking to keep their home currency weak.)

- is a **favourable** exchange rate movement when **importing**. A strengthening of the home currency will reduce the cost of imports if a foreign supplier has invoiced in a foreign currency

- **reduces the value of overseas assets and liabilities** when translated at the year end, or when sold. An asset in the United States owned by a French company worth $1.2m, for example, would be worth €1.0m in euro when translated at $1.20 per €1. If the rate changed to $1.50 per €1, however, the same asset would only be worth €0.8m in euro.

Of course the opposite is true when the home currency weakens.

Exam tip – Stengthening & weakening currencies

Students need to be able to confidently discuss the impact of a strengthening or a weakening of a currency on a business in a scenario.

To prepare for an exam it is best to learn the impact that, for example, a strengthening would have, and then remember that everything is the opposite for a weakening! If all else fails make up a little example with numbers.

EXCHANGE RATE THEORY

In this section we cover the ways in which exchange rates are quoted, and also various theories about exchange rate movements (sorry – a little bit more theory is needed).

Finance terminology explained

Spot rate

This is the term given to the exchange rate available for immediate conversion from one currency into another. If, for example, dollars can be converted into euro at $1.20 per euro today, then we can say that today's spot rate is $1.20 per euro.

The spot rate is always quoted by dealers or banks as two separate rates. The difference between the two rates is the dealers '**spread**' which effectively provides the dealer with a profit to cover the risk that a dealer faces of holding currency that loses value. The size of the dealers spread relates mainly to the risk, or volatility, of the exchange rate between the currencies.

A spot rate between the dollar and the euro might, for example, be quoted as:

$$\$1.1453 - \$1.1678 \text{ per } €1$$

Which rate will be used for a transaction? Suppose a French company, for example, had to pay $100,000 to a supplier in the United States, what would be the cost in euro to the French company?

The key to getting the right rate in an exam question is to understand that there are really two separate transactions going on. The first transaction is that the French company needs to pay $100,000 to the supplier in the United States. The second transaction is that the French company needs to buy these dollars from a foreign exchange dealer in order to be able to pay the supplier.

Let's look at these transactions graphically:

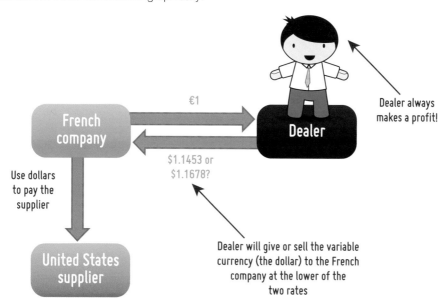

The exchange rate is quoted as the amount of dollars (which is therefore the variable currency) per one euro (which is therefore the fixed currency). The French company needs dollars from the foreign exchange dealer. This means that the dealer will be selling the dollar to the French company and buying the euro.

The question is then – for every one euro that the dealer buys (the fixed currency) how many dollars will the dealer give to the French company? Well – the dealer will always make the gain on the difference between the two rates and therefore the dealer will give the lower amount of dollars to the French company - $1.1453.

If the dealer had been buying dollars from the French company then the dealer would buy $1.1678 for every €1 given back.

In general we can therefore say:

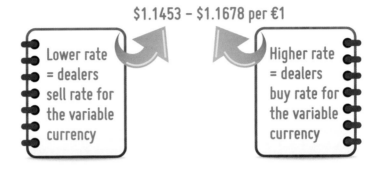

$1.1453 – $1.1678 per €1

| Lower rate = dealers sell rate for the variable currency | Higher rate = dealers buy rate for the variable currency |

Finance terminology explained

Purchasing power parity theory (PPPT)

Purchasing power parity is sometimes called the law of one price. It is an exchange rate theory that suggests that goods and services that are sold in different currencies should cost the same price irrespective of the currency in which they are sold.

If the price was different in different currencies then market forces would impact on the exchange rate to push the prices closer together.

Suppose a car costs $8,000 in the United States and the exchange rate today is $1.28 per euro. Purchasing power parity theory suggests that if the same car was on sale in the Eurozone (e.g. in France) then it should cost $8,000/$1.28 = €6,250. If it cost more than €6,250 in France then French consumers who want to buy the car would (ignoring transportation costs!) buy the car in the United States and import it into France. If all consumers did this – the price in France would quickly drop to €6,250.

Purchasing power parity theory and inflation

How does inflation impact on the exchange rate (or spot rate)?

If we take the example of purchasing a car that we saw above. Suppose inflation was 6% per annum in the United States, and 4% per annum in the Eurozone, what would be the impact of this on the spot rate in one years' time?

A car costing $8,000 today in the United States would be expected to cost $8,000 x 1.06 = $8,480 in one year's time. Similarly a car costing €6,250 in France would be expected to cost €6,250 x 1.04 = €6,500 in one year's time. If purchasing power parity theory still holds then the spot rate in one year's time should be $8,480/€6,500 = $1.3046 per €1.

Need to know!

Under purchasing power parity theory, the currency of the country with the higher rate of inflation is expected to weaken over time.

In this case, inflation is higher in the dollar, and the dollar is weaker in 12 months' time compared to the current spot rate.

Purchasing power parity formula

There is a formula that can be used to estimate the future spot using PPP:

$$S1 = S0 \times \frac{1 + inf_c}{1 + inf_b}$$

Where:

S1 = estimated spot rate in 1 years' time

S0 = spot rate now

inf_c = inflation in the counter currency (the counter currency is the currency which varies)

inf_b = inflation in the base currency (the base currency is the currency that is fixed)

For the example above the exchange rate is quoted as $ per €, and therefore the dollar is the counter currency (that is the currency that varies) and the euro is the base currency (that is the currency that is fixed). Using the formula:

$$S1 = \$1.2800 \times \frac{1 + 0.06}{1 + 0.04}$$

S1 = $1.3046 per euro

Accuracy of purchasing power parity forecast

Purchasing power parity predicts future exchange rates on the basis of one variable only – inflation.

Of course, in practice many factors other than inflation have an impact on exchange rates.

- The level of economic growth in an economy.

- The balance of trade and balance of payments figures.

- The degree of government intervention to manipulate exchange rates.

- Speculation (!).

Despite this, many economists feel that purchasing power parity does provide a reasonably accurate estimate of long term changes in exchange rates.

Finance terminology explained

Interest rate parity theory (IRPT)

The forward market is a market where an exchange rate is quoted today for future delivery. It is possible, for example, to obtain a quote today for an exchange rate to convert dollars into euros in 6 months' time. The quote is today but the delivery or conversion will not happen until 6 months from today.

The forward market can be used to reduce exchange rate risk. It is possible to sign contracts with an exchange rate dealer today, for conversion of currency at a future date, using the rate agreed today. We will see how this works later.

To avoid creating arbitrage opportunities for speculators (that is the ability to make gains through buying and selling), the forward rate needs to reflect interest rate differences between currencies. There is a formula to use for calculating the forward rate which is:

Need to know!

$$F0 = S0 \times \frac{1 + int_c}{1 + int_b}$$

where:

$F0$ = forward rate

$S0$ = spot rate now

int_c = interest rate in the counter currency (which is the variable currency)

int_b = interest rate in the base currency (which is the fixed currency)

This formula is mathematically the same as the purchasing power parity formula but the aim is different. Rather than predicting a future spot rate we use this formula to find a forward rate that can be used in forward exchange contracts. It is possible to prove that unless a forward rate is set at this level in a forward exchange contract there is a possibility for a speculator to make a riskless gain at the expense of a foreign exchange dealer – the proof is beyond the scope of this book!

Example 1

Suppose the current spot rate is $1.1000 per euro. If interest rates are 7% per annum in the dollar and 3% per annum in the euro, what is the one year forward rate that would be quoted by an exchange rate dealer?

Solution 1

Using the formula we will end up with the following one year forward rate:

$$F0 = \$1.1000 \times \frac{1 + 0.07}{1 + 0.03}$$

$S = \$1.1427$

Finance terminology explained

The International Fisher effect

The Fisher effect is a relationship between interest rates in an economy and the levels of inflation. The effect suggests that currencies in which inflation levels are high will generally have higher interest rates, and similarly currencies in which inflation levels are low will generally have lower interest rates.

There are a number of reasons for this. A central bank, for example, using interest rates to control demand led inflation, will raise interest rates when inflation levels rise.

If the Fisher effect holds true, it could be argued that the forward rate (determined using interest rate parity) and the estimated future spot rate (determined using purchasing power parity) will give very similar results. If this is the case then it could also be argued that the forward rate is a good estimate of the future spot rate. This is the international fisher effect.

INTERNAL HEDGING TECHNIQUES — TRANSACTION RISK

The next thing for us to consider is the way in which companies can hedge transaction foreign currency risk using internal techniques.

What is meant by hedging?

Hedging is a general term for a **risk reduction technique**. We can say that risk can be reduced, or hedged, by taking a particular course of action. All of the techniques that we cover in this section, and the next, allow us to hedge or reduce risk to some extent. Most hedging techniques reduce downside risk but also reduce upside risk (that is the potential to benefit from a favourable exchange rate movement). Options, which we cover later are the exception to this.

What are the internal techniques that a company could use to hedge?

There are a range of possibilities which include the following.

Invoice in home currency

In this case a company seeks to invoice all customers in the home currency when they export and seeks to be invoiced in the home currency when they import. This effectively passes any foreign currency risk to the other party to the transaction.

The ability to do this depends, to a large extent, on the strength of the company in relation to its customers and its suppliers. If, for example, a customer in a foreign market has a choice of potential suppliers, and other suppliers are willing to invoice the customer in the customers own currency, it would be very difficult to compete in that market place if a company sought to invoice in their home currency.

Leading and lagging

This involves **bringing forward or delaying the transaction**. The purpose of this technique is to be able to take advantage of forecast exchange rate changes. Leading means bringing forward a receipt or a payment whereas lagging means delaying a receipt or a payment.

This is more a technique to take advantage of a company's forecasting ability rather than strictly to manage risk. As it is based on forecasts, those forecasts could, of course, be wrong!

Direct matching

If a business has receipts and payments at the same point in time, and in the same foreign currency, then it would be sensible to match the receipt with the payment.

If a German company is due to receive from a customer $3 million in 4 months' time, and pay to a supplier $2 million in 4 months' time, it would make sense to use the anticipated receipt to make the payment. This would leave a net receipt of $1 million. There is clearly still transaction risk on that net receipt but that could be hedged using other methods.

Foreign currency accounts and matching

If a business has a significant volume of receipts and payments in the same foreign currency, rather than direct matching it would make sense to open a bank account in the foreign currency, deposit all receipts into that bank account and use the account to make all of the foreign currency payments. The net balance could then be converted into the home currency at a time when the exchange rate is favourable.

EXTERNAL HEDGING TECHNIQUES — TRANSACTION RISK

External hedging means that a company uses an outside party in some way to hedge the transaction risk that arises. The main techniques that could be used are as follows.

1 Forward exchange contracts.
2 Money market hedging.
3 Financial futures.
4 Option contracts.
5 Currency swaps.

In this chapter we will consider how forward exchange contracts and money market hedging could be used to manage transaction risk. Futures, options and swaps, which are more advanced and more complex techniques, are considered in later chapters.

Finance terminology explained

Forward exchange contract

A forward exchange contract is a contract, or agreement, to buy or to sell a certain amount of foreign currency at a certain future date using the forward rate. We saw earlier that the forward rate was calculated using interest rate parity theory.

Forward contracts are widely available to companies of all sizes, and for transactions of any amount. The contract is an over-the-counter (OTC) contract between a company and a dealer which means that it will be tailored to the company's specific needs.

The contract is legally binding on both parties.

Example 2

Noodles is a company based in the United States that sells advanced scanning equipment used in hospitals. All of its orders are unique. It has just secured an order for a new scanner which will be delivered to a hospital in Spain in 6 months' time. The scanner will be sold for €8m and the hospital will pay when the scanner is delivered.

Exchange dealers in the United States have quoted the following rates:

Current spot rate   €0.9237 - €0.9456 per $1
Six month forward rate   €0.9563 - €0.9722 per $1

How much will Noodles receive from the sale of this scanner if the transaction is hedged using a forward contract?

Solution 2

The forward rate is quoted as euro per dollar. Noodles will receive euro from the customer which it will then sell to an exchange dealer for dollars. The dealer will therefore be buying the variable currency, the euro, and will buy at the higher rate.

The relevant forward rate is therefore €0.9722 per $1.

The receipt in $ will be €8m/0.9722 = $8,228,760.

Some points to note about forward exchange contracts

- A forward contract is a perfect currency hedge – it eliminates exchange rate risk. In the above example Noodles knows that when the €8m is received it can convert this into exactly $8,228,760.

- A normal forward contract has no flexibility in terms of the date upon which it is used. If, in the above example, the customer did not pay on the due date – this creates a problem. The forward contract is a binding contract between Noodles and the dealer and therefore Noodles will still need to honour the transaction with the foreign exchange dealer on the due date even if the customer does not pay.

- Because of the lack of flexibility forward contracts are best used to hedge single large known transactions such as the sale or purchase or a large piece of machinery, or the payment or receipt of interest in a foreign currency on a due date.

- It is possible to build some flexibility into the dates of a forward exchange contract by entering into an option dated forward exchange contract.

An option dated forward exchange contract

This is a binding forward contract but one which allows some flexibility in terms of the dates upon which it can be used. Noodles, for example, may have been able to enter into a forward contract which could be used between 6 and 7 months from now.

The downside of having the flexibility is that the rate offered would be the worst forward rate across the range of dates offered.

Money market hedging

Money markets are markets available for borrowing and investing money on a short term basis in different currencies. A company can use the money markets to create a transaction risk hedge. By using the money markets a company can bring forward the conversion from one currency to another so that the money can be converted at today's spot rate, and thereby avoid currency risk.

The approach to using the money markets to create a hedge is slightly different depending on whether we are hedging a foreign currency cash receipt or a foreign currency cash payment.

Hedging for a future foreign currency cash payment

The approach here is to convert some **home** currency (which will need to be borrowed) into the **foreign** currency today on the spot market and put that money on deposit in the foreign currency until it is needed to make the future payment. By converting cash from the home currency into the foreign currency today, rather than in the future, a company can avoid exchange rate risk.

Need to know!

To hedge a future foreign currency cash **payment** a company needs to:

- **invest** in the **foreign currency** and

- **borrow** in the **home currency**.

The hedge is created in the following way.

1   Determine the amount of **foreign currency to invest** today. When a company invests in the foreign currency it will earn interest. Taking the interest into account it can therefore invest less in the foreign currency today than the amount that will be needed to make a future payment in that foreign currency.

2   Determine the **cost in the home currency today**, assuming that the foreign currency needed is purchased at today's spot rate.

3   If we assume that we need to **borrow** an amount in the **home currency** today, in order to purchase the foreign currency, we can determine the total cost of the hedge on the date that the payment needs to be made.

Example 3

Milan Crystal, a manufacturer of glass crystal based in Italy, has just purchased a large amount of material used in the glass manufacturing process from a supplier in the United Arab Emirates. The supplier requires a payment of $600,000 in six months' time.

The following information is available.

Money Market rates (annual equivalent)

	Borrowing	Deposit
Euro	6.0%	5.1%
Dollars	5.2%	4.0%

Spot rate = $1.3245 - $1.3541 per €1

Determine the cost of the purchase, in six months' time, in euro, assuming that Milan Crystal hedges its exposure using the money markets.

Solution 3

The money market hedge can be illustrated as follows:

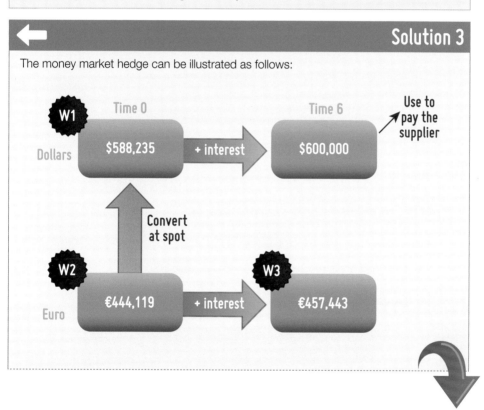

Working 1

The amount that is invested in dollars today should be the present value of the payment that Milan needs to make in six months' time.

Interest rates are always quoted on an annual equivalent basis. Milan Crystal will only invest for a six month period and therefore the interest earned would, on a simple basis, be the annual interest x 6/12.

The interest earned would be = 4.0% x 6/12 = 2.0% = 0.02 as a decimal.

The present value of $600,000 would therefore be $600,000/(1 + 0.02) = $588,235.

Working 2

To invest $588,235 in dollars today, Milan Crystal needs to purchase this amount from a dealer today. Milan needs to buy the dollars today in order to invest and therefore the dealer will sell the dollar (the variable currency) to Milan at the lower rate.

The cost to Milan today in euros is therefore $588,235/1.3245 = €444,119.

Working 3

In order to pay €444,119 to an exchange dealer today, we will assume that Milan will need to borrow this amount for six months.

The interest paid on borrowings over a six month period would, on a simple basis, be:

6.0% x 6/12 = 3% = 0.03 as a decimal.

If €444,119 is borrowed today this will grow to be a loan of €444,119 x (1+0.03) = €457,443 in six months' time.

After six months Milan will use the investment in dollars to pay the supplier.

The cost in euros in six months' time of paying this supplier is therefore €457,443.

The predicted result of the money market hedge can then be compared to the predicted result of other hedging techniques e.g. a forward exchange contract to determine which is likely to provide the most favourable result.

Exam tip – Pro-rata of annual interest rates

When working through a money market hedge calculation it is necessary to pro-rata the annual interest rates that will be given in the question.

Unless told otherwise it is generally acceptable to pro-rata these rates on a simple basis which was the approach adopted in the solution to example 3. An examiner may, alternatively expect the pro-rata to be determined on a compound basis. If so, this would need to be approached in the way illustrated in chapter 2.

Hedging a future foreign currency cash receipt

The approach here is to convert some **foreign** currency (which will need to be borrowed) into the **home** currency today on the spot market and put that money on deposit in the home currency. The future cash receipt in the foreign currency can then be used to repay the amount borrowed. By converting cash from the foreign currency into the home currency today, rather than in the future, a company can avoid exchange rate risk.

Need to know!

To hedge a future foreign currency cash **receipt** a company needs to:

* **borrow** in the **foreign currency** and

* **invest** in the **home currency.**

The hedge is created in the following way.

1 Determine the amount of **foreign currency to borrow** today. A company will pay interest on any amount borrowed. The amount borrowed today will be the present value of the future cash receipt.

2 Convert the amount borrowed in the foreign currency into **the home currency today using today's spot rate**.

3 Invest the amount converted in the **home currency** today. The value of the investment at the time when the receipt is due, will be the hedged receipt.

Example 4

Milan Crystal has an export contract with a wholesaler based in the UK, who then sells the glass crystal to UK retailers. The wholesaler settles the amount outstanding on a quarterly basis in sterling (pounds). The next receipt of £350,000 is due in three months' time. The following information is available:

Money Market rates (annual equivalent)

	Borrowing	Deposit
Euro	6.0%	5.1%
Sterling	4.2%	3.7%
Spot rate = €1.1235 - €1.1578 per £1		

Determine the result of hedging the next quarterly receipt by using a money market hedge.

The money market hedge can be illustrated as follows:

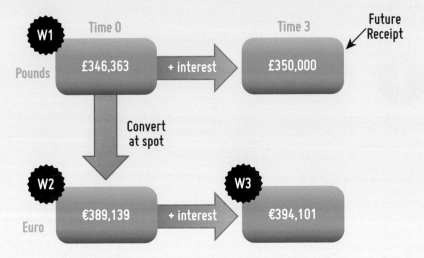

Working 1

The amount that is borrowed in pounds (sterling) today should be the present value of the receipt due in three months' time.

Interest rates are again quoted on an annual equivalent basis. Milan Crystal will only borrow for a three month period and therefore the interest would on a simple basis be:

4.2% x 3/12 = 1.05% = 0.0105 as a decimal.

The present value of £350,000 would therefore be £350,000/(1 + 0.0105) = £346,363

Working 2

When Milan Crystal borrows in pounds today, it can convert the cash borrowed into euro today. Milan will need to buy the euro. The dealer will therefore be selling the euro (the variable currency) and will sell at the lower rate.

The receipt today in euro is therefore £346,363 x 1.1235 = €389,139.

Working 3

The cash is then invested in euro for 3 months. The interest received on the investment will be 5.1% x 3/12 = 1.275% = 0.01275 as a decimal.

The value of the investment in euro in 3 months' time is therefore:

€389,139 x (1 + 0.01275) = €394,101

The receipt of £350,000 from the customer is then used to repay the loan taken out in sterling. This leaves us with a receipt in euro of €394,101.

Some points to note about money market hedging

- Like a forward contract a money market hedge is a **perfect currency hedge**. Provided we can fix the rates of interest at which we can borrow or invest in different currencies we will know exactly how much we will receive or pay in the home currency.

- A money market hedge should give a very **similar result to a forward exchange contract** hedge because of interest rate parity. The forward rate is based on interest rate differences between currencies and the money market is based on borrowing and investing at different interest rates in different currencies.

- A money market hedge does, however, provide more flexibility than a forward contract. If, for example, a customer pays late following a foreign currency sale, it may be possible to extend the loan in the foreign currency so that the receipt can still be used to repay the loan.

Chapter 19
key points summary

- A strengthening currency is an adverse exchange rate movement when exporting and a favourable exchange rate movement when importing.

- There are three types of exchange rate risk:

    - transaction risk – when currency is converted following a transaction

    - translation risk – risk in the financial statements from translation

    - economic risk – long term – impact on the present value of future cashflows.

- Exchange rate – the dealer will always sell the variable currency at the lower rate and buy the variable currency at the higher rate.

- Purchasing power parity:

    - same good priced at same true amount in different currencies

    - higher inflation leads to a weakening of that currency

    - formula $\Rightarrow$ $S1 = S0 \times \dfrac{1 + \text{inf}_c}{1 + \text{inf}_b}$

- Interest rate parity:

    - forward rate in forward contracts ins based on this

    - formula $\Rightarrow$ $F0 = S0 \times \dfrac{1 + \text{int}_c}{1 + \text{int}_b}$

- External hedging techniques covered in this chapter:

    - forward contract – lock into contract at the forward rate

    - money market hedge

        - if foreign currency receipt $\Rightarrow$ borrow in the foreign currency and invest in the home currency

        - if foreign currency payment $\Rightarrow$ invest in the foreign currency and borrow in the home currency.

Introduction
what is this chapter about?

Options and futures are types of derivative contracts. They have a wide range of potential applications in finance and financial management including the management of currency risk and interest rate risk. In this chapter options and futures are introduced, and some basic applications are covered.

Key areas of the chapter are ....

1. **Introduction to options** – what is an option contract and what are the potential gains and losses that can arise from taking a position on an option contract?

2. **Black Scholes model** – the Black Scholes option pricing model offers a way to value an option when there is a period of time before the option expires? What are the main variables that determine the value of an option under the Black Scholes model and how are these used within the model?

3. **Real options** – one useful application of option theory is in investment appraisal. When considering new investments using NPV analysis, often 'real options' arise as a result of undertaking the investment. What are these real options and how are they valued?

4. **Futures** – what are futures contracts and how can they be used to hedge risk?

INTRODUCTION TO OPTIONS

Finance terminology explained

What is an option?

An option is an agreement or contract that gives the holder the right to buy or sell a specific quantity of an asset on or before an agreed future date, at a predetermined price.

Options are available on a whole range of assets including shares, stock market indicies, currency, interest rates and commodities (e.g. sugar, cocoa, wheat).

Option holder and option writer

All option contracts involves a holder and a writer. The option writer will create the option contract and sell it to someone who then becomes the option holder.

The option holder then has the option to buy or sell a specific quantity of the asset at a future date.

Don't confuse the positions of an option writer and an option holder. The position of each in terms of gains and losses is quite different.

Fred is an option trader at a major bank. He has just created (written) an option which allows the holder to buy one share in Lowcost Airlines in 3 months' time for 500c. Fred is prepared to sell this option for 10c.

Alice decides to buy this option. She pays Fred, the option writer, 10c and as a result **becomes the option holder**.

In 3 months time, Alice **could** pay 500c cash to Fred, the writer of the option, and in return get one share in the company.

The word 'could' is key – the holder has the **right** to buy the share but there is **no obligation** to go ahead and exercise the option. If the option holder exercises the option to buy the share, the option writer must then sell the share at that price to the option holder.

What would happen if the shares in Lowcost Airlines are trading at 440c in 3 months' time?

It would make far more sense for Alice, the option holder, to buy the share on the stock market rather than through exercising her option. In this case Alice would allow the option to **lapse** (i.e. do nothing).

What would happen if the shares in Lowcost Airlines are trading at 580c in 3 months' time?

In this case it would be advantageous for Alice to buy the share at the option price. In this instance Alice would **exercise** the option (i.e. exercise her right under the option to buy the share for 500c). Fred, the option holder would then have to sell one share to Alice for 500c.

What is the point of holding options?

There are two main ways in which options like this could be used by a holder:

1   To speculate (or gamble!!)

Alice, in the example above was able to buy the option from Fred for 10c. When the share price went up to 580c we saw that Alice would excercise her option to buy the share for 500c. Should could then sell the share for 580c on the stock market making a profit of 80c. If we deduct the 10c cost of the option the net profit would be 70c. This is a massive 700% return on the cost of the option.

The risk is very high, however, because if the share price fell to 440c we saw that the option would not be worth exercising. The 10c that Alice paid for these share would therefore have been lost.

2 To hedge risk (much more sensible!)

Suppose a coffee importer needs to buy a certain amount of coffee in 3 months' time, and needs to be certain that the price will not be more than a certain amount.

The coffee importer could purchase an option (and become an option holder) to buy the coffee at a certain price exercisable in 3 months' time. If the coffee rises in price the importer could exercise the option and buy the coffee at that guaranteed price. If the price falls, the option holder could, however, allow the option to lapse and pay less than this. By paying a small amount to purchase the option the holder can therefore guarantee a maximum price that would have to be paid for the coffee.

Finance terminology explained

Some important option terminology

Term	What it means
Call option	The right to buy an asset
Put option	The right to sell an asset
Exercise or strike price	The price at which an asset can be bought or sold if the option is exercised
European option	An option that can only be exercised on the expiry date
American option	An option that can be exercised at any time up to the expiry date
Premium	The cost, or value of an option

What is the value of an option?

The value of an option is the amount that an option writer could sell an option for, or the amount that a potential option holder is prepared to pay to hold the option.

This value is sometimes called the cost of an option, or, alternatively, it is sometimes called the option premium.

Need to know!

The terms **option premium, cost of an option**, and **value of an option** all mean the same thing! The terms all essentially refer to the amount that an option (or, more specifically, the rights in the option) will be worth to a holder.

Options are a form of **derivative**. This means that they derive their value from the value of an underlying asset. The key to understanding options (and other derivative products) is to understand that the option is a separate instrument to the underlying asset (e.g. a share) **but** that its value is always dependent on the value of the underlying asset.

There are two elements to the value of any option.

1   The intrinsic value.

2   The time value.

The intrinsic value is relatively straightforward to determine. The time value is much more complicated!

The intrinsic value of a call option

The basic value of an option is called the intrinsic value. This is always the **value**, or worth of the option **on the expiry date** (i.e. on the last date that it can be used).

If we take the example of Alice being the holder of an option to **buy** a share (a call option) in a company for 500c (the exercise price). The table below shows us what the intrinsic value of the option would be, given possible market share prices on the date that the option has to be used.

Share Price	440c	500c	580c
Exercise Price	500c	500c	500c
Intrinsic Value	**NIL**	**NIL**	**80c**

<table>
<tr><td align="center">↑</td><td align="center">↑</td><td align="center">↑</td></tr>
<tr><td align="center">Out of the money</td><td align="center">At the money</td><td align="center">In the money</td></tr>
</table>

If the share price was 500c or less the option is worthless to Alice on the date of expiry. There would be no benefit in exercising the option and paying 500p for the share, if the share can be bought on the stock market for this amount or less.

If, however, the share price was 580c, as we saw earlier, Alice could exercise the option for 500c, and then the share that she receives could be sold for 580c on a stock market, netting a profit of 80c.

- **In the money** – this is where the share price is above the exercise price and the option has a positive intrinsic value to the holder.

- **At the money** – this is where the share price is equal to the exercise price and the intrinsic value is nil.

- **Out of the money** – this is where the share price is below the exercise price and the intrinsic value is nil.

The **intrinsic value** of the call option can be shown graphically as follows:

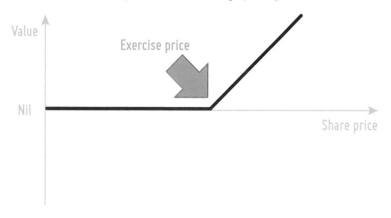

The intrinsic value of a put option

If we take the same example as above but let's assume that in this case the option is a right to sell a share for 500c i.e. a **put** option.

What would the intrinsic value be at different share prices?

Share Price	440c	500c	580c
Exercise Price	500c	500c	500c
Intrinsic Value	**60c**	**NIL**	**Nil**

Given that it is a right to sell and not a right to buy, if the share price is less than 500c, then the option will have a value – or will be 'in the money'. If the share price is 440c, an option holder could buy the share for 440c on the stock market and then sell it for 500c by exercising the option. The option is therefore worth 60c.

If the share price was 580c – in this case the option is worthless. There is no point selling a share for 500c by exercising the option if the share can be sold on the stock market for 580c.

The intrinsic value of the put option can be shown graphically as follows:

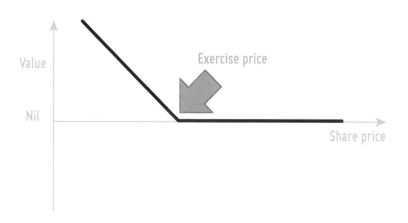

One additional point about this graph – the maximum intrinsic value of a put option is also the exercise price. If the share is worthless, or the share price is nil, a holder of the put option could buy the share for nothing and sell it (by exercising the option) for the exercise price.

Other aspects of the intrinsic value

We do not have the ability in a publication such as this to consider further aspects of the intrinsic value.

More detailed publications on option theory will consider other aspects of the intrinsic value such as the value from the point of view of the writer rather than the holder, or the profit or loss position to a writer or a holder when a premium paid is taken into account.

Don't confuse these other aspects with the basic intrinsic value of a call and a put option to an option holder. The graphs that we have seen so far show the intrinsic value to someone that already holds a call or a put option.

THE BLACK SCHOLES MODEL

What is the value of an option if there is a period of time to go before the expiry date?

This presents an interesting problem. Suppose a holder owned a call option that was currently at the money (and therefore had no intrinsic value) but which was to be exercised in 3 months' time rather than today. If the share price was higher in 3 months' time than it is today the option would be 'in the money' on the expiry date. There must be a significant possibility that the share price would rise before the expiry date and therefore despite an intrinsic value of zero should the option have a value today?

In 1973 Fisher Black and Myron Scholes developed a mathematical model which allowed an option to be priced or valued 'correctly' even when there was a period of time to go before the option expiry date. Robert Merton then refined and developed the model.

The key to the model was an understanding that every share option position could effectively be 'simulated' by borrowing and buying and selling shares on the stock market.

The Black Scholes model provides a means of valuing a call option.

The variables underlying the Black Scholes model

The mathematics behind the Black Scholes model involves some complex differential calculus using probability theory. Most students studying financial management, even at an advanced level, will not need to understand the mathematics behind the model.

Even students who have to calculate the value of an option using the Black Scholes model will often find that it becomes a rather mechanical process of putting the variables into a formula given by an examiner, following a series of repetitive steps and producing a result on a calculator.

All students who study option theory should, however, be aware of the variables that the Black Scholes model is based upon. They are:

Variable	Explanation
Current price of the asset	For example the current price of a share for a share option.
Exercise price	The price at which the option can be exercised. For a call option this is the price at which a holder can buy the asset.
Risk free rate of interest	The rate of interest charged for risk free borrowing.
Time to expiry	The length of time before the expiry date of the option.
Standard deviation of the asset	This measures the volatility or risk of the underlying asset e.g. the volatility of share price movements for a share option.

(The first two variables are bracketed as **Intrinsic value**; the last three as **Time value**.)

The Black Scholes model is therefore based on five variables. The difference between the first two variables is the intrinsic value as we have already seen. The time value element, or the extra value because there is a period of the time to the expiry of the option, is made up of three additional variables.

How would a change in any of the variables affect the value of a call option?

If any of the variables underlying the Black Scholes model were to change then this would affect the value of the option. Let's see how an increase in any of the variables affects the value of a call option.

Variable	Impact of an increase in the variable on the value of the option	Explanation
Current price of the asset	Increase	The higher the current price of the asset the greater the intrinsic value of a call option.
Exercise price	Decrease	The higher the exercise price the lesser the intrinsic value of the call option.
Risk free rate of interest	Increase	This is a complex point. In essence there is a time value of money benefit from holding a call option – the greater the risk free rate of interest the greater the time value of money benefit.
Time to expiry	Increase	This is a similar explanation to the risk free rate. If there is a time value of money benefit from holding a call option – the greater the time to expiry the greater the time value of money benefit.
Standard deviation of the asset	Increase	To the holder of a call option the greater the standard deviation of the underlying asset the greater the chance of the option being 'in the money' on expiry and the further 'in the money' the option could be.

Exam tip – Change in Black Scholes variables

An easy way to remember the way in which a change in any of the five variables affects the value of the call option is to remember that the exercise price is the one that stands out as being different!

An increase in the exercise price will decrease the value of the option. An increase in any of the other four variables will increase the value of the option.

The same pattern is also true in reverse i.e. if there was a decrease in any of the variables.

The Black Scholes formula

Don't be put off by the formula if you have to use it in an exam. It will always be given to you and with practice the calculations can be performed quickly. The formula, where C represents the value of the call option is:

$$C = Ps\,N(d_1) - Pe\,N\,(d_2)e^{-rt}$$

Where:

$$d_1 = \frac{\ln\,(Ps/Pe) + (r + 0.5s^2)t}{s\sqrt{t}}$$

and

$$d_2 = d_1 - s\sqrt{t}$$

The variables are:

Ps = Current price of the asset

Pe = Exercise price

r = risk free rate of interest

t = time to expiry (as a proportion of a year)

s = standard deviation of the asset

Example 1

Andy owns a call option on a share. The share is currently trading at 200c. The option allows Andy to buy a share for 150c in 6 months' time. The risk free rate is 5% and the standard deviation of the share is 20%. How much is the option worth?

There is a bit of alegbra involved in finding the solutions to each part of the formula. If you are not confident with this make sure that you run through the steps with a classroom tutor.

The variables are:

Ps = 200c
Pe = 150c
r   = 5% or 0.05
t   = 6 months = 0.5 (in years)
s   = 20% or 0.20

Working 1 – Calculate d_1

$$d_1 = \frac{\ln(200c/150c) + (0.05 + 0.5 \times 0.20^2)0.5}{0.20\sqrt{0.5}}$$

$d_1 = 2.28$

Working 2 – Calculate d_2

$d_2 = 2.28 - 0.20 \times \sqrt{0.5}$

$d_2 = 2.14$

Working 3 – calculate $N(d_1)$ and $N(d_2)$

This involves using the normal distribution tables in appendix 2 at the back of the book. There is a guide to using the tables in appendix 2.

From the tables:

$N(d_1) = 0.5 + 0.4887 = 0.9887$

$N(d_2) = 0.5 + 0.4838 = 0.9838$

Working 4 – the value of the call option

We now use the main formula to find the value of the call option

$C = 200c \times 0.9887 - 150c \times 0.9838 \times e^{-(0.05 \times 0.5)}$

$C = 53.81$ cents

The value of the call option is therefore **53.81 cents**.

The value is made up of the intrinsic value and the time value. We know that the intrinsic value must be (200c-150c) and therefore the time value must be (53.81c - 50c) = 3.81c.

This is the extra value attached to the option because of the time to expiry.

The put call parity relationship

The Black Scholes model provides a way of valuing a call option. To find the value of a put option we firstly need to value a call option using the Black Scholes formula. The value of the equivalent put option can then be found by default because the following relationship must hold true:

The position of an investor who buys a call option on a share, and at the same time sells a put option at the same exercise price, is **exactly the same** as an investor who borrows the present value of the exercise price and buys a share.

From this relationship the following equation can be derived:

$P = C - Ps + Pe \times e^{-rt}$

The definition of the terms are the same as in the Black Scholes formula. P represents the value of a put option.

Example 2

Using the information from example 1 and the solution to example 1, what would be the value of a put option with exactly the same terms as the call option given?

Solution 2

Using $P = C - Ps + Pe \times e^{-rt}$

$P = 53.81c - 200c + 150c \times e^{(-0.05 \times 0.5)}$

$P = 0.11c$

An equivalent put option is therefore only worth 0.11c.

The fact that the put option is worth a lot less than the call option based on the information in example 1 should not be a surprise. As a call option the intrinsic value is 'in the money' but as a put option it is 'out of the money' (and by a significant amount). For the put option to be worth anything on expiry the share price would need to fall to below 150c.

The assumptions underlying the Black Scholes model

To derive the model a number of important simplifying assumptions were made. Even though the Black Scholes model is widely used in real life to value options the assumptions are also limitations, and provide a basis for criticism of the result obtained. What are these assumptions?

Assumption	What it means
The option is a European call	The model assumes that the option is a call option that can only be exercised on the expiry date i.e. it is a European style option.
An investor can borrow at the risk free rate	The model is based on recreating the option position by borrowing money to buy a share. It assumes that an investor pays exactly the risk free rate on any amount borrowed.
The risk free rate and the standard deviation of the underlying asset are constant	The model assumes that there will be no change in either of these variables before the expiry date.
No dividend is payable before the expiry date of the option	A key difference between owning a share and owning an option to buy a share in the future, is that the holder of an option will only receive a dividend after the option is exercised.
The range of possible share prices follows the pattern of a log normal distribution	The model uses probability theory based on a log normal distribution.
There are no transactions costs	Fees are avoided if borrowing money or buying or selling shares.

Types of option contract

There are two main types of option contract available:

1   An OTC (over-the-counter) option

This is a contract that is written specifically for the holders needs by a financial institution e.g. a bank. This is a tailor-made contract. There is no secondary market in this type of contract.

2   An exchange traded option

This is a option created by dealers on an option market. Contracts are standardised rather than tailor-made and there is an active secondary market for buying and selling contracts.

REAL OPTIONS

Option theory can be applied not just to options that are created by the financial services industry. It can also be applied to real life situations where an option appears to exist because of a particular set of circumstances. One such situation is the the application of option theory to an investment appraisal scenario.

Finance terminology explained

What are real options?

These are options on real assets that can be exercised through the decision making of finance managers within a company. They are options to buy or sell real assets such as property, machinery or even subsidiary companies at certain dates in the future.

Real options often arise when considering an investment appraisal exercise using NPV techniques. When the information relating to a new investment is analysed, as well as the direct cashflows from the investment, the possibility of real options sometimes emerges.

What are the main types of real option available to a company?

The main types of real option are as follows.

1   Expansion option ('follow-on' option)

Suppose a manufacturing company is considering purchasing a plot of land to build a new factory. The plot of land is 30,000 square feet in size. Given current production and sales plans the company only intends to use 20,000 square feet to construct the factory. The terms of the purchase are that the company must, however, purchase the full 30,000 square feet if it wishes to go ahead with the construction of the factory. Because of access issues it would not be possible for the company to sell the additional 10,000 square feet that it does not need. The only possible use of the land is that the factory could be expanded at a future date if demand for the product increases.

When carrying out an NPV evaluation on the proposed new investment the possible expansion using the extra 10,000 square feet would be ignored. There is considerable uncertainty relating to the expansion and therefore the cashflows relating to this should be ignored in the NPV evaluation.

The possible expansion is however a **real call option**. The option could be 'exercised' by spending the amount necessary to expand the factory (equivalent to the cost of buying a share if a share option is exercised). After constructing the expanded part of the factory the company would receive future net cash inflows from the extra production and sales that would be generated.

2   Option to delay

This is where there would be an option to delay capital expenditure. Suppose a manufacturing company makes an assumption that a major piece of machinery will need replacing after 10 years of the life of a new potential project. This will be the assumption that will be used in the NPV evaluation.

If, however, there was an option to refurbish the equipment after 10 years for a small capital outlay which would delay the need to replace for a further 5 years, this option could be valued using option theory.

This is again a **call option**. The option is exercised by spending the amount needed to refurbish the factory. The benefit of exercising the option in this case would be the time value of money impact of delaying the purchase of the major new piece of machinery.

3　Option to abandon

A company is considering an investment in a foreign country. The investment has a projected life of 25 years, but as an incentive to invest let's suppose that the Government in the foreign country has offered to buy the investment for a certain amount after 5 years. The company therefore has an option to sell the investment after 5 years or alternatively can continue with the investment for its 25 year life.

The option in this case is a **put option**. The company can exercise the put option by selling the investment but will then lose the future net cashflows that would have arisen over the remaining life of the project.

How are real options incorporated into an NPV appraisal?

The approach is to:

1　Calculate the project NPV using the known forecast cashflows.

2　Use the Black Scholes model to value the real option. The three variables that make up the time value would be similar to the variables if using the the model to value a share. Care needs to be taken, however, with the two variables that make up the intrinsic value. In the case of an expansion option, for example:

● the cost of expansion = the exercise price (Pe).

● the present value of net cash inflows from the expansion = price of the underlying asset (Ps).

3　Add the value of the option to the project NPV to give the strategic NPV.

	$
Project NPV	X
Value of real option	X
Strategic NPV	**X**

The decision to invest should then be based on the strategic NPV rather than the project NPV alone.

FUTURES

A futures contract is an alternative to taking out a option contract as a way to hedge risk. Unlike an option contract, however, a futures contract is binding on both parties i.e. it must be honoured by both parties to the contract.

Finance terminology explained

What is a futures contract?

A futures contract is a standardised contract between two parties to buy or sell a certain amount of an asset at a certain date in the future at a price agreed today.

All futures contracts are exchange traded contracts. This means that they are created by dealers on a futures exchange, regulated by a futures exchange, and settled on the futures exchange.

A user of the futures market can sign contracts agreeing to buy the asset in the future (a buy futures contract), or can agree to sell the asset in the future (a sell futures contract). A commitment to buying an asset in the future is called a long position whereas a commitment to selling an asset in the future is called a short position.

How are futures contracts settled?

A key feature of the way in which a futures exchange works is that there is flexibility in terms of the way in which futures contracts can be settled.

Futures contract can be settled in three main ways.

1   **On expiry by physical delivery** – in this case the futures contract is settled on the settlement date by physical delivery of the goods. A buyer of orange juice futures, for example, could, on the settlement date, pay the seller the agreed price, and the seller would then physically deliver the agreed quantity of orange juice to the buyer. This is the same as the way in which forward exchange contracts for currency risk were settled in chapter 19.

2   **On expiry by calculation of the gain or loss** – some futures contracts are notional. This means that although there is a contract to buy or sell an asset at a future date it is not possible to physically deliver that asset. An example is a stock market index future. When the index changes, the value of a contract to buy or sell the index changes and creates a gain or loss which is settled on the expiry date.

3   **Prior to expiry - closing out** – in this case the futures contracts are effectively closed out by entering into a reversing contract at any time before the settlement date. A buyer of orange juice futures could, for example, sign additional futures contracts to sell orange juice before the settlement date. The two contracts cancel each other out although a cash profit or loss will be generated from the difference in price between the two types of contract.

Need to know!

The ability to settle futures contracts prior to expiry via closing out is the feature that makes futures contracts very attractive to users. It means that the futures contract can really be used to hedge a transaction that takes place **any time** up to the expiry date. This provides a large amount of timing flexibility.

Exam questions involving futures, as we will see in the next two chapters, will almost certainly require settlement prior to expiry via closing out.

Example 3

Sunny Outlook is a company that specialises in buying frozen concentrated orange juice in bulk quantities. The orange juice is then defrosted, reconstituted and repackaged, and sold to major retailers throughout the world. Sunny Outlook sources the orange juice from suppliers in Florida and Mexico. The price of the concentrated orange juice is very volatile and Sunny Outlook therefore wishes to hedge the price risk by using futures contracts.

Now it is January 1st. Sunny Outlook wishes to hedge the import of 60,000 lb of frozen orange juice planned for September 12th. The following information is available from ICE (Intercontinental exchange) futures US:

Standard contract size = 15,000 lb of orange juice solids

Price on January 1st for delivery on September 12th = $1.60 per lb.

Requirement

(a) What is the result of the hedge if we assume physical delivery of the orange juice on September 12th?

(b) What is the result of the hedge if we assume that the price of orange juice futures on both the futures and the spot market is $1.70 per lb on September 12th and that the futures contracts are settled through closing out just before the contract period ends?

Solution 3

Part (a)

The futures contracts are only available in standard sizes of 15,000 lb. To use the futures market to hedge, Sunny Outlook must therefore enter into multiples of this number of contracts. Sunny Outlook wants to hedge the purchase of 60,000 lb of orange juice and will therefore enter into:

$$\frac{60,000}{15,000} = 4 \text{ contracts}$$

These will be contacts to buy the commodity, or buy futures.

If the contracts are physically deliverable, on September 12th Sunny Outlook will pay:

4 contracts x 15,000 lb x $1.60 = $96,000 for the orange juice.

555555555555553333333

222222222222222222222222222222

Part (b)

In this case, Sunny Outlook will still buy 4 futures contracts on January 1st. On September 12th, however, Sunny Outlook will close out the futures contracts and then buy the orange juice at the spot price on the spot market.

Closing out the futures

This is achieved by signing 4 new reversing futures contracts at the new futures price i.e. 4 sell futures at $1.70, or agreements to sell orange juice to a futures dealer at $1.70. These contracts cancel out the original contracts but, because the price has changed, the difference in price is settled up with the dealer.

Because Sunny Outlook has a contract to buy orange juice from a dealer at $1.60 per lb and then sell it back to the dealer at the higher price of $1.70 per lb, the dealer will pay Sunny Outlook the value of the difference between the rates to settle up.

Sunny Outlook will therefore receive from the dealer:

4 contracts x 15,000 lb x ($1.70 - $1.60) = $6,000

This one payment of $6,000 by the dealer to Sunny Outlook settles both contractual obligations. This means that Sunny Outlook will not physically buy orange juice from the dealer or sell orange juice to the dealer.

Buy orange juice at spot

Sunny Outlook must now, however, buy the orange juice on the spot market at the new spot rate of $1.70. The cost of the orange juice will be:

60,000 lb x $1.70 = $102,000

Net result

The net result of the hedge in part (b) is therefore:

	$
Gain on the futures market	6,000
Cost of orange juice on spot market	(102,000)
Net cost of the orange juice	**(96,000)**

The financial result i.e. the cost of the orange juice to Sunny Outlook is therefore **exactly the same in both cases**.

Some other characteristics of futures contracts

- **Standardised contracts** - all futures contracts are created by exchange dealers and are traded on an exchange. To make this feasible all futures contracts are standardised in terms of amounts, settlement dates, and, in the case of commodity futures, the quality and consistency of the product.

- **Margins** – users of futures contracts must pay an initial margin to a dealer, and a variation margin on a daily basis. These are amounts that meet the potential exposure existing at the end of each trading day. If the price changes such that one party will potentially make a loss when futures contracts are settled, that party must deposit an amount in a 'margin account' to meet that loss.

- **Speculation or hedging** – like options, futures contracts can be used to hedge or to speculate. The scenario in example 1 involved using futures contracts to hedge. A speculator could, however, have taken a long position on futures (buy futures) in the hope that the price would rise. If the price rises the speculator would buy the orange juice on the futures market and sell it at a higher price on the spot market. Of course the contract is binding and so if the price fell the speculator would be tied into making what could be a significant loss.

Chapter 20
key points summary

- An option gives the holder the right to buy or sell an asset.

- The cost of the option is a premium which has two elements:

    - the time value – the difference between the price of the asset and the exercise price

    - the time value – based on the risk free rate, the time to expiry and the standard deviation of the asset.

- A call option is valued using the Black Scholes model.

- Real options are options on physical assets rather than financial assets. The strategic NPV of an investment adds the value of any real options that arise to the NPV of the forecast project cashflows.

- Futures contracts are binding obligations to buy or sell an asset in the future. They can be settled:

    - on expiry by physical delivery or calculation of gain or loss

    - prior to expiry by closing out.

Introduction
what is this chapter about?

This chapter builds on the risk management techniques covered in chapters 19 and 20. In the chapter we look at how futures contracts and option contracts can be used to hedge currency risk. A word of warning – some of the calculations are quite heavy going but if you work through each step carefully, and read my comments about why we carry out each step, you should understand the process.

Exam tip – Complex currency questions

When reading through the information in a complex currency risk management question examples in this chapter) it is important to think about three things. They are:

1   where is a company based (for example the United States)

2   how is the currency quoted (for example dollars per euro)

3   what does the company want to do (for example buy euro from a dealer to pay a supplier in euro).

Key areas of the chapter are ....

1   **Currency futures** – how can currency futures be used to hedge currency risk? Will using currency futures to hedge currency risk always give a perfect result?

2   **Currency options** – how could currency options be used to hedge currency risk? Under what circumstances would this be a better method of hedging than using currency futures?

CURRENCY FUTURES

A currency future is a **binding** contract to exchange one currency for another at an agreed price (that is exchange rate) on an agreed future date.

Currency futures are therefore similar to forward contracts (seen in chapter 19) in many respects. Both contracts are binding on both parties and both can be used to fix the amount at which one currency is converted into another on a future date.

Forward contracts are, however, OTC (over-the- counter) contracts which means that they are written specifically for the needs of the user whereas futures contracts are standardised exchange traded contracts. This means that futures contracts, as we saw in chapter 20, are only available in standard sizes (for example £62,500) and for settlement on standard dates.

Most currency futures contracts have physical delivery like the orange juice futures seen in chapter 20. This means that on the expiry date the two parties to the contract will convert the currencies at the agreed rate. In practice, however, the vast majority of currency futures are settled prior to the expiry date of the contract through **closing out**.

Calculating the results of a futures and a traded options hedge

In exam questions involving the use of futures or traded options (which will be covered later in the chapter) to hedge currency risk you are likely to be asked to show the result of a hedge when the transaction being hedged arises **before the expiry date** of the contract being used. The settlement will therefore be via the closing out procedure.

If this is the case – how should we structure an answer?

Exam tip – Answering futures and traded options questions

The process is very similar for futures and traded options hedging with some important differences which we will see through examples.

For futures:

Step 1 – Contract set up

- **T**ype of contract – buy or sell
- **E**nd – when will the contract end – when is the expiry date
- **N**umber of contracts to enter into

Step 2 - Close out contract

Step 3 – Convert at spot

For traded options:

Step 1 – Contract set up

- **T**ype of contract – buy (call) or sell (put)
- **E**nd – when will the contract end – when is the expiry date
- **N**umber of contracts to enter into

Step 2 – Cost of the option – the premium

Step 3 - Close out contract

Step 4 – Convert at spot

The approach is therefore the same in both cases apart from the need to calculate a cost for the option.

In summary – to remember:

3 'C's and TEN for futures!
4 'C's and TEN for traded options!

Example 1

Brecon is a UK based whisky distiller whose home currency is the pound. A significant proportion of its sales are exports to the United States. Now is January 1st. It expects a major customer in the United States to settle a significant number of transactions through a payment of $1,200,000 to Brecon on August 1st. It wishes to hedge the currency risk through using currency futures offered on the Chicago Mercantile Exchange (CME). Rates are quoted as dollars per £1.

The following information is available about futures contracts on the CME

Standard contract size	£62,500
June settlement futures price on 1st January	$1.5766
September settlement futures price on 1st January	$1.5508

Assume that all currency futures contracts on the CME are settled on the third Wednesday of the month.

Requirement

Determine the result of the futures contract hedge if, on August 1st, the spot rate is $1.6802 and the September settlement contract price on the CME is $1.6798.

Step 1 – Contract set up - on 1st January

(a) Type of contract

With currency futures, the 'commodity' being bought or sold is the standard contract. In this example Brecon can contract to buy or sell amounts of £62,500. This means that a buy future will allow Brecon to buy blocks of £62,500 and a sell future will allow the company to sell blocks of £62,500.

Brecon will need to sell dollars and therefore buy pounds following the receipt. Given that the standard contract is £62,500 and Brecon wishes to buy pounds, the relevant contracts will be buy futures.

(b) End - The expiry date

On January 1st, the prices are given for both June and September settlement. We want to use the currency futures contract to hedge a receipt due on August 1st. As this does not coincide with an official settlement date we will use the closing out procedure. For this to work, the formal settlement date must be **after** the date of the receipt so that we can close out before we reach this date.

We will therefore use September settlement contracts to hedge the receipt on August 1st.

(c) Number of contracts to buy or sell

Brecon wishes, ideally to hedge the full $1,200,000 receipt. This may not be possible because of the need to buy futures in multiples of £62,500.

The equivalent of $1,200,000 at the September futures rate on January 1st is

$$\frac{\$1,200,000}{\$1.5508} = £773,794$$

Dividing this by the standard contract size would give $\dfrac{£773,794}{£62,500} = 12.38$ contracts

We can only buy whole numbers of futures contracts and therefore need to decide whether to round up or round down. Neither is perfect and either would be acceptable in an exam. If we assume that we round to the nearest whole number we will round down to 12 contracts.

Step 2 – Close out futures contract - on 1st August

To close out the futures contracts before the settlement date Brecon needs to reverse the original contracts entered into. The original contracts were buy futures (to buy the standard contract i.e. £62,500), which were taken out in January with a price of $1.5508.The reverse position therefore will be to take out the same number of sell futures contracts at the price on 1 August which is $1.6798. Because the price has changed this will create a gain or a loss.

Brecon therefore now enters into 12 new September settlement sell futures.

We now look at the difference in rates:

	$
Sept contracts signed on 1st Jan to buy £1 – cost in dollars =	1.5508
Sept contracts signed on 1st Aug to sell £1 – receipt in dollars =	1.6798
Gain to Brecon	0.1290

To understand this part of the calculation it is important to remember that the 'commodity' being trade is £1 (because the standard contract size is in that currency). Think of £1 as being the equivalent of 1lb of orange juice in chapter 20. The price at which this as 'commodity' is bought or sold is therefore in the dollar.

The net effect of the two contracts is that Brecon has contracted to pay a futures dealer the lower amount of dollars and receive the higher amount of dollars from trading the 'commodity' – this is therefore a net gain to Brecon

The futures dealer will therefore pay Brecon the following to settle the contractual obligations:

12 contracts x £62,500 x $0.1290 = $96,750

Because the futures market used is the CME, the gain is in dollars. As a result Brecon needs to convert this gain into pounds on the spot market at the spot rate on August 1st.

The gain in pounds is therefore $\dfrac{\$96,750}{\$1.6802} = £57,582$

Step 3 –Convert the receipt at spot - on 1st August

The receipt from the customer can now be converted into pounds on the spot market using the spot rate on August 1st.

Receipt in pounds on August 1st $= \dfrac{\$1,200,000}{\$1.6802} = £714,201$

The net result of the hedge will therefore be:

	£
Gain on the futures market	57,582
Receipt at spot	714,201
Net receipt in £	**771,783**

The net receipt is therefore at an effective exchange rate of $\dfrac{\$1,200,000}{\$771,783} = \$1.5548$

The key point is that this is very close to the original September futures rate and therefore the hedge has worked even though we have closed out the contract early to match the timing of the receipt. The result is not perfect – we will look at why this is the case in due course.

Two points to note about the above calculations

1 The futures contract is binding. If the rates had moved the other way a loss would have been made when the futures were closed out in step 2. The receipt is step 3 would, however, have been greater and the overall result would have been similar to the one above.

2 The solution above is very lengthy – mainly because each of the steps has been explained in some detail. After a bit of practice, your confidence and understanding should improve to the extent that it should be possible to produce a solution quickly in the way shown below.

Alternative – shortcut solution to example 1

	$	£
Contract set up		
Sept buy futures – No of contracts = $\dfrac{\$1,200,000}{\$1.5508} \div £62,500 = \mathbf{12}$ approx		
Close out futures		
Contracts set up on 1st Jan – Buy £1 – cost	1.5508	
Contracts set up on 1st Aug – Sell £1 – receipt	1.6798	
Gain on futures	0.1290	
Gain in £ – 12 contracts x £62,500 x $0.1290 ÷ $1.6802 =		57,582
Convert receipt at spot		
Receipt in £ at spot - $1,200,000 ÷ $1.6802 =		714,201
Net receipt in £		**771,783**

Currency futures compared to forward contracts

- **Flexibility**

  Currency futures are more flexible to use than forward contracts. Through the close out method futures contracts can be used at **any time** up to the expiry date. Standard forward contracts can only be used on the expiry date itself. In addition – a company does not have to use all of the futures contracts at the same time. If a company took out 12 contracts, for example, the company could close out 3 contracts in one month, 2 in the next month and in this way match the timing of receipts and payments from significant amounts of international trade.

- **Perfect result?**

  Currency futures do not give a perfectly predictable result whereas the result of a forward contract is always known with absolute certainty. There are two reasons why the result of a futures hedge **may not be perfect.**

  - The number of contracts required may have been rounded up or down.

  - The movement in the futures rate compared to the spot rate may not have been exactly as predicted. This is known as **basis risk** and is covered in more detail in the next chapter.

CURRENCY OPTIONS

There are two types of currency option.

1   An OTC (over- the- counter) or negotiated option.

2   Traded option.

There is a greater volume of trade, worldwide, in negotiated currency options than in traded currency options. Let's see how each of these instruments work.

OTC currency option

This is an option contract that is negotiated or agreed with a financial institution – normally a bank. The contracts are not standardised but instead are written specifically for the needs of the purchaser of the option.

Negotiated options are **always settled via physical delivery**, that is, on the settlement date one currency is exchanged for another.

Example 2

Ellen is a clothing retailer based in Chicago in the United States. It has purchased some clothing from Italy and is due to pay the supplier €600,000 in 3 months' time. The current spot rate is €0.7296 per $1. Ellen is concerned about a potential weakening of the dollar before the payment is made and is considering the use of a negotiated option to hedge the risk.

The Chicago Bank has offered Ellen a put option on the dollar (a right to sell the dollar which will be the same thing as a call option on the euro – a right to buy the euro) with an expiry date in 3 months' time at an exercise price (or exchange rate) of €0.7300 per $1. For an option to convert dollars into the full €600,000 needed the bank will charge a premium of $12,300.

Requirements

(a)   What will be the result of the options hedge if the spot rate in 3 months' time is €0.6504 per $1?

(b)   What will be the result of the options hedge if the spot rate in 3 months' time is €0.7867 per $1?

Solution 2

An option is a right to convert without the obligation. Ellen can therefore wait and see what the exchange rate will be in three months' time before deciding whether to use the option. The downside is that the premium has to be paid whether the option is used or not.

Part (a) – spot rate is €0.6504

Ellen is purchasing euro to pay the supplier. In this case the option rate will be more favourable than the spot rate and therefore Ellen will exercise the option.

The net cost would therefore be:

	$
Cost of euro under option - $\dfrac{€600,000}{0.7300}$	(821,918)
Premium payable	(12,300)
Net total cost of hedge	**(834,218)**

Part (b) – spot rate is €0.7867

In this case the spot rate is a more favourable rate than the option rate and therefore Ellen will allow the option to lapse.

The net cost would therefore be:

	$
Cost of euro at spot - $\dfrac{€600,000}{0.7867}$	(762,680)
Premium payable	(12,300)
Net total cost of hedge	**(774,980)**

The option has therefore provided protection against an adverse movement in exchange rates whilst at the same time allowing Ellen to take advantage of a favourable movement in exchange rates.

Exam tip – Currency options

Whenever currency options are being compared to other currency risk management techniques in a solution to an exam question, there are some key points that an examiner would always expect students to make. They are:

1   an option protects against an adverse movement in exchange rates but allows a company to take advantage of a favourable movement in exchange rates (**benefit** of an option)

2   an option is much more expensive than other currency risk management techniques (**drawback** of an option).

Traded currency option

Traded currency options are available on a range of markets around the world. They operate in a similar way to futures contracts except that, by definition, they do not have to be exercised.

Most exchanges offer both American-style (can be exercised at any time up to the expiry date) and European-style currency options (can be exercised only on the expiry date). In practice, even if the traded options are American-style they tend to be sold on the exchange rather than exercised before expiry. This is because the time value of an option means that they are worth more if sold before expiry than if exercised.

Like currency futures, traded currency options can either be settled on the expiry date by physical delivery, or, if the date of the transaction being hedged is prior to the expiry date, they can be settled via closing out.

Traded currency options — puts and calls

In a traded currency option the standard contract size will be in one currency. The standard contract is the equivalent of the commodity that is being bought or sold. Pricing, that is the exercise price or the spot price, will then be in the other currency.

If a question, for example, says that for a dollar-euro traded option the **standard contract is €10,000** (which is the standard contract size for these options on the Philadelphia exchange - NASDAQ OMX PHLX) this really means that the options are for buying or selling blocks of €10,000. A **put option** is therefore a **right to sell €10,000** (that is sell euro) whereas a **call option is a right to buy this amount of euro**. The pricing, and the calculation of value, such as the intrinsic value will then be in the dollar.

Need to know!

Closing out traded currency options prior to expiry

The key to understanding how traded currency options are closed out prior to expiry is to remember how an option is valued. The value is made up of an **intrinsic value** and a **time value**.

If we wish to use an option to hedge a transaction prior to the settlement date of the option the approach is to sell the option on the traded option exchange. The option could be sold for its value on that day, which, in exam questions is always assumed (to keep the calculations manageable) to be its intrinsic value.

If, for example, we held a dollar-euro **call option** on the Philadelphia exchange with a standard contract size of €10,000 and an exercise price of $1.30 per euro, the relationship between the spot rate and the intrinsic value would be as follows:

	$	$	$
Spot rate – market price to buy €1 =	1.22	1.30	1.56
Exercise price – option price to buy €1 =	1.30	1.30	1.30
Intrinsic value	NIL	NIL	0.26

The option is a call option on the standard contract currency – which is the euro. This means that the option holder can buy €1 (the commodity, or asset) at a cost of $1.30. If the spot rate was $1.56 the option holder would be better off using the option and 'paying' only $1.30 for each euro rather than paying $1.56 at the spot rate. The intrinsic value is therefore $0.26. The option could therefore be sold, prior to expiry for this amount.

An option will never have a negative value to a holder. When a traded currency options contract is closed out prior to expiry, there will be a gain, or we assume that the value will be nil.

One other small point about traded options!

On most currency traded option exchanges, the intrinsic value is based on a comparison of the exercise price with the **spot rate** – that is the relevant exchange rate on the spot market.

Some traded option exchanges, however, most notably the Chicago Mercantile Exchange (CME), work slightly differently and base the intrinsic value on the difference between the exercise price and the relevant **futures rate** on the exchange.

In an exam question – read the question carefully to determine how the intrinsic value is calculated. If the question doesn't say anything you can assume either (but state your assumption).

Example 3

Jonathan is a company based in France that exports goods to the United States. Now is July 1st. Jonathan is due to receive $9,400,000 on 1st December following the sale of goods to a US customer. The company wishes to use traded currency options available on the Chicago Mercantile Exchange (CME) to hedge. The current spot rate is $1.3300 per €1 and Jonathan wants to ensure that the conversion rate in December is no worse than this.

The following information is available about option contracts on the CME:

Standard contract size- €125,000
Style - American

Premium payable ($ per € of contract)

Exercise price	Calls Sept	Calls Dec	Puts Sept	Puts Dec
$1.3000	0.0124	0.0145	0.0041	0.0053
$1.3300	0.0077	0.0098	0.0083	0.0114
$1.3500	0.0035	0.0072	0.0154	0.0173

Assume that the expiry of the contract is on the third Friday of the relevant month. The value of the traded option on any date prior to expiry is calculated by comparison to the futures contract rate.

Requirement

What is the result of the option hedge if the spot rate on December 1st is $1.3984 per €1 and the futures rate is the same?

Solution 3

We will follow the approach suggested earlier in the chapter, that is 4 'C's and **TEN** for traded options.

Step 1 – Contract set up - on July 1st

- **Type** – The option will be to buy or sell the currency of the standard contract which is the euro. Jonathan wishes to buy euro and therefore the relevant option is a **call option** on the euro. Protection is needed at the current spot rate and therefore Jonathan will select the option at **$1.3300** per euro.

- **End** – the settlement date must be after the date of the transaction therefore we will use **December** settlement options.

- **Number** – The number of contracts needed will be $\dfrac{\$9,400,000}{\$1.3300} \div €125,000 =$ 56.54 therefore approx. 57 contracts.

Step 2 – Cost – on July 1st what is the premium?

- The cost of the **premium** will be 57 contracts x €125,000 x $0.0098 = $69,825

This will be payable by Jonathan on July 1st and therefore the cost in euro on

July 1st will be $\dfrac{\$69,825}{1.3300} = €52,500$

With currency option questions there is a lot of work to do at the contract set up stage – the mark allocation in an exam question should reflect this!

Step 3 – Close out the options- on Dec 1st

The option pricing is in dollars. The option is a call option on the euro. This means that Jonathan can buy one euro ('the commodity') and pay $1.3000 for that commodity.

The intrinsic value (rates are dollars per 1 euro).

	$
Spot/futures rate – market price to buy 1 euro =	1.3984
Exercise price – option price to buy 1 euro =	1.3300
Intrinsic value	**0.0684**

The option has an intrinsic value because it allows the holder to buy the commodity (1 euro) at a cheaper price in dollars than the market price on December 1st. If the market price had been below the exercise price on December 1st the option would have had an intrinsic value of nil.

Jonathan could therefore sell the option contracts on Dec 1st for:

57 contracts x €125,000 x $0.0684 = $487,350

Step 4 – Convert at spot – on Dec 1st

The receipt from the customer and the gain from trading the option can both now be converted into euro on December 1st as follows;

	$	€
Receipt from customer	9,400,000	
Gain from trading options	487,350	
Net amount of dollars	**9,887,350**	
Converted at spot on 1st December	÷ 1.3984 =	7,070,473
Less premium paid		(52,500)
Net receipt		**7,017,973**

Summary of the differences between the main currency risk management techniques

	Forward Contract	Money Market Hedge	Futures	OTC Option	Traded Options
Perfect result	✓	✓	✗	✓	✗
Simple to set up	✓	✓	✗	✓	✗
Exchange traded	✗	✗	✓	✗	✓
OTC (over-the-counter)	✓	✓	✗	✓	✗
Protect adverse movement	✓	✓	✓	✓	✓
Take advantage of favourable movement	✗	✗	✗	✓	✓
Expensive (premium)	✗	✗	✗	✓	✓

Chapter 21
key points summary

- Currency futures are all exchange traded. Most contracts are closed out before the settlement date. To show the full result of a hedge:

  - **C**ontract set up – **T**ype/**E**nd date/**N**umber of contracts
  - **C**lose out contract – reverse contracts – gain or loss
  - **C**onvert at spot
  - remember 3 'C's and TEN!

- Futures are binding like forward contracts. They are more flexible than forward contracts in terms of the date upon which then can be used – but they may not give a perfect result.

- Currency options – two types – OTC – written specifically for the user, and exchange traded.

- Currency options protect against an adverse movement but allow the holder to take advantage of a favourable movement. Currency options cost more than futures – the premium.

- Exchange traded currency options. To show the full result of a hedge:

  - **C**ontract set up – **T**ype/**E**nd date/**N**umber of contracts
  - **C**ost of the option – the premium
  - **C**lose out contract – intrinsic value
  - **C**onvert at spot
  - remember 4 'C's and TEN!

INTEREST RATE RISK MANAGEMENT 22

Introduction
what is this chapter about?

There are many situations where a business may be exposed (meaning – suffer some adverse consequence) if interest rates change. A business, for example, that has borrowed money at a floating (or variable) interest rate might pay greater amounts of interest than expected if interest rates rise. Alternatively a business that has invested some surplus cash and earns a floating rate of interest on that cash may earn less interest than expected on the investment if interest rates fall.

In this chapter we consider techniques that a business can use to manage exposure to interest rate risk on both the financing and the investing side.

Key areas of the chapter are ....

1   **Basic techniques** – Under what circumstances might a business be exposed to interest rate risk? What are the basic techniques that could be used by a business to manage that exposure?

2   **Interest rate futures & exchange traded interest rate options** – how could interest rate futures and exchange traded interest rate options be used to manage interest rate risk?

BASIC TECHNIQUES

Interest rate risk – the exposure!

There is a wide range of situations where a company may be exposed in some way to interest rate risk, or the risk of interest rate changes. These include the following.

1   A company has **borrowed money at a floating rate of interest** – the risk is of future cash interest payments being greater than anticipated because of a rise in interest rates.

2   A company has **invested money at a floating rate of interest** – the risk is of future cash interest receipts being less than anticipated because of a fall in interest rates.

3   A company plans to **issue a fixed rate bond (and therefore raise debt finance) at a future date** – although the interest rate will be fixed when the bond is issued, there is still interest rate risk. Why? This is because, in order to sell the bond to investors the company needs to offer a yield (or return) that investors are looking for on the date that the bond is issued. This means that if interest rates rise before the bond is issued a company will have to offer a higher yield than originally planned for, and once the bond is issued it will continue to pay the higher rate for the duration of the borrowing period.

4   **A change in the fair value of a fixed rate debt investment (asset) or a fixed rate loan (liability)** because of a change in interest rates. The accountants amongst you will be very excited by this one! Suppose a company, for example, has invested a large amount of surplus cash in government bonds. A rise in interest rates would reduce the fair value of these assets, and may therefore have a significant impact on the financial statements of the company.

OK. What about interest rate risk management? Before we look at how the exposure to interest rate changes can be managed we need to consider some more terminology.

Finance terminology explained

Interbank offered rates

In exam questions the variable or floating rate of interest quoted is often an interbank offered rate. What is this?

An interbank offered rate is the rate at which term deposits (meaning deposits of money for a period of time – or a term) are offered by one prime bank to another within a particular currency zone.

Two of the most important interbank offered rates are:

EURIBOR (The Euro Interbank Offered Rate) - this is the interbank offered rate for euro within the Eurozone

LIBOR (London Interbank Offered Rate) – this is the interbank offered rate offered in London. As well as a LIBOR for pounds, a LIBOR rate for term deposits in London, in nine other currencies is also available!

The rates are very significant because a lot of large scale bank lending is tied to the relevant offered rate – a bank may, for example, lend a large amount of pounds to a company for 3 months at LIBOR + 1%. This means that the interest payable by the borrower will be the 3 month LIBOR rate plus an additional 1%.

They are also significant because most interest rate hedging instruments including futures and traded options are based around the relevant interbank offered rate.

Finance terminology explained

Basis point

1 basis point = 0.01%.

Interest rates are often quoted in basis points instead of percentages e.g. LIBOR + 1% might be quoted as LIBOR + 100 basis points

The main interest rate risk management techniques

The main techniques that can be used are as follows:

1   Forward rate agreement.

2   Interest rate guarantee.

3   Interest rate futures.

4   Exchange traded interest rate options.

5   Interest rate swaps.

We will cover the first two of these techniques in this section. Futures and exchange traded interest rate options will be covered later in the chapter. Interest rate swaps are covered in chapter 23.

Finance terminology explained

Forward rate agreement (FRA)

An FRA is an agreement to pay or receive a certain rate of interest, from a certain date, for a certain period of time, and on a certain amount of notional capital. The term 'notional capital' is important. It means that under an FRA capital is not borrowed or invested – the only transfer of cash from one party to another is in respect of interest payments on a notional or nominal amount of capital.

The effect of the FRA is to fix an interbank rate at a certain level.

The agreement is negotiated directly with a bank, and is therefore tailor made to the needs of a company.

An FRA is quoted in this way:

3-7 FRA at 5.67 – 5.21

- The 3-7 is the number of months until the borrowing period covered by the FRA begins and the number of months until the borrowing period ends. In this case borrowing will begin in 3 months and end in 7 months (i.e. it will be for a period of 4 months).

- The 5.67 – 5.21 are the interbank rates of interest that can be 'fixed'. The borrowing rate is always the higher rate. In this case the FRA could be used by a borrower to fix the interbank rate at 5.67%, or it could be used by an investor to fix interbank rate on an investment at 5.21%.

Example 1

Andrew wishes to borrow €6m for 5 months beginning in 3 months' time. Andrew can borrow at Euribor + 40 basis points for the period, but is concerned about a significant rise in the Euribor rate over the next 3 months.

The following Euribor FRA's are available from Andrew's bank:

2-7 FRA at 4.51 – 4.26

3-8 FRA at 4.93 – 4.72

Requirements

(a) What is the result of hedging using an FRA if the Euribor borrowing rate is 7.00% for the duration of the loan?

(b) What is the result of hedging using the FRA if the Euribor borrowing rate is 3.00% for the duration of the loan?

Solution 1

Part (a)

Andrew wishes to borrow for 5 months beginning in 3 months' time therefore the relevant FRA is 3-8. If Andrew is borrowing, the relevant rate is the higher rate of 4.93%.

The FRA is a Euribor FRA – this means that it fixes the Euribor rate at 4.93%. If Euribor rises above this rate the bank will pay Andrew the difference between the Euribor rate and 4.93%. If the rate falls below this rate Andrew will have to pay the difference to the bank.

If Euribor is fixed at 4.93% this means that the interest that Andrew will pay will be fixed at (4.93% + 40 basis points) = 5.33%. (40 basis points = 0.40%)

The result of the FRA hedge will be:

		€
Interest paid on loan	€6m x (7.00% + 0.4%) x $\dfrac{5}{12}$ =	(185,000)
Recovered under FRA	€6m x (7.00% – 4.93%) x $\dfrac{5}{12}$ =	51,750
Net interest paid		**(133,250)**

$$\text{€6m} \times (4.93\% + 0.4\%) \times \frac{5}{12} = \text{€133,250}$$

The net interest paid is the equivalent of borrowing at (4.93% + 0.4%) = 5.33%.

Part (b)

Because Euribor has fallen below the FRA rate – in this case Andrew would need to pay the difference between Euribor and the FRA rate to the bank.

The result of the FRA if Euribor falls to 3% will be as follows:

		€
Interest paid on loan	€6m x (3.00% + 0.4%) x $\dfrac{5}{12}$ =	(85,000)
Recovered under FRA	€6m x (4.93% – 3.00%) x $\dfrac{5}{12}$ =	(48,250)
Net interest paid		**(133,250)**

$$€6m \times (4.93\% + 0.4\%) \times \frac{5}{12} = €133,250$$

The net interest paid is the equivalent of borrowing at (4.93% + 0.4%) = 5.33%

The results are the same however the EURIBOR rate moves between now and three months' time when Andrew takes out the loan, and hence is an example of a perfect hedge as uncertainty is eliminated.

Finance terminology explained

Interest rate guarantee (IRG)

An interest rate guarantee is a negotiated interest rate option. It gives the holder (remember the holder is the "buyer" of the option) the right, without the obligation, to pay or receive a certain rate of interest, from a certain date, for a certain period of time, and on a certain notional amount of capital.

It works in exactly the same way as an FRA except that the holder of the option does not have to use it. Because of this flexibility a premium is payable for the option.

Example 2

We will use the same scenario as example 1.

Andrew wishes to borrow €6m for 5 months beginning in 3 months' time. Andrew can borrow at Euribor + 40 basis points for the period, but is concerned about a significant rise in the Euribor rate over the next 3 months.

A Euribor IRG is available from Andrew's bank with the following details:

3-8 IRG at 4.93 - 4.72

Premium payable = 100 basis points (1% of the amount borrowed or invested).

Requirements

(a) What is the result of hedging using the IRG if the Euribor borrowing rate is 7.00% for the duration of the loan?

(b) What is the result of hedging using the IRG if the Euribor borrowing rate is 3.00% for the duration of the loan?

Solution 2

Part (a)

As with the FRA – if Andrew is using the IRG to protect against a rise in interest rates when borrowing the rate offered will be the higher rate of 4.93%

Like the interest payable – if Andrew is only borrowing for 5 months, the premium quoted is pro-rata'd.

If Euribor rises to 7.00%, Andrew will exercise the option with the following result:

		€
Interest paid on loan	€6m x (7.00% + 0.4%) x $\dfrac{5}{12}$ =	(185,000)
Recovered under IRG	€6m x (7.00% – 4.93%) x $\dfrac{5}{12}$ =	51,750
Premium paid	€6m x 1% x $\dfrac{5}{12}$ =	(25,000)
Net interest paid		(158,250)

Part (b)

If Euribor falls to 3%, Andrew will allow the option to lapse with the following result:

		€
Interest paid on loan	€6m x (3.00% + 0.4%) x $\frac{5}{12}$ =	(85,000)
IRG lapses		NIL
Premium paid	€6m x 1% x $\frac{5}{12}$ =	(25,000)
Net interest paid		**(110,000)**

If Euribor rises the IRG protects Andrew against the rise in rates. Whatever the rise in rates, Andrew will not pay more than €158,250 of interest. This is, however, a greater amount than would be paid under the FRA because of the premium.

If Euribor falls this would be a favourable interest rate movement for Andrew. The IRG, like all options allows Andrew to take advantage of the favourable movement and pay less interest.

INTEREST RATE FUTURES

Interest rate futures are similar to other futures contracts in that they are standardised contracts that are traded on a futures exchange.

They are contracts to borrow or invest a certain amount of money at a certain rate of interest for a certain period of time. They are therefore similar to FRA's except for the fact that FRA's are OTC contracts whereas futures contracts are exchange traded.

They are available on a number of major futures markets and in a variety of currencies. On the Chicago Mercantile Exchange (CME), for example, the interest rate futures that are available include the following.

- Three month Eurodollars.
- One month LIBOR.
- Euro yen.
- Mexican Treasury Bills.
- One month Fed Funds.

Interest rate futures contracts that are available on futures markets always relate to significant active markets for borrowing and investing money. Eurodollars are where US dollars are held on deposit in banking institutions outside of the United States (it has nothing in this context, to do with euro the currency!). Companies outside of the United States who trade in US dollars, or invest in US dollars often use the Eurodollar market. The borrowing rates charged by the banks are normally based on the Eurodollar LIBOR rate – for example LIBOR + 30 basis points.

Because so much borrowing and investing of Eurodollars at a floating rate of interest takes place there is significant demand for hedging instruments such as three month Eurodollar futures.

Some key points about interest rates futures

1   **Pricing** – Interest rate futures are always priced at 100 less the relevant market interest rate as a percentage (normally an interbank offered rate). Three month Eurodollar futures on the CME, for example, are priced at 100 less the Eurodollar LIBOR rate. A contract offering a Eurodollar LIBOR rate of 6.24%, for example, would be priced at (100-6.24) = 93.76.

2   **Link between price and interest rate** – The pricing structure leads to a second important point. There is an **inverse relationship** between a change in the interest rate and the price of the future. If Eurodollar LIBOR rose to 7.12% for example, the price of a Eurodollar future would fall to (100-7.12) = 92.88.

3   **Creating a hedge** – The pricing structure means that we **create a hedge** as follows:

  - To hedge a **rise in rates** when borrowing ➡ **sell** futures when setting up the hedge. This means that if rates rise, the price of the future will fall and futures can be bought at a lower price to create a gain when closing out the position.

  - To hedge a **fall in rates** when investing ➡ **buy** futures when setting up the hedge. This means that if rates fall, the price of the future will rise and futures can be sold at a higher price to create a gain when closing out the position.

4   **Adjusting the number of contracts** – A three month Eurodollar future means a commitment to borrow or invest on the futures market for three months from a future date. If a user wishes to hedge for a longer or shorter period than three months, the number of contracts must be adjusted to make the hedge effective.

Quick reminder!

In chapter 21 we looked at how to approach currency futures. The same approach of **3 'C's and TEN** can be used to tackle interest rate futures questions. It might be worth reviewing this approach in chapter 21 before looking at the example that follows.

Example 3

Alice is a major international pharmaceutical company which has a headquarters in London. It owns research and manufacturing facilities around the world including significant operations in the United States.

Part of the operation in the United States is financed by a US dollar loan. The current Eurodollar loan is due for repayment on January 1st 20X2 and will be replaced by a new six month Eurodollar loan of $40million. Alice can borrow at a rate of Eurodollar LIBOR + 50 basis points.

Now is September 1st 20X1 and the current Eurodollar LIBOR rate is 6%.

Alice wishes to hedge by using March 20X2 three month Eurodollar futures on the CME. The price of these futures on September 1st is 93.72. The CME has a standard contract size of $1 million for Eurodollar futures.

Requirement

What will be the net amount of interest payable on the new loan if on January 1st 20X2 LIBOR is 8% and March futures are priced at 91.88?

Solution 3

Step 1 – Contract set up - on September 1st 20X1

- **T**ype of contract – Selling futures commits us to borrowing (in theory) for 3 months from the settlement date. We therefore sell futures.

- **E**nd – the end date must be after the date that we wish to borrow from i.e. 1st January. We therefore use March futures (the only possibility anyway in this example).

  The price of March futures on September 1st is 93.72 which means a LIBOR rate of (100 – 93.72) = 6.28%. This means that by selling March futures we are committed to borrowing at 6.28% from the settlement date of the futures contract in March.

- **N**umber of contracts taken out will be $\dfrac{\$40,000,000}{\$1,000,000} \times \dfrac{6 \text{ months}}{3 \text{ months}} = 80$ contracts

We need to pro-rata the number of contracts by 6 months/3 months. This is because the futures hedge works by making gains or losses on the futures contracts to compensate for movements in LIBOR. Alice wants to borrow for 6 months on the Eurodollar market and therefore to make the hedge work Alice needs to take out 80 contracts rather than 40 contracts.

Step 2 – Close out futures contracts - on 1st January 20X2

Alice does this by reversing the contracts. This means that Alice will buy 80 new March settlement futures at the new price on January 1st 20X2 of 91.88. This, in theory, commits Alice to investing for 3 months from the settlement date in March at a rate of (100-91.88) = 8.12%.

The contractual position can therefore be summarised as:

	Futures LIBOR rate
Contracted to borrow at	6.28%
Contracted to invest at	8.12%
Gain	**1.84%**

If Alice is contracted to invest at a higher rate of LIBOR than the borrowing rate this must be a gain.

The gain will be settled by cash which then ends the contractual obligations – the company will not then borrow or receive interest for three months from the end of March.

Because the futures are only 3 month contracts this means that the cash settlement will only be 3 months' worth of the annual interest rate.

The gain to Alice will therefore be:

80 contracts x $1,000,000 x 1.84% x 3/12 = $368,000

Step 3 – Convert at spot – on 1st January 2OX2 (for interest rate futures this means borrowing on the relevant debt market – in this case Eurodollars)

The interest payable by Alice will be LIBOR + 50 basis points. This is LIBOR + 0.5%. If LIBOR on 1st January 20X2 is 8% then Alice will pay (8% + 0.5%) = 8.5%

The interest payable over a 6 month period will be:

$40,000,000 x 8.5% x 6/12 = $1,700,000

The net result of the hedge will therefore be:

	$
Gain on futures contracts	368,000
Interest payable on loan	(1,700,000)
Net interest payable	**1,332,000**

This is the net interest payable on the 6 month loan of $40 million. This works out to be an effective annual interest rate of:

$$\frac{1,332,000}{40,000,000} \times \frac{12}{6} = 6.66\%$$

If Alice is borrowing at LIBOR + 0.5% then this is an effective LIBOR rate of (6.66% - 0.5%) = 6.16%. The hedge has allowed Alice to 'lock into' this rate of LIBOR. Whatever happens to LIBOR Alice should always pay approximately this amount of interest.

Exchange traded interest rate options

All exchange traded interest rate options are options on futures contracts. This means that the intrinsic value is always based on the difference between the exercise price and the **futures rate** on the same market (and not the spot rate) - and if you have forgotten what the intrinsic value is – it would be sensible to have a quick review of options in chapters 20 and 21.

Some points to note about traded interest rate options.

1   A **put option** is a right to **sell a future** – we therefore take out a put option to protect against a rise in interest rates when borrowing. Similarly a **call option** is a right to **buy a future** and we therefore take this out to protect against a fall in interest rates when investing.

2   A **premium is payable**. This will be quoted as an interest rate percentage and is dealt with in the same way as the gain or loss on the futures contracts.

Another quick reminder!

In chapter 21 we looked at how to approach currency options. The same approach of **4 'C's and TEN** can be used to tackle interest rate futures questions.

Example 4

We will use exactly the same information as in example 3 – Alice.

Let's assume that in this case, however, a 3 month Eurodollar option is available at 94.00 for a premium of 60 basis points.

What will be the result of the options hedge if on 1st January 20X2 LIBOR is 8% and March futures are priced at 91.88?

Solution 4

Step 1 – Contract set up - on September 1st 20X1

Because traded interest rate options are options on futures, the contract size is exactly the same as with futures. This means that, as with futures contracts will want to enter into 80 contracts. These need to be contracts to borrow and will therefore be put options at 94.00 = 6.00%.

Step 2 – Cost – on September 1st 20X1 calculate the premium payable

This is quoted as an annual rate and therefore like the gain or loss on futures we need to pro-rata the rate to determine the actual amount to pay. The premium would therefore be:

80 contracts x $1,000,000 x 0.60% x 3/12 = $120,000

Step 3 – Close out the options contract - on 1st January 20X2

This is done by calculating the intrinsic value of the option as follows

The position can therefore be summarised as:

	Rate
Futures price	8.12%
Exercise price (borrow)	6.00%
Intrinsic value	**2.12%**

This is the futures rate on January 1st from example 3

Remember that this is a put interest rate option which is an option to borrow. If Alice is able to borrow at 6.00% this is better than borrowing at 8.12% therefore the option has an intrinsic value. The value of these option contracts is worked out in the same way as the gain or loss on futures, and the premium.

The option contracts could therefore be sold for:

80 contracts x $1,000,000 x 2.12% x 3/12 = $424,000

Step 4 – Convert at spot - on 1st January 20X2

This is exactly the same as step 4 with the futures hedge – i.e.: borrow the $40 million.

The interest payable over a 6 month period will again be:

$40,000,000 x 8.5% x 6/12 = $1,700,000

The net result of the hedge will therefore be:

	$
Intrinsic value of options	424,000
Interest payable on loan	(1,700,000)
Premium payable	(120,000)
Net interest payable	**(1,396,000)**

This works out to be an effective annual interest rate of:

$$\frac{1,396,000}{40,000,000} \times \frac{12}{6} = 6.98\%$$

In this case the effective interest rate is 6.98%. The option is therefore more expensive than the future when we compare the answers to example 3 and example 4.

Comparing interest rate options with futures – some important points to note!

- In example 3 and 4, the scenario was based on LIBOR rising from 6% to 8%. This is a significant adverse movement in interest rates. In such a scenario we would expect the result of an options hedge to be worse than the result of a futures hedge because of the significant cost of the premium.

- If the scenario had, however, suggested a **significant fall in LIBOR**, the result of the options hedge would have been better than the result of a futures hedge. In step 2 under a futures hedge if the futures LIBOR rate on January 1st fell significantly we would make a loss and would have to pay a dealer. With an option hedge, however, we could allow the option to lapse and therefore there would not be a loss.

Basis – predicting a second futures rate

A futures rate on any futures market is really a prediction of the spot rate on the settlement date. If, for example, on January 1st there is a futures price of 93.20 for June settlement three month Eurodollar interest rate futures, this means that traders who use the futures market expect the three month LIBOR rate to be (100-93.20) = 6.80% on the futures settlement date in June.

Finance terminology explained

What is basis?

The term basis refers to the difference between the current LIBOR rate and the current futures rate. It is also therefore the difference between the current LIBOR rate, and the market's expectation of the LIBOR rate on the settlement date of the futures contracts. If the current LIBOR rate was, for example, 8.00%, and June settlement futures were currently trading at 6.80%, then the basis would be (8.00%-6.80%) = 1.20%. This means that traders expect LIBOR to fall from the current level of 8.00% to 6.80% by the settlement date of the futures contracts in June.

Now - on the date that the futures contracts expire the spot rate and the futures rate must be the same, that is, the basis must be nil. If this wasn't the case it would create an arbitrage opportunity (here we go – arbitrage again!) Suppose the June dollar LIBOR futures expire on the last day of June. If the LIBOR rate was lower on the spot market than it was on the futures market an investor could make a no risk gain by borrowing for three months on the spot market and investing at the higher rate on the futures market.

The basis can therefore be assumed to diminish linearly from a current level down to nil by the expiry date of a contract.

Exam tip – Predicting future rate on the close out date

If the futures rate on the close out date of a contract is not given an examiner may expect students to use this concept of the basis diminishing in a linear fashion to predict a futures rate on a close out date. The predicted futures rate on the close out date can then be used to calculate the result of a futures hedge.

Example 5

On January 1st the dollar LIBOR spot rate is 8.00% and the June dollar LIBOR futures are trading at 93.20 (implying a LIBOR rate on the futures market of 6.80%). Assume that June LIBOR futures expire on the last day of June.

If the dollar LIBOR spot rate is 6.00% on May 1st what would be the expected June LIBOR futures rate on May 1st?

Solution 5

To find the futures rate on May 1st we need to set up a basis table. The futures rate on May 1st will then be the balancing figure.

	Jan 1st	May 1st	June 30th
Spot rate (LIBOR)	8.00%	6.00%	
Futures rate (LIBOR)	6.80%	5.60%	
Basis	1.20%	0.40%	NIL

This is the balancing figure. 6.00% – 0.40% = 5.60%

The remaining basis on May 1st must be:
1.20% x 2/6 = 0.40%

This will always be nil on the expiry date of the futures contract

The difference between the futures rate on the date that a contract is taken out (6.80%) and the futures rate on the close out date (5.60%) can then be used to determine the gain or loss on the futures hedge in exactly the same way as we determined earlier in the chapter.

Chapter 22
key points summary

- Forward rate agreement (FRA) – like a forward contract for currency risk.

    - Fixes the rate of interest for borrowing or investing for a period of time.

- Interest rate guarantee (IRG) – an OTC option.

    - Holder can protect against an adverse interest rate movement but take advantage of a favourable movement.

    - A premium is payable – more expensive than an FRA.

- Interest rate futures are all exchange traded. These contracts must be closed out before the settlement date. To show the full result of a hedge:

    - **C**ontract set up – **T**ype/**E**nd date/**N**umber of contracts

    - **C**lose out contract – reverse contracts – gain or loss

    - **C**onvert at spot

    - remember 3 'C's and TEN!

- Options on futures – these are exchange traded interest rate options – the value is based on the corresponding futures rate. To show the full result of a hedge:

    - **C**ontract set up – **T**ype/**E**nd date/**N**umber of contracts

    - **C**ost of the option – the premium

    - **C**lose out contract – intrinsic value

    - **C**onvert at spot.

    - Remember 4 'C's and TEN!

- Basis – difference between the futures rate and the relevant market rate (e.g. 3 month Eurodollar LIBOR).

    - Can assume that basis decreases linearly to predict futures rate at close out date.

SWAPS 23

Introduction
what is this chapter about?

Swaps are used for a variety of purposes and in a variety of different financial situations. The market is an over-the-counter (OTC) market, that is, unlike futures or options, there is no formal exchange where swaps are bought and sold. As a result, a wide variety of swaps exist and the range of products is constantly evolving.

In this chapter we explore two types of swap that are particularly useful to companies and to investors.

Key areas of the chapter are ....

1   **Interest rate swaps** – how does an interest rate swap work and what are the benefits of entering into an interest rate swap?

2   **Currency swaps** – There are a number of different types of currency swap. What are the different types and how do these differ from an interest rate swap?

INTEREST RATE SWAPS

Finance terminology explained

What is an interest rate swap?

This is a contract between two counterparties to exchange one stream of interest payments for another. This means that two parties agree to pay each other a certain amount of interest on an agreed amount of debt finance. This agreed amount of debt finance is called the principal and is notional (in that it only exists on paper as the amount of debt finance upon which interest is charged). Only the interest payments are exchanged - there is no exchange of principal.

The essence of a swap arrangement is to swap one type on interest payment (such as fixed interest) for another (such as floating rate interest).

Company X, for example, might agree to pay Company Y a fixed amount of 8% per annum on a notional amount of debt finance of $5million. Company Y (the counterparty) would therefore receive this amount. In exchange company Y would agree to pay company X a floating rate of LIBOR (and remember we defined this in chapter 22) per annum on a notional amount of $5million.

The two counterparties might be two companies or a company and a bank. It will last for an agreed number of years. An interest rate swap will always be a fixed to floating (variable) rate interest swap.

What are the potential benefits of using an interest rate swap?

1   **To obtain new finance at a cheaper rate** than would be possible by borrowing directly. Suppose a company wishes to issue a certain amount of fixed rate debt. It may find that by issuing floating rate debt and then swapping this for fixed, it will a pay a lower net fixed rate of interest than is available from borrowing directly at a fixed rate.

    Most calculations in exam questions revolve around this benefit (see example 1 below).

2   **To reduce risk**. Interest rate swaps can be used to reduce risk in a number of different ways. A bank offering fixed rate mortgages (from which it will receive interest) but with floating rate savings accounts (where it will need to pay interest) can reduce the risk of interest rates rising (which would reduce its profits) by converting the fixed rate mortgage interest received into floating rate interest received through a swap.

3   **To take advantage of forecast interest rate changes**. A company may, for example, swap from fixed to floating interest rate payments on a loan because it believes that interest rates may fall in the future. Of course, this is speculation and taking a position of this nature could result in considerably higher interest payments if interest rates rise!

4   **To gain access to a particular type of debt finance**. Some smaller businesses, for example, may find it difficult to raise fixed rate finance directly, but can obtain fixed rate finance through issuing floating rate debt and then swapping that for fixed rate debt.

Example 1

Sinclair Engineering wishes to raise $80 million of debt finance to carry out further investment in research and development. The directors of Sinclair wish to pay a floating rate of interest as they believe that there is a significant possibility of interest rates falling over the next 5 years.

A bank advising Sinclair has suggested that they could raise this finance at a floating rate of LIBOR + 2%. Alternatively, if Sinclair were to issue fixed rate debt instead it would be possible to raise the finance at a rate of 6%.

Watford Property wishes to raise a similar amount of debt finance to expand its property portfolio. The directors of Watford, however, are concerned about the impact on cashflow of a rise in interest rates and therefore would like to fix the interest rate.

The bank advising Watford have suggested that if it were to borrow at a fixed rate then it would need to pay 8% interest, but if it were to borrow at a floating rate instead it could raise the finance at LIBOR + 3%.

Requirement

Demonstrate how an interest rate swap could result in a saving of interest payable whilst still allowing both companies to pay the type of interest required.

Solution 1

The best approach to take to answer a question like this is split the workings into the following three steps:

Step 1

Suppose each company issues $80 million of the '**right type**' of finance i.e. paying interest of the type that each company wishes to pay. Although each company pays interest completely independently of the other, the total amount of interest paid by the two companies together to their investors would be:

Sinclair Engineering pays floating	(LIBOR + 2%)
Watford Property pays fixed	(8%)
Total combined interest	**(LIBOR + 10%)**

Step 2

Suppose, as an alternative, each company were to issue the '**wrong type**' of debt i.e. Sinclair issues fixed rate debt despite the fact that it would prefer to issue floating rate debt, and Watford issues floating rate debt despite the fact that it would prefer to issue fixed rate debt. The total interest paid by the two companies together would be:

Benefit = 1%

Sinclair Engineering pays fixed	(6%)
Watford Property pays floating	(LIBOR + 3%)
Total combined interest	**(LIBOR + 9%)**

The total interest paid by the two companies together is, in this case, 1% better than if each company issues the 'right' type of debt. This is because of 'comparative advantage'. Sinclair Engineering has a better credit rating than Watford Property, that is, it pays less interest on its debt whether it issues fixed or floating rate debt finance. There is, however, a greater benefit, or greater difference between the two companies on fixed rate debt compared to floating rate debt and it is this that we can take advantage of with a swap.

The total benefit of both companies issuing the wrong type of debt is 1%. We can arrange for both companies to borrow and pay the 'wrong type' of interest and then a swap so that both parties benefit by 0.5%. It would be possible to split the benefit in a different way but the total benefit cannot exceed 1%.

Step 3 – the terms of the swap

Each company borrows the wrong type of debt (meaning that they pay the wrong type of interest). In this case therefore Sinclair will pay a fixed rate of interest of 6% and Watford will pay a floating rate of interest of LIBOR + 3%.

The swap is then arranged between the two companies. Under the swap arrangement each company will contract to pay the other a certain amount of interest. In practice, one side of the swap tends to be LIBOR exactly, and the other side will be the balancing figure to give the right overall result. The swap, when combined with the interest that each company pays on their borrowings should result in each party saving interest compared to issuing debt of the right type.

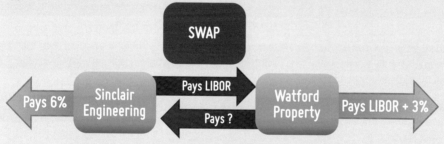

To make the swap work the amount that Watford Property will pay Sinclair Engineering must be the **balancing figure** and is determined as follows:

Sinclair Engineering		Watford Property	
Pays on borrowings	(6%)	Pays on borrowings	(LIBOR + 3%)
Receives from Watford	4.5%	Receives from Sinclair	LIBOR
Pays to Vicarage	(LIBOR)	Pays to Sinclair	(4.5%)
Net interest	**(LIBOR + 1.5%)**	**Net interest**	**(7.5%)**

Balancing figure

This is a **floating** rate of interest (the type that Sinclair wishes to pay) and is **0.5% better** than the best floating rate normally available to Sinclair

This is a **fixed** rate of interest (the type that Watford wishes to pay) and is **0.5% better** than the best fixed rate normally available to Watford

The net interest must provide each company with a 0.5% benefit. To make the swap work, the balancing figure must be a payment of 4.5% from Watford to Sinclair.

In practice, because the payments from Sinclair to Watford and Watford to Sinclair are in the same currencies, the amounts will be netted off against each other and the net difference will be settled through a payment from one company to the other.

Using an intermediary for an interest rate swap

Most interest rate swaps in practice are arranged through an intermediary, for example a merchant bank.

If this is the case a bank would charge a fee for the arrangement and then take a percentage of the potential benefit that is available, leaving less potential benefit available to each company.

CURRENCY SWAPS

Finance terminology explained

What is a currency swap?

A currency swap is an agreement between two parties to exchange either principal or interest payments in one currency for the equivalent in present value terms in another currency.

Like interest rate swaps, currency swaps are an over-the-counter instrument, that is they are arranged directly between the two counterparties (one of which is normally a bank) rather than through a formal market.

Currency swaps are similar to interest rate swaps except that they always involve two different currencies and they can involve an exchange of principal as well as an exchange of interest payments.

What are the potential benefits of using currency swaps?

1   **To hedge currency risk**

A currency swap could be used to hedge transaction, translation or long term economic currency risk.

2   **To obtain new finance at a cheaper rate than is available from borrowing directly in a foreign currency**

A company may wish to raise finance in a foreign currency in order to invest in the same foreign currency. By matching the currency of the finance with the currency of the investment it can reduce exchange rate risk.

Companies will often, however, find that it is advantageous, in terms of interest rates payable, to borrow in their own currency rather than in another currency. A swap can allow a company to raise finance in their own currency whilst at the same time achieve the exchange rate risk reduction effect that would be available from borrowing in the foreign currency.

What types of currency swap are available?

There are three main types of currency swap.

Finance terminology explained

Exchange of principal only (plain 'vanilla' currency swap or forex swap)

This is the most basic type of currency swap. It is sometimes called a plain 'vanilla' currency swap, and sometimes called a forex swap. In this case a certain amount of cash (principal) in one currency is exchanged for a certain amount of cash in another currency.

This type of currency swap can involve a single exchange of cash but normally involves two legs or transactions. They are an immediate exchange of currency now (first leg) with an agreement to reverse the transaction (second leg) at some future date.

1 Exchange of principal only

This type of currency swap allows a company to hedge currency risk. Let's see how this works.

Barak is a company based in the United States that has some surplus cash available (all dollars). It wishes to use some of this cash to undertake a unique investment opportunity that has become available in France. The investment is for one year and would require an investment of €100,000. The investment is expected to generate a profit of €20,000 at the end of the one year period. A bank offers Barak a one year currency swap on the €100,000 with both legs at a fixed exchange rate of $0.80 per euro.

This means that Barak could:

(a) convert $80,000 (€100,000 x $0.80) into €100,000 immediately **(first leg of the swap)**

(b) invest this for one year in the euro

(c) after one year convert €100,000 back into $80,000 **(second leg of the swap)**.

The company is therefore protected against the transaction currency risk that would arise when the €100,000 in converted back into dollars in a years' time. The profit of €20,000 is not protected from transaction risk through the swap in this case (because both legs are for exactly €100,000) although Barak could hedge the €20,000 profit by using a forward exchange contract.

A swap of this type has the same effect as converting dollars into €100,000 on the spot market immediately and then converting €100,000 into dollars on the forward market in a years' time. The **first leg** of the swap would therefore **normally be at the current spot rate and the second leg would normally be at the forward rate** to prevent arbitrage opportunities.

2   Exchange of principal and exchange of interest payments

This is a combination of a plain 'vanilla' currency swap with an interest rate swap. With the interest rate swap element, because the interest payments are in different currencies the amounts are not netted off. Each company instead pays the other the full amount agreed.

Suppose Barak did not have any surplus cash available to finance the investment. Let's assume that Barak decides to borrow to finance the investment. In order to minimise currency risk Barak would prefer to borrow in euro. The best interest rate available if Barak borrows €100,000 directly is 9% per annum. Barak could, however, borrow $80,000 (the equivalent in dollars) at 7% per annum. The bank has offered Barak a currency swap with the same exchange of principal as before but in this case the bank is also prepared to pay **7% interest in dollars** to Barak if Barak pays **interest to the bank in euro at 8%**.

This means that Barak could:

(a)   borrow $80,000 immediately (and pay 7% interest in dollars)

(b)   convert $80,000 (€100,000 x $0.80) into €100,000 immediately **(first leg of the swap)**

(c)   invest this for one year in the euro

(d)   the bank would then pay interest to Barak at 7% in dollars (which directly matches, or cancels out the interest that Barak pays on its loan in dollars). Barak would then pay interest in euro at 8% to the bank **(exchange of interest payments under the swap)**

(e)   after one year convert €100,000 back into $80,000 **(second leg of the swap)**

(f)   use the $80,000 to repay the loan.

This type of currency swap therefore allows Barak to hedge transaction risk but also pay 1% (9%-8%) less interest in euro than if it had borrowed the euro directly.

3   Exchange of interest payments

In this case there is no exchange of principal. Only the interest payments are exchanged on a notional amount of principal. This type of currency swap is the same as an interest rate swap except that the interest payments from one party to another and vice versa are in different currencies.

Exam tip – Type of currency swap

When reading the requirements and information in an exam question relating to a currency swap it is very important to understand what type of currency swap an examiner is referring to – that it – does it involve an exchange of principal, an exchange of interest or both?

If a currency swap involves both (the second of the three types outlined above) it is then important to understand whether the focus of the question requirements is on reducing transaction risk or, alternatively, on the interest saved under the swap compared to borrowing directly in the foreign country.

Plain 'vanilla' currency swap compared to a forward contract

A plain 'vanilla' currency swap, as we saw above, involves an exchange of principal but not an exchange of interest. How does this type of swap compare to a forward contract as a means of reducing currency risk?

The swap is a less efficient way of hedging short term currency transaction risk than a forward contract. Because the swap is an over-the-counter agreement, each contract arranged is unique and is therefore more costly and difficult to arrange than a forward contract.

Swaps can, however, be arranged for much longer periods of time than forward contracts (often up to 10 years) and for long term hedges they become a much more efficient hedging instrument. Additionally, because swaps are tailor made instruments they also allow greater flexibility than forward contracts. In the example that we considered earlier, rather than the second leg of the currency swap being a single exchange of €100,000 back into $80,000 in 1 year's time, the second leg could be a series of equal exchanges (for example 4 quarterly exchanges of €25,000 into an equivalent of dollars). The rate of conversion, and hence the amount of dollars received would need to be worked out so that the present value of dollars received under the swap would be the same as the present value of the dollars received under a series of forward contracts – again to prevent arbitrage opportunities!

Example 2

A Dubai based construction company, Hugo, wins a contract to construct a new 'sub-tropical' swimming pool and sports complex in London.

The total cost of constructing the pool has been estimated to be £20 million. Although construction will take place over a 12 month period, for NPV purposes we can assume that this is all payable immediately. The local council, who commissioned the complex, have agreed to pay Hugo an amount of £25 million on completion of the complex in 12 months' time. This should provide Hugo with a healthy profit margin, ignoring currency fluctuations, of 20%.

Hugo's local currency is the dollar. The current spot rate is $1.5300 per £1. The 1 year forward rate is $1.5500 per £1. Hugo's bank has offered Hugo a two leg plain 'vanilla' currency swap on £20 million and the equivalent in dollars. The swap involves an exchange of principal only. The first leg of the swap would be at the current spot rate and the second leg would be at the forward rate.

The treasurer at Hugo has been assessing the risk of exchange rate fluctuations and believes that given economic conditions, there is a significant chance of the pound falling in value. In the worst case scenario the pound will weaken to $1.3100 per £1.

Hugo's cost of capital is 10%.

Requirements

(a) What is the NPV of the investment in dollars if the worst case scenario outlined by Hugo's treasury team arises and the investment is not hedged?

(b) What would the NPV be if the investment was hedged using the currency swap?

Part (a)

The NPV based on the worst case scenario would be:

Time	Cashflow (£)	Exchange Rate	Discount Rate (10%)	Present value ($)
0	(20,000,000)	X 1.5300	X 1.000	30,600,000
1	25,000,000	X 1.3100	X 0.909	(29,769,750)
			NPV =	(830,250)

In this case, the weakening pound would wipe out the profit margin in the original contract.

Part (b)

The swap will be arranged so that Hugo will initially swap $ into £ at $1.5300 per £1. It will then use the pounds to finance the £20 million investment. In one years' time it will swap the £20 million back into $ at the forward rate. The £5m profit will need to be converted at the spot rate at the time.

Time	Cashflow (£)	Exchange Rate	Discount Rate (10%)	Present value ($)
0	(20,000,000)	X 1.5300	X 1.000	(30,600,000)
1	20,000,000	X 1.5500	X 0.909	28,179,000
1	5,000,000	X 1.3100	X 0.909	5,953,950
			NPV =	3,532,950

First leg

Second leg

The currency swap would therefore protect the investment from a weakening of the pound.

Other types of swap

There are many other types of swap that can be used in finance to achieve different financial effects. These are beyond the scope of this book.

Chapter 23
key points summary

- Interest rate swaps – main benefits:

    - obtain new finance at a cheaper rate

    - reduce risk

    - take advantage of forecast interest rate changes

    - gain access to a particular type of debt finance.

- Interest rate swaps – approach to questions:

    - total cost if each company issues the 'right' type of debt

    - total cost if each company issues the 'wrong' type of debt

    - terms of swap based on benefit of comparing the total costs.

- Currency swap – benefits:

    - hedge foreign currency risk

    - obtain new finance at a cheaper rate than available if borrowing directly.

- Currency swap – 3 types:

    - exchange of principal only (plain 'vanilla' currency swap or forex swap)

    - exchange of principal and interest

    - exchange of interest only.

"Earnings can be as pliable as putty when a charlatan heads the company reporting them."

Warren Buffett

VALUATION

Introduction
what is this chapter about?

Many key finance decisions depend on being able to estimate accurately the value of a business, and the value of the equity within the business.

Valuation is not an exact science! In this chapter we explore a number of techniques that could be used to estimate a value, or range of values, for a business. Each technique has its own strengths and weaknesses – none of them give us a perfect answer.

Key areas of the chapter are ....

1   **Equity valuation** – what are the main techniques that allow us to place a value on the equity of a business?

2   **Valuation in a takeover** – a special case - what is the difference between the valuation of equity in a takeover scenario and the valuation of equity in another business scenario?

3   **Debt valuation** – how is a bond valued? What is the relationship between a change in the yield and a change in the value of a bond?

EQUITY VALUATION

The difficulty of valuing equity accurately and realistically

There are many cases in corporate history where businesses have seemingly spectacularly overpaid for target companies during an acquisition process.

This may be as a result of incorrect valuations in the first place, increasing an offer above a realistic valuation during a takeover battle, failure of due diligence to identify valuation issues, or failure of post-takeover integration of the two businesses. The cases do, however, demonstrate the difficulties of valuing a business accurately and realistically.

Real life illustration – RBS and ABM Amro

In October 2007, a consortium led by the Royal Bank of Scotland (RBS) succeeded in acquiring ABM Amro for €71bn (£63bn). This had followed a long and protracted takeover battle with Barclays. In 2008, RBS reported a loss of £24.1bn, the largest annual loss in UK corporate history. The loss included a massive £16.2bn write-down of assets, a significant part of which related to the acquisition of ABM Amro.

In 2009, the former chairman of RBS, Sir Tom McKillop, told the Treasury Select Committee:

"We bought ABN Amro at the top of the market. In fact, we are sorry we bought ABN Amro. The bulk of what we paid for ABN Amro will be written off as goodwill."

Value per share or total value of the equity?

When you are asked to value equity in an exam question it is important to be clear as to whether you are aiming to value

- each individual share or

- the total value of the equity – which is the value of all of the ordinary share capital in the company.

In order to go from one to the other it is a simple case of either dividing or multiplying by the number of ordinary shares that the company has in issue.

If, for example, the total value of the equity was $200,000, and the company has 25,000 ordinary shares in issue, the value of each individual share is:

$$\frac{\$200,000}{25,000} = \$8 \text{ per share}$$

Exam tip – Value per share or total value of the equity?

In an exam question it is sometimes easier and quicker to value one individual share, and sometimes easier and quicker to find the total value of the equity. With the DVM method, for example, it is often easier to determine the value per share based on the information that is provided, whereas with an asset based valuation it is often easier to find the total value of the equity.

When reading the question, consider the easiest way to value, and then determine the value in that way. If necessary, you can then divide or multiply by the number of shares is issue to present the result to the examiner.

Finance terminology explained

What does market capitalisation mean?

The term market capitalisation sometimes causes confusion. It simply means the total market value of the equity of a company on a stock market. If we were to say, for example that a company had 100 million shares and that each share was trading at $4.00 it would be worth $400m on the stock market. We could say that the market capitalisation of the company was $400m.

The term is often used by examiners to mean the total value of the equity. If an examiner asks you to determine the market capitalisation – you just need to value the equity using an appropriate method.

When is a valuation of equity needed?

There are many business scenarios in real life that would require an estimate of the value of equity. The most common exam scenarios are:

- **Takeover**

    - An estimate of the value of the equity of a target company (that is the company being acquired) by a bidding company (that is the company doing the acquiring) prior to the bidding company making an offer **or**

    - An estimate of the value of the equity of a group following a takeover.

- **Flotation**

    - An estimate of the value of the equity of a company prior to an initial public offering (IPO). The price at which the shares will be offered for sale will be based on this valuation.

- **Management buyout**

    - An estimate of the value of a company, or a division, prior to its purchase by a management led team.

- **Demerger or another form of business reorganisation**

    - There are many possible scenarios around this theme. An example might be an estimate of the value of a division of a company if it was separated from the rest of the organisation and sold.

The main methods of equity valuation

There are four main valuation methods that are commonly used to value equity.

1 **Dividend valuation model (DVM)** – value is based on future expected dividends.

2 **Earnings basis** – value is based on future expected earnings.

3 **Asset basis** – value is based on the assets that the company owns.

4 **Present value of future cashflows** – value is based on future expected cashflows.

Each of the four methods therefore focuses on a different element of business value – dividends, earnings, assets and cashflows.

In this chapter we will consider the first three of these methods. The fourth method, and an additional more complex method based on option theory will be considered in chapter 25.

Dividend valuation model (DVM)

In chapter 9 we used the dividend valuation model to estimate the cost of equity. We can use exactly the same model to value a company's shares.

Need to know!

The DVM formula is:

$$Po = \frac{Do\,(1 + g)}{ke - g}$$

Where

Po = the ex-div share price

Do = the latest or current dividend

g = the estimated future growth rate

Ke = the cost of equity

To use this formula to value a share, the cost of equity needs be known or estimated. The cost of equity may be given in an exam question or an examiner may expect a student to use CAPM to calculate the cost of equity.

Example 1

Ryan, an investor, is considering buying a 20% stake in an unquoted company, Ben. The company has just paid a dividend of 12c per share. Over the past 5 years dividends have consistently grown at 4% per annum on a compound basis and this growth is expected to continue for the forseeable future.

The risk free rate of return is 6% per annum and the equity risk premium is 3%. Ben, being an unquoted company, does not have a published beta factor. It is known, however, that the equity beta of a similar quoted company to Ben is 1.2.

How much should Ryan offer for each share in Ben?

We firstly need to estimate the cost of equity using CAPM. The CAPM formula covered in chapter 11 is:

$$Ke = Rf + \beta(Rm-Rf)$$

Where:

Rf	=	6% or 0.06
β	=	1.2
(Rm-Rf)	=	3% or 0.03
Ke	=	0.06 + 1.2 x 0.03
	=	0.096 or 9.6%

We then use the DVM to value each share

Do	=	12c
g	=	4% or 0.04

$$Po = \frac{12c\,(1 + 0.04)}{0.096 - 0.04} = 223c \text{ or } \$2.23$$

Ryan should therefore be prepared to offer up to $2.23 for each share in Ben.

Some points to note about a DVM valuation

- It is the best method, theoretically, for valuing shares. In a perfect market shares should be correctly priced by the DVM (more on this later).

- A significant criticism of the DVM as a valuation technique is that the value depends on the assumptions made about growth rates and the cost of equity. A small change in the assumptions made about either of these variables could significantly affect the value obtained.

- The method is particularly suitable in a valuation scenario when an investor is buying less than 50% of the equity of a company.

Earnings basis

This approach estimates the value of a share by applying a suitable price/earnings (P/E) ratio to the earnings per share (EPS) of the company being valued.

Need to know!

Estimated share price = The EPS of the company being valued x suitable P/E ratio

The P/E ratio is a key investors' ratio for quoted companies. It is calculated as the price per share divided by earnings per share and tells the investor how much a share is trading at in relation to the latest published EPS figure. For quoted companies their P/E ratios are readily available in the financial press. The P/E ratio is influenced by many factors, but in general, high potential future growth in earnings, and lower levels of risk attached to those future earnings, tends to lead to higher P/E ratios.

Because growth potential and risk tend to be based to a significant extent on industry factors, we often find that companies in the same industry have similar P/E ratios. A quick glance through the financial press will confirm this. Supermarket chains, for example, often have P/E ratios in the region of 12 to 14.

This creates a useful method of valuing an unquoted company. If P/E ratios are similar for companies in the same industry, we could apply an industry average quoted P/E, or the P/E of a similar quoted company, to the unquoted company that we are seeking to value.

The EPS of the unquoted company will then be multiplied by the suitable P/E ratio.

Adjustments to P/E ratio and EPS when valuing

To obtain the most accurate estimate of the value of a share when using this method it may be sensible to adjust both the P/E ratio and the EPS for known or likely differences.

If it is known, for example, that a company being valued has

- has a **lower growth** potential than the industry average

- is **more risky** than an industry average

- is a **private company** and therefore has less marketable shares.

it would be sensible to adjust the P/E ratio used **downwards** to reflect this. The extent of the adjustment will be subjective.

Similarly, if it is know that the latest EPS of the unquoted company being valued is lower or higher than normal, perhaps because of an exceptional loss or exceptional gain, it would be sensible to adjust the EPS figure to reflect this.

Example 2

Blue Airways is a private airline company offering low cost flights within the European Union. It's latest financial statements show a profit after tax of €350,000, and that it has 2 million shares in issue. It is considering an IPO on a European stock market and wants to estimate a suitable price at which the shares should be offered for sale.

The latest financial statements include an exceptional loss of €50,000 due to the closure of unprofitable routes. The industry average P/E ratio for airlines on the relevant European stock market is 18.

Estimate a suitable price at which the shares should be offered for sale.

The latest earnings of Blue Airways should be adjusted to remove the impact of the exceptional loss. As this is not expected to recur, adjusting in this way will give a more realistic valuation.

	€
Latest earnings	350,000
Add back exceptional loss	50,000
Adjusted earnings	400,000

The revised EPS can then be calculated

$$\text{Revised EPS} = \frac{€400,000}{2,000,000 \text{ shares}} = €0.20 \text{ or } 20c$$

The industry average P/E ratio is 18. The only known difference between Blue Airways and other companies in the same industry is the fact that Blue Airways is currently unquoted. The shares are currently less marketable and may be perceived as being more risky – it would therefore be sensible to adjust the P/E ratio downwards slightly e.g, by 10%.

A suitable P/E would therefore be:18 x 90% = 16.2 or approx 16.

The estimated share price would be:

20c x 16 = 320c per share or $3.20 per share.

In this example there is no absolutely 'correct' answer. Credit would be given by an examiner for any **reasonable** assumptions about earnings and the P/E ratio that are used to arrive at your valuation.

Exam tip – P/E valuation of a quoted company

A common mistake that infuriates examiners (!) is when a student uses a circular argument to 'value' a company's equity at the current quoted share price. The mistake works in this way:

1 Students calculate the current P/E ratio of the company by dividing the current quoted share price by the current EPS.

2 The same P/E ratio is then applied to the current EPS to 'value' the shares using the earnings method.

The earnings based valuation method is only useful if a suitable P/E ratio (from elsewhere) is applied to the earnings of the company being valued to give some additional information about the estimated value of the company's equity.

Asset basis

Under this method we estimate the value of the equity by considering the value of the assets in the company's statement of financial position.

The total value of the equity is estimated as follows:

	$
Estimated value of the company's total assets	X
Less the value of the company's liabilities	(X)
Total value of the equity	X

Value of the assets

To find the most accurate value we need to estimate the most up to date, realistic value of the company's assets.

Given the popularity of 'fair value' accounting, a reasonable value of the company's assets might be obtained by simplying using the information from the company's latest statement of financial position.

Some points to note about an asset valuation:

1   An examiner may suggest in a question that adjustments need to be made to the asset values provided in the latest statement of financial position e.g. a question may state that 20% of the inventory is obsolete and needs to be written off.

2   The latest statement of financial position will not include the value of intangibles such as goodwill that fail to meet the recognition criteria for an asset under Accounting Standards.

3   Because of the difficulty of valuing many intangible assets, the asset valuation tends to undervalue a business and is therefore often perceived as providing a **minimum value**.

4   An asset based valuation is not suitable for valuing a company in the service industry where the value of tangible assets tends to be very small in relation to the true worth of the company.

Valuing a quoted company

You may be asked to estimate the value of either an unquoted company or company whose shares are quoted on an existing stock market.

Of course, if valuing a quoted company there is already an existing share price. This could be incorporated by an examiner into an exam question in two different ways.

1   Undervalued or overvalued shares.

In a perfectly efficient market, a share should, in theory, always be trading at the correct value (see chapter 14 on market efficiency). An examiner could therefore ask you to value an existing share and **compare your value to the current quoted share price** to determine whether the shares are currently undervalued or overvalued. The DVM is the most suitable valuation method to use in this case as it is theoretically the best model.

If, for example, we were to value a share using the DVM at $2.50, and the share is currently trading at a price of $2.20 on a stock market we could conclude that a share is undervalued, and is therefore worth buying at $2.20. We could also conclude that the stock market is not efficient.

2   As a benchmark in a takeover scenario.

In a takeover scenario, if the target company is a quoted company, a bidding company will need to offer a premium on the existing quoted share price to have any chance of being successful in a takeover bid. Existing shareholders could clearly sell their shares on the open market at the current share price, and therefore to persuade the existing shareholders of a target company to accept, for example, a share for share exchange from a bidding company, the offer would need to be at a significant premium to the current share price.

A premium of 20% to 30% on the quoted pre-bid share price is commonly offered in takeover bids. The bidding company will be able to offer this because of the synergy gains expected from the takeover.

Real life illustration – Morrisons & Safeway

In 2003, Morrisons, the UK supermarket chain successfully acquired supermarket rival Safeway after a year-long takeover battle. The final successful takeover offer was at 283p per share (or £3bn for the total equity). This represented a 33% premium on the closing price of Safeway's shares on the day before the initial bid was launched.

At the time of the announcement of the deal, the board of Morrisons also announced that it expected to find annual cost savings of around £215m.

Real life illustration – L'Oreal and Body Shop

In 2006, French cosmetics firm L'Oreal completed a successful takeover of Body Shop. The agreed offer was at 300p per share which represented a 34% premium on the share price of Body Shop prior to speculation in the press about a possible takeover bid.

VALUING EQUITY IN A TAKEOVER – A SPECIAL CASE!

Why?

There are two key additional issues to deal with when valuing in a takeover situation. They are:

1   **The impact of synergy**. This is the extra value gained from combining two businesses e.g.cost savings, greater marketing power, cross selling of products etc.

2   **The way that the takeover is financed**. This will have an impact on the value of the group post-takeover and on the share price of the bidding company post-takeover.

The impact of synergy

If a bidding company expects to benefit from synergy following a takeover, this should be taken into account when valuing a target company. Synergy also allows both the bidding company's shareholders and the target company's shareholders to benefit from the takeover.

Cornwall is a company that sells budget package holidays. It is considering making an offer for a smaller privately owned rival company, Devon. Both companies offer a similar product and have similar future growth expectations.

Cornwall's latest earnings are $55m and it currently has a quoted P/E ratio of 12, giving it a market capitalisation of $660m ($55m x 12). It has 40m shares in issue. Devon's latest earnings are $10m and it has 8m shares in issue.

The takeover is expected to result in synergistic benefits equivalent to an increase in annual earnings of $5m.

Requirement

What is the maximum amount that Cornwall should be prepared to offer for the total equity of Devon?

 Solution 3

The only feasible valuation method that can be used in this case is the earnings basis. Given that Cornwall and Devon operate the same type of business, and have similar growth expectations, it is reasonable to use Cornwall's P/E ratio to value Devon.

When Cornwall buys Devon it is gaining access not only to Devon's own earnings but also the extra earnings generated by the group as a result of synergy.

The relevant annual earnings are therefore:

	$
Devon's pre-takeover earnings	10m
Extra earnings from synergy	5m
Total	15m

Applying Cornwall's pre-takeover P/E ratio to the extra earnings, the value of Devon's equity to Cornwall would be:

$15m x 12 = $180m

This is the maximum amount that Cornwall should be prepared to offer for Devon.

The way that the takeover is financed

A takeover can be financed in one of three ways.

1   **Share for share exchange**. The target company shareholders can be **given shares** in the bidding company in **exchange** for the shares that they currently own in the target company.

2   **Cash for share exchange**. The target company shareholders can be **given cash** in **exchange** for the shares that they currently own in the target company.

3   **Bond for share exchange**. The target company shareholders can be **given bonds** issued by the bidding company in **exchange** for shares that they currently own in the target company.

We will see how the different forms of consideration impact on post-takeover value by looking at an example.

Example 4

We will use the **information from example 3**.

Let's assume that after some negotiation, a offer of $160m is made by Cornwall for Devon, and that this offer is accepted by the shareholders of Devon. (Remember – the $180m valuation in example 3 would be the maximum amount that Cornwall would be prepared to pay for Devon. It would seek to buy Devon for less than this amount.)

Requirements

Using the information from example 3 determine:

(a) the total equity value of Cornwall post takeover, and the value of each share in Cornwall post-takeover, assuming that Cornwall **pays cash** for Devon. Assume that Cornwall has sufficient cash in its current assets to finance the takeover

(b) the total equity value of Cornwall post-takeover, and the value of each share in Cornwall post-takeover, assuming that Cornwall finances the takeover through a **share for share exchange**.

Solution 4

Part (a)

If cash is being used to finance the takeover it is important to note that post-takeover:

•   Cornwall will now own the whole of Devon (Devon becomes a wholly owned subsidiary of Cornwall) which will increase the value of Cornwall

•   the cash given to Devon's shareholders will, however, **reduce Cornwall's value**

•   Cornwall will **not issue** any new ordinary shares.

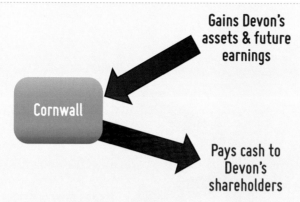

Gains Devon's assets & future earnings

Cornwall

Pays cash to Devon's shareholders

The total value of the equity of Cornwall post-takeover would therefore be:

	$
Pre-takeover value of Cornwall ($55m x 12)	660m
Value placed on Devon in example 3	180m
Less cash paid for Devon	(160m)
Post-takeover value of Cornwall	680m

Given that the takeover is financed by cash, there is no change in the number of Cornwall shares in issue.

The **post-takeover value per share** is therefore $\dfrac{\$680m}{40m} = \$17.00$ per share.

The pre-takeover value of each Cornwall share was $\dfrac{\$660m}{40m} = \$16.50$ per share.

There would therefore be an expected gain per share in Cornwall of $0.50 if the takeover was financed in this way.

The total gain to Cornwall's shareholder is $20million. This is because Cornwall has paid $160million cash to gain assets (Devon) worth $180million.

The gain to each shareholder in Cornwall would therefore be

$\dfrac{\$20million}{40million\ shares} = \$0.50$ per share.

Part (b)

If shares are used to finance the takeover it is important to note that post-takeover:

- Cornwall will now own the whole of Devon (Devon becomes a wholly owned subsidiary of Cornwall) which will increase the value of Cornwall

- Cornwall **does not use up any assets** to pay for the takeover

- Cornwall will issue new ordinary shares to offer as consideration to the shareholders of Devon, and therefore there will be a **dilution** of control for Cornwall's existing shareholders.

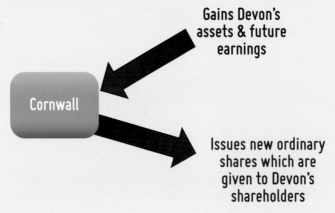

The **total value of the equity** of Cornwall post-takeover would therefore be:

	$
Pre-takeover value of Cornwall ($55m x 12)	660m
Value placed on Devon in example 3	180m
Post-takeover value of Cornwall	840m

This is $160m greater than in part (a) because Cornwall does not need to use any of its assets to finance the takeover.

Given that the takeover is financed by shares, we need to work out the number of new shares that would be issued to finance the takeover.

If each share in Cornwall was worth $16.50 before the takeover, the number of new shares issued would be:

$$\frac{\$160m}{\$16.50} = 9{,}696{,}970.$$

The total number of Cornwall shares in issue post-takeover is therefore:

40,000,000 + 9,696,970 = 49,696,970 shares

The **post-takeover value per share** is therefore $\dfrac{\$840{,}000{,}000}{49{,}696{,}970} = \$16.90$ per share.

In this case there is therefore an expected gain of ($16.90 - $16.50) $0.40 per share to Cornwall's shareholders.

The total gain from the takeover is still $20 million ($180 million - $160 million). In the case of a share for share exchange, however, the gain is split between the shareholders of Cornwall and the shareholders of Devon.

Key points to note about valuation in a takeover

- Some synergy is always expected in a takeover. This means that the value of the group post-takeover should be greater than the sum of the bidding company and target company pre-takeover.

- The existence of synergy means that the shareholders of both the bidding company and the target company can benefit from the takeover.

- The method of financing the takeover can impact on the total value of the equity of the bidding company post-takeover, and on the expected bidding company share price post-takeover.

- If financing a takeover by cash, the value of the bidding company's assets will fall by the amount of cash used.

- If financing a takeover by issuing shares, there will be dilution of the bidding company's share capital.

DEBT VALUATION

The valuation of marketable debt, or bonds, is much more straightforward than the valuation of equity.

Need to know!

What is the value of a bond?

The value of a bond is always assumed to be equal to the present value of the future cashflows from that bond discounted at the investor's required rate of return.

When discussing the value of a bond it is important to remember from the chapter on raising long term finance (chapter 8) and the cost of capital (chapter 9) that:

- the terms: investors required rate of return, pre-tax cost of debt, and yield all mean the same thing

- the terms: bond, debenture, marketable debt and loan stock also all essentially mean the same thing

- there were two types of straight bond – an irredeemable bond and a redeemable bond.

The value of an irredeemable bond

An irredeemable bond is a perpetuity – in other words, an investor buying an irredeemable bond will receive a constant stream of cashflows from time 1 to infinity. We can use the following formula, based on a perpetuity to find the value of a bond:

Need to know!

$$P_0 = \frac{I}{r}$$

Where:

P_0 = the market value of a bond per $100 nominal value

I = the interest payment per $100 nominal value

r = the investors required return (expressed as a decimal).

This formula is just a rearrangement of the formula that we used to determine the pre-tax cost of debt in chapter 9.

Example 5

A potential investor in an irredeemable bond with an 8% coupon rate is seeking a yield of 9% on the investment. How much would the investor be prepared to pay for the bond?

Solution 5

In chapter 9 we saw that the calculations will be worked out per $100 nominal value of debt.

In this example:

I = 8% x $100 = $8

r = 9% = 0.09

Therefore:

$$P_0 = \frac{\$8}{0.09} = \$88.89$$

The investor would therefore be prepared to pay $88.89 per $100 nominal value of the bond. By doing so the investor will receive a yield of 9%.

The value of a redeemable bond

To find the value of a redeemable bond we need to go back to first principles of discounting. There isn't a formula to use in this case – instead we discount the future cashflows that the investor expects to receive having purchased the bond.

Example 6

A company has in issue 11% redeemable bonds. The bonds are redeemable in 5 years' time at par value. Investors are currently demanding a yield of 10% on these bonds. What will be the market value of these bonds?

In this case we know that an investor buying the bond today will receive:

- Interest of 11% x $100 = $11 per annum from time 1 to time 5.

- A redemption value of $100 at time 5.

Like irredeemable debt – all the calculations are based on a nominal value of $100

The market value is then determined as follows:

Time	Narrative	Cashflow ($)	DF @ 10%	Present value ($)
T1 – T5	Interest payments	$11	3.791	41.70
T5	Redemption value	$100	0.621	62.10
	Total			**103.80**

The market value is therefore $103.80 per $100 nominal value.

Note – tax and the market value of a bond

When we work out the market value of a bond we ignore corporate tax because all of the cashflows and returns are considered from an investors point of view. The discount rate used is the yield (or **pre-tax cost of debt**) and interest payments are the **gross amount** that the investor will receive.

Chapter 24
key points summary

- There are 4 main ways of valuing equity:

  - dividend valuation model (DVM) formula - $P_o = \dfrac{D_o(1 + g)}{K_e - g}$

  - earnings basis

  - asset basis

  - present value of future cashflows.

- In a perfectly efficient market the quoted share price should equal the value obtained by using the DVM.

- Valuation of equity in a takeover presents extra complications.

  - The value of synergy needs to be considered.

  - The financing of the takeover affects the total value of equity and the estimated post-takeover share price.

- The value of a bond is always equal to the present value of future cashflows discounted at the investors required rate of return.

  - Straight bond formula - $P_o = \dfrac{I}{r}$

  - Redeemable bonds – discount future cashflows.

ADVANCED BUSINESS AND EQUITY VALUATION **25**

Introduction
what is this chapter about?

In chapter 24 we estimated the value of equity using three different methods of valuation: the dividend valuation model, earnings based valuation and asset based valuation. In this chapter we consider how we can value equity using free cashflows and also look at how option theory can be applied to the valuation of equity.

Key areas of the chapter are ....

1. **Free cashflow valuation** – How can discounted cashflow techniques be applied to the valuation of equity? What are the differences between using discounted cashflow techniques in the valuation of equity compared to using these techniques to appraise a new investment?

2. **Valuing equity as an option** – Can investing in equity be equivalent to taking out an option on the assets of a company? When is option theory useful to use as a method of valuation?

FREE CASHFLOW VALUATION

In section 1 of the book we considered how discounted cashflow techniques could be used to appraise new investments, or projects, that a business was considering. The main technique used was the net present value technique (NPV). If the NPV was positive then the new investment was considered to be worthwhile and shareholder wealth would increase as a result of undertaking the new investment.

The NPV approach to investment appraisal can also be used to value existing businesses. Using this approach, the value of a business is the present value of future cashflows that would be generated, discounted at a required rate of return. Using this approach to value a business is therefore consistent with the way in which we 'value' or appraise new investments.

What is free cashflow?

When using this approach to value a business we need to be careful about which cashflows are included in the valuation exercise and how those cashflows are then used to obtain a value for the equity of a business. The cashflow that we focus on is the free cashflow.

There are a number of different definitions of free cashflow but the term really means the cashflow that is available to distribute to the providers of capital, or to the long term investors in the company.

If the free cashflow for one accounting period is determined by adjusting the published financial information then the best way of estimating that free cashflow is as follows:

	$
Operating profit (Profit before interest and tax)	X
Add back depreciation	X
Deduct tax on operating cashflows	(X)
Deduct increase in working capital	(X)
Deduct necessary capital expenditure	(X)
Free cashflow	**X**

The idea is that we focus on the cashflow that a business **is able** to distribute to its investors in the form of interest payments (and redemption values if debt is redeemed in the accounting period) to the providers of debt capital and dividends to the providers of equity capital. A business may choose not to distribute all the free cashflow in an accounting period, for example, cashflow available to shareholders may be retained and reinvested rather than distributed (see chapter 15 on dividend policy) but the important point is that this is a **choice** that the managers of a company will have made as to how the free cashflow will be used.

If a business needs to increase its working capital, or invest in new non-current assets to maintain the current projected level of future operating profit, then the expenditure on these items must be deducted before we reach a free cashflow figure. Without this expenditure the projected future operating profit and hence projected future free cashflow would not be achieved.

Free cashflow (FCF) and free cashflow for equity (FCFE)

When using free cashflows to value, these future free cashflows are forecast and then discounted at at an appropriate required rate of return.

In order to value equity, we then need to consider how the investment that the providers of debt capital have in the business is taken into account. There are two ways in which this can be done.

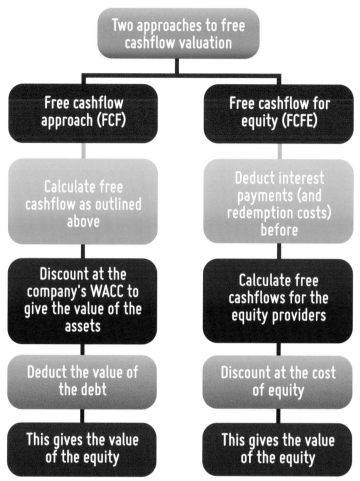

Under the free cashflow approach interest payments and redemption values on debt are ignored when determining the **free cashflow**. The free cashflows are therefore those that are available to all of the providers of long term capital of the company. There are discounted at the WACC to give the overall value of the company's assets. We then deduct the value of the debt to give the value of the equity.

Under the free cashflow for equity approach interest payments and redemption values are deducted from cashflows before ariving at the free cashflow in each accounting period. The free cashflow after these deductions in therefore the free cashflow available to the shareholders, or the **free cashflow for equity**. This is then discounted at the cost of equity to give the value of the equity.

Exam tip – FCF or FCFE?

An examiner should make it clear as to whether an FCF approach or an FCFE approach is required in an exam question. If not, either approach is technically correct and therefore either approach could be used. Make sure that you state any assumptions that you make.

Discounted cashflow complications

In chapter 4 we looked at more complex discounted cashflow situations including perpetuities, annuities, growing perpetuities and delayed growing perpetuities. These complexities will sometimes feature in exam questions that require a free cashflow valuation.

Growing perpetuities and delayed growing perpetuities in particular often feature in a cashflow valuation. This is because, when valuing an existing business, unlike an investment, we expect the existing business to continue generating cashflows to some infinite date in the future.

In preparing to answer a question on discounted cashflow valuation it is important therefore to be able to deal with these complications – therefore a quick revision of chapter 4 might be appropriate before going any further.

Example 1

A business expects to generate a free cashflow for equity of $140,000 in the next accounting period. The WACC is 9%, the cost of equity is 10% and the free cashflow for equity is expected to grow at 5% per annum to infinity.

What is the value of the equity of the business?

Solution 1

This is a free cashflow for equity (FCFE) valuation scenario as the $140,000 must be the cashflow after deducting interest payments to the providers of debt capital. The cost of equity is the relevant discount rate to use. The future cashflows are a growing perpetuity and therefore we will value by using the formula for a growing perpetuity.

From chapter 4 the formula for a growing perpetuity is:

$$\frac{1}{r - g}$$

Where:

r = the discount rate (expressed as a decimal)

g = the constant annual rate of growth in future cashflows (expressed as a decimal)

The value of the equity is therefore:

$$\$140,000 \times \frac{1}{(0.10 - 0.05)}$$

= $2,800,000

Let's now look at a more complex example. In a more complex example the information will often be presented in a very similar way to an NPV investment appraisal exercise.

Example 2

Francesca is a private company that is considering listing its shares on a stock market in the near future. The finance director wishes to value the equity of the company using the free cashflow approach. The following forecast information has been produced:

	Year 1 ($,000)	Year 2 ($,000)	Year 3 ($,000)
Sales revenue	85,000	92,000	102,000
Costs excluding depreciation	(45,000)	(49,000)	(58,000)
Depreciation	(12,000)	(13,000)	(17,000)
Finance cost	(11,000)	(11,000)	(11,000)
Capital expenditure	(3,000)	(32,000)	(5,000)

The corporate tax rate is 30%, payable in the same year as the cashflow itself. No capital allowances are claimable. The capital expenditure is expenditure that is necessary to achieve the forecast sales revenue.

Beyond year 3, the free cashflow is expected to grow steadily at 3% per annum to infinity. The company's WACC is 11% and the cost of equity is 14%. The value of the company's long term debt is $70 million.

Requirement

Determine the value of the company's equity using the free cashflow valuation method.

 Solution 1

The approach to take in this example is a free cashflow valuation method. Interest payments (finance cost) are therefore ignored when determining the cashflows and the relevant discount rate to use is the company's WACC.

Working 1 – Present value of free cashflows from time 1 to time 3

We will separate out the cashflows from time 1 to time 3 from the cashflows beyond time 3. Depreciation is ignored in the calculations because it is not a cash flow.

	Year 1 ($,000)	Year 2 ($,000)	Year 3 ($,000)
Sales revenue	85,000	92,000	102,000
Costs excluding depreciation	(45,000)	(49,000)	(58,000)
Net taxable cashflows	**40,000**	**43,000**	**44,000**
Tax @ 30%	(12,000)	(12,900)	(13,200)
Capital expenditure	(3,000)	(32,000)	(5,000)
Free cashflow	**25,000**	**(1,900)**	**25,800**
DF @ 11%	0.901	0.812	0.731
Present value	**22,525**	**(1,543)**	**18,860**

The present value of the cashflows from time 1 to time 3 is therefore ($22,525K – $1,543K + $18,860K) = $39,842K

> **Working 2 – Present value of the free cashflow from T4 to infinity**
>
> This is a deferred growing perpetuity. Using the technique covered in chapter 4 the present value of the deferred growing perpetuity can be determined as follows:
>
> The cashflow at time 4 will be:
>
> $25,800K x (1 + 0.03) = $26,574K
>
> The present value at time 3 of the cashflows from time 4 to infinity is:
>
> $$\$26,574K \times \frac{1}{(0.11 - 0.03)}$$
>
> = $332,175K
>
> We then discount this back to time 0 by treating it as a 'single' cashflow arising at time 3.
>
> The present value at time 0 is therefore:
>
> $332,175 x 3 year DF @ 11%
>
> = $332,175 x 0.731
>
> = $242,820K
>
> **Working 3 – The value of the assets**
>
> This will be the sum of the value of the cashflows from time 1 to time 3 and the value of the cashflows from time 4 to infinity.
>
> The value of the assets = $39,842K + $242,820K = $282,662K.
>
> **Working 4 – The value of the equity**
>
> We then deduct the value of the debt ($70million) to find the value of the equity.
>
> The value of the equity is therefore ($282,662K - $70,000K) = $212,662K.

VALUING EQUITY AS AN OPTION

In chapter 21 we saw how option theory can be used to value real options, that is options on real assets within an investment appraisal situation. Another important possible application of option theory is to use option theory to value equity.

Warning – if you are dipping into different chapters of the book – please make sure that you read chapter 21 before attempting to work through the next section – if you don't the next section will not make any sense!

Need to know!

When can option theory be used to value equity?

There are two conditions which must exist for option theory to be used to value equity. They are:

1   **Limited liability**. Investors in equity must have limited liability. In the event of a liquidation of a company shareholders must be able to walk away having lost, at worst, only the capital that is invested in the company.

2   **Debt financing**. The company must be financed partly by debt capital.

How can option theory be used to value equity?

If a company is partly financed by debt, shareholders effectively have a **call option** on the company's assets.

On the date that the debt matures, or is to be redeemed, if the assets of the company are worth more than the redemption value of the debt, the debt will be redeemed and the shareholders will own the remainder of the assets. The shareholders would therefore benefit from any growth in the value of the company's assets.

If, however, on the date of redemption, the value of the assets is less than the redemption value of the debt (and hence the company is technically insolvent), the shares would be worthless, and the debt providers would sell the assets of the company to recover as much of the amount owed as possible. Although the shareholders would lose the value of the capital that they put into the company, because of limited liability they would not use any of their personal wealth.

This is a call option scenario. If the debt is redeemed, the shareholders are **exercising their option** to buy the assets of the company. If the company is insolvent and the assets of the company are passed to the debt holders, the **option is allowed to lapse**. The amount that an investor should be prepared to pay for the equity today therefore would be the value of, or premium payable for this option.

If on the date of redemption:

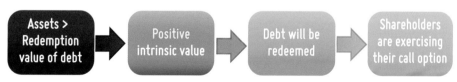

If, alternatively, on the date of redemption:

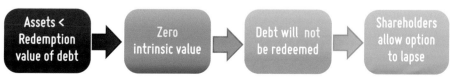

Determining the variables to use in the Black Scholes model

In chapter 20 we saw that the Black Scholes option pricing model was based on 5 variables. If the model is used to value equity in this way, what would the 5 variables be:

	Variable	Option to value equity in a company with debt finance
Intrinsic value	**Current price of the asset**	The current value of the firm's assets.
	Exercise price	The total redemption value of the outstanding debt.
Time value	**Risk free rate of interest**	The rate of interest charged for risk free borrowing.
	Time to expiry	The length of time until the debt is to be redeemed.
	Standard deviation of the asset	The standard deviation of the firm's assets.

One complication with the application of the option pricing model to this scenario is that in order to successfully redeem the debt on maturity, the company must pay any interest on the due dates as well as the redemption value on maturity.

To deal with this complication we assume that the debt is zero coupon, that is, the only return that an investor would receive would be the redemption value on maturity. No interest would be payable prior to redemption.

If the debt is not zero coupon the approach would be to work out the equivalent redemption value of zero coupon debt that offers the same yield to the investor as the debt that is in issue.

Example 2

A company has an asset value currently estimated to be worth $110 million. It is financed by equity and $60million of 10% straight bonds. The current market value of each bond is $95. The bonds are redeemable at par in 5 years time. It is also known that the standard deviation of the asset value is 25% per annum and that the risk free rate of return is 5%.

Requirements

(a) What is the current value of the equity using an asset based valuation?

(b) What is the yield on the straight bond that is in issue?

(c) If a zero coupon bond was in issue that had the same yield, and the same current market value as the straight bond, what would its redemption value be?

(d) What is the current value of the equity using the Black Scholes option pricing model?

Part (a)

The current market value of the debt is $60 million x $\dfrac{\$95}{\$100}$ = $57 million

The asset based value of the equity would therefore be the value of the company's assets less the value of the debt = ($110 million - $57 million) = $53 million

Part (b)

This is a redeemable straight bond. The yield is therefore the IRR of the cashflows. This is found by using trial and error and then the formula for linear interpolation (covered in chapter 9).

Po (current market value) = $95 per $100 nominal value

I (annual interest) = 10% x $100 = $10

RV (Redemption Value) = $100

To calculate the current yield on the bond we therefore discount at two different discount rates e.g. 5% and 15%

Time	Cashflow ($)	DF @ 5%	NPV ($) @ 5%	DF @ 15%	NPV ($) @ 15%
T0	(95)	1.000	(95)	1.000	(95)
T1 – T5	10	4.329	43.29	3.352	33.52
T5	100	0.784	78.40	0.497	49.70
			26.69		**(11.78)**

To calculate the IRR:

$$IRR = 5\% + \dfrac{26.69}{(26.69 + 11.78)} \times (15\% - 5\%)$$

IRR = 11.94% or 0.1194

Therefore the yield on the straight bond is approximately 12%.

Part (c)

If the bond was zero-coupon the redemption value would be the single cashflow that an investor in the bond would receive on redemption to give the same 12% yield as that available on the current straight bond. This is found by compounding up the current market value of the bond for 5 years at 12%.

Redemption value on zero coupon bond = $95 x $(1 + 0.12)^5$ = $167 per $100 nominal.

The total redemption value would therefore be $60million x $\dfrac{\$167}{\$100}$ = $100.2 million.

Part (d)

We can now use the Black Scholes model to value the equity following the steps that were covered in chapter 20.

The variables are:

Ps = $110million (the value of the assets)

Pe = $100.2million (the redemption value of an equivalent zero coupon bond)

r = 5% or 0.05

t = 5 (in years)

s = 25% or 0.25

Working 1 – Calculate d_1

$$d_1 = \frac{\ln\left(\frac{110M}{100.2M}\right) + (0.05 + 0.5 \times 0.25^2)5}{0.25 \times \sqrt{5}}$$

$d_1 = 0.89$

Working 2 – Calculate d_2

$d_2 = 0.89 - 0.25 \times \sqrt{5}$

$d_2 = 0.33$

Working 3 – calculate N(d1) and N(d2)

This involves using the normal distribution tables in appendix 2 at the back of the book. There is a guide to using the tables as part of the black scholes formula in appendix 2.

From the tables

$N(d_1) = 0.5 + 0.3133 = 0.8133$

$N(d_2) = 0.5 + 0.1293 = 0.6293$

Working 4 – the value of the call option

We now use the main formula to find the value of the call option

C = 110 million x 0.8133 - 100.2 million x 0.6293 x $e^{-(0.05 \times 5)}$

C = 40.35 million

The value of the equity using an option based valuation is therefore $40.35million.

In this example the estimate of value using an option based valuation is therefore lower than the asset based valuation by ($53 million - $40.35 million) = $12.65 million

When is an option based equity valuation method useful?

This method is particularly useful as a valuation method when there is a need to value companies that have experienced dramatic changes in the value of assets, cashflows, earnings and dividends and where the more conventional methods of valuation are difficult to use accurately.

A good example of this would be the banking and financial services industry in 2008 and 2009. The dramatic collapse in the value of the assets and earnings of a number of major banks resulted in liabilities exceeding the assets (which would mean a zero asset based valuation) and the collapse in earnings made predicting future cashflows, earnings or dividends very difficult.

An option based valuation of the equity takes into account asset volatility. Even if assets are worth less than liabilities at the date of valuation, if the asset value is volatile, and there is a period of time before the liabilities mature, there is a possibility that before maturity the assets will be worth more than the liabilities and the option to redeem the liabilities is 'in the money'. The option based valuation therefore works well when attempting to value companies that have experienced financial distress.

Chapter 25
key points summary

- Free cashflow valuation – two approaches.

  - Free cashflow (FCF)

    - do not deduct interest

    - discount at WACC

    - gives value of assets

    - deduct value of debt

    - to get value of equity.

  - Free cashflow for equity (FCFE)

    - deduct interest

    - discount at cost of equity

    - gives value of equity.

  - May need to calculate the present value of a growing perpetuity:

    - Cashflow at T1 $\times \dfrac{1}{r-g}$

- Valuing equity as an option.

  - Can be used if:

    - limited liability

    - some debt financing.

  - Equity holder has a call option on assets of the company

    - if debt is redeemed – option is exercised

    - if debt not redeemend – option lapses.

APPENDIX

Single period discount factor table

Period	1%	2%	3%	4%	5%	6%	7%	8%	9%	10%
1	0.990	0.980	0.971	0.962	0.952	0.943	0.935	0.926	0.917	0.909
2	0.980	0.961	0.943	0.925	0.907	0.890	0.873	0.857	0.842	0.826
3	0.971	0.942	0.915	0.889	0.864	0.840	0.816	0.794	0.772	0.751
4	0.961	0.924	0.888	0.855	0.823	0.792	0.763	0.735	0.708	0.683
5	0.951	0.906	0.863	0.822	0.784	0.747	0.713	0.681	0.650	0.621
6	0.942	0.888	0.837	0.790	0.746	0.705	0.666	0.630	0.596	0.564
7	0.933	0.871	0.813	0.760	0.711	0.665	0.623	0.583	0.547	0.513
8	0.923	0.853	0.789	0.731	0.677	0.627	0.582	0.540	0.502	0.467
9	0.914	0.837	0.766	0.703	0.645	0.592	0.544	0.500	0.460	0.424
10	0.905	0.820	0.744	0.676	0.614	0.558	0.508	0.463	0.422	0.386

Period	11%	12%	13%	14%	15%	16%	17%	18%	19%	20%
1	0.901	0.893	0.885	0.877	0.870	0.862	0.855	0.847	0.840	0.833
2	0.812	0.797	0.783	0.769	0.756	0.743	0.731	0.718	0.706	0.694
3	0.731	0.712	0.693	0.675	0.658	0.641	0.624	0.609	0.593	0.579
4	0.659	0.636	0.613	0.592	0.572	0.552	0.534	0.516	0.499	0.482
5	0.593	0.567	0.543	0.519	0.497	0.476	0.456	0.437	0.419	0.402
6	0.535	0.507	0.480	0.456	0.432	0.410	0.390	0.370	0.352	0.335
7	0.482	0.452	0.425	0.400	0.376	0.354	0.333	0.314	0.296	0.279
8	0.434	0.404	0.376	0.351	0.327	0.305	0.285	0.266	0.249	0.233
9	0.391	0.361	0.333	0.308	0.284	0.263	0.243	0.225	0.206	0.194
10	0.352	0.322	0.295	0.270	0.247	0.227	0.208	0.191	0.176	0.162

How to use?

The discount factor needed to find the
present value of a single cashflow at time 6
(period 6) at 11%, for example, is this figure
i.e. 0.535.

Annuity factor table(equal annual cashflow from period 1 to period n)

Period	1%	2%	3%	4%	5%	6%	7%	8%	9%	10%
1	0.990	0.980	0.971	0.962	0.952	0.943	0.935	0.926	0.917	0.909
2	1.970	1.942	1.913	1.886	1.859	1.833	1.808	.1783	1.759	1.736
3	2.941	2.884	2.829	2.775	2.723	2.673	2.624	2.577	2.531	2.487
4	3.902	3.808	3.717	3.630	3.546	3.465	3.387	3.312	3.240	3.170
5	4.853	4.713	4.580	4.452	4.329	4.212	4.100	3.993	3.890	3.791
6	5.795	5.601	5.417	5.242	5.076	4.917	4.767	4.623	4.486	4.355
7	6.728	6.472	6.230	6.002	5.786	5.582	5.389	5.206	5.033	4.868
8	7.652	7.325	7.020	6.733	6.463	6.210	5.971	5.747	5.535	5.335
9	8.566	8.162	7.786	7.435	7.108	6.802	6.515	6.247	5.995	5.759
10	9.471	8.893	8.530	8.111	7.722	7.360	7.024	6.710	6.418	6.145

Period	11%	12%	13%	14%	15%	16%	17%	18%	19%	20%
1	0.901	0.893	0.885	0.877	0.870	0.862	0.855	0.847	0.840	0.833
2	1.713	1.690	1.668	1.647	1.626	1.605	1.585	1.566	1.547	1.528
3	2.444	2.402	2.361	2.322	2.283	2.246	2.210	2.174	2.140	2.106
4	3.102	3.037	2.974	2.914	2.855	2.798	2.743	2.690	2.639	2.589
5	3.696	3.605	3.517	3.433	3.352	3.274	3.199	3.127	3.058	2.991
6	4.231	4.111	3.998	3.889	3.784	3.685	3.589	3.496	3.410	3.326
7	4.712	4.564	4.423	4.288	4.160	4.039	3.922	3.812	3.706	3.605
8	5.146	4.968	4.799	4.639	4.487	4.344	4.207	4.078	3.954	3.837
9	5.537	5.328	5.132	4.946	4.772	4.607	4.451	4.303	4.163	4.031
10	5.889	5.650	5.426	5.216	5.019	4.833	4.659	4.494	4.339	4.192

How to use?

The annuity factor needed to find the present value of a 10 year annuity (that is an equal annual cashflow from time 1 to time 10) at 12%, for example, is this figure i.e. 5.650.

Standard normal distribution table

	0.00	0.01	0.02	0.03	0.04	0.05	0.06	0.07	0.08	0.09
0.0	.0000	.0040	.0080	.0120	.0159	.0199	.0239	.0279	.0319	.0359
0.1	.0398	.0438	.0478	.0517	.0557	.0596	.0636	.0675	.0714	.0753
0.2	.0793	.0832	.0871	.0910	.0948	.0987	.1026	.1064	.1103	.1141
0.3	.1179	.1217	.1255	.1293	.1331	.1368	.1406	.1443	.1480	.1517
0.4	.1554	.1591	.1628	.1664	.1700	.1736	.1772	.1808	.1844	.1879
0.5	.1915	.1950	.1985	.2019	.2054	.2088	.2123	.2157	.2190	.2224
0.6	.2257	.2291	.2324	.2357	.2389	.2422	.2454	.2486	.2518	.2549
0.7	.2580	.2611	.2642	.2673	.2704	.2734	.2764	.2794	.2823	.2852
0.8	.2881	.2910	.2939	.2967	.2995	.3023	.3051	.3078	.3106	.3133
0.9	.3159	.3186	.3212	.3238	.3264	.3289	.3315	.3340	.3365	.3389
1.0	.3413	.3438	.3461	.3485	.3508	.3531	.3554	.3577	.3599	.3621
1.1	.3643	.3665	.3686	.3708	.3729	.3749	.3770	.3790	.3810	.3830
1.2	.3849	.3869	.3888	.3907	.3925	.3944	.3962	.3980	.3997	.4015
1.3	.4032	.4049	.4066	.4082	.4099	.4115	.4131	.4147	.4162	.4177
1.4	.4192	.4207	.4222	.4236	.4251	.4265	.4279	.4292	.4306	.4319
1.5	.4332	.4345	.4357	.4370	.4382	.4394	.4406	.4418	.4430	.4441
1.6	.4452	.4463	.4474	.4485	.4495	.4505	.4515	.4525	.4535	.4545
1.7	.4554	.4564	.4573	.4582	.4591	.4599	.4608	.4616	.4625	.4633
1.8	.4641	.4649	.4656	.4664	.4671	.4678	.4686	.4693	.4699	.4706
1.9	.4713	.4719	.4726	.4732	.4738	.4744	.4750	.4756	.4762	.4767
2.0	.4772	.4778	.4783	.4788	.4793	.4798	.4803	.4808	.4812	.4817
2.1	.4821	.4826	.4830	.4834	.4838	.4842	.4846	.4850	.4854	.4857
2.2	.4861	.4865	.4868	.4871	.4875	.4878	.4881	.4884	.4887	.4890
2.3	.4893	.4896	.4898	.4901	.4904	.4906	.4909	.4911	.4913	.4916
2.4	.4918	.4920	.4922	.4925	.4927	.4929	.4931	.4932	.4934	.4936
2.5	.4938	.4940	.4941	.4943	.4945	.4946	.4948	.4949	.4951	.4952
2.6	.4953	.4955	.4956	.4957	.4959	.4960	.4961	.4962	.4963	.4964
2.7	.4965	.4966	.4967	.4968	.4969	.4970	.4971	.4972	.4973	.4974
2.8	.4974	.4975	.4976	.4977	.4977	.4978	.4979	.4980	.4980	.4981
2.9	.4981	.4982	.4983	.4983	.4984	.4984	.4985	.4985	.4986	.4986
3.0	.4987	.4987	.4987	.4988	.4988	.4989	.4989	.4989	.4990	.4990

How to use?

The first column is the standard deviation to one decimal place and the top row is the second decimal place. The figures in the middle of the table are probabilities.

Suppose we wish the find the probability associated with a standard deviation of 2.43. This standard deviation needs to be read as a combination of 2.4 and 0.03. We then find the figure at the intersection of the row 2.4 and the column 0.03. The corresponding probability is therefore 0.4925.

If the standard deviation is positive, and the tables are being used as part of the Black Scholes Model, then 0.5 must be added to the figure from the tables.

INDEX